90 0509594 5

Post Keynesian Econometrics, Microeconomics and the Theory of the Firm

THE POST KEYNESIAN ECONOMICS
STUDY GROUP

Post Keynesian Econometrics, Microeconomics and the Theory of the Firm and *Keynes, Uncertainty and the Global Economy* are the outcome of a conference held at the University of Leeds in 1996 under the auspices of the Post Keynesian Economics Study Group. They are the fourth and fifth in the series published by Edward Elgar for the Study Group.

The essays in these volumes bear witness to the vitality and importance of Post Keynesian Economics in understanding the workings of the economy, both at the macroeconomic and the microeconomic level. Not only do these chapters demonstrate important shortcomings in the orthodox approach, but they also set out some challenging alternative approaches that promise to lead to a greater understanding of the operation of the market mechanism. The papers make important contributions to issues ranging from the philosophical and methodological foundations of economics to policy and performance.

The Post Keynesian Study Group was established in 1988 with a grant from the Economic and Social Research Council and has flourished ever since. At present (2002), there are four meetings a year hosted by a number of 'old' and 'new' universities throughout Great Britain. These are afternoon sessions at which three or four papers are presented and provide a welcome opportunity for those working in the field to meet and discuss ideas, some of which are more or less complete, others of which are at a more early stage of preparation. Larger conferences, such as the one from which these two volumes are derived, are also held from time to time, including a conference specifically for postgraduates. There are presently over five hundred members who receive the Post Keynesian Study Group electronic newsletter and details of seminars. The Study Group has established a number of international links.

As the present convenor of the Post Keynesian Study Group, I should like to thank Sheila Dow and John Hillard for the not inconsiderable time and effort they have spent in editing the proceedings and making these important papers available to a wider audience.

John McCombie
Downing College, Cambridge, UK

Post Keynesian Econometrics, Microeconomics and the Theory of the Firm

Beyond Keynes, Volume One

Edited by

Sheila C. Dow

Professor of Economics, University of Stirling, UK

and

John Hillard

Director of Taught Postgraduate Programmes, Leeds University Business School, UK

IN ASSOCIATION WITH THE POST KEYNESIAN ECONOMICS STUDY GROUP

Edward Elgar
Cheltenham, UK • Northampton, MA, USA

© Sheila Dow and John Hillard 2002

All rights reserved. No part of this publication may be reproduced, stored in
a retrieval system or transmitted in any form or by any means, electronic,
mechanical or photocopying, recording, or otherwise without the prior
permission of the publisher.

Published by
Edward Elgar Publishing Limited
Glensanda House
Montpellier Parade
Cheltenham
Glos GL50 1UA
UK

Edward Elgar Publishing, Inc.
136 West Street
Suite 202
Northampton
Massachusetts 01060
USA

A catalogue record for this book
is available from the British Library

ISBN 1 85898 584 6 ✓

Printed and bound in Great Britain by Biddles Ltd, *www.biddles.co.uk*

UNIVERSITY OF PLYMOUTH		
Item No.	9005095945	
Date	− 2 JUL 2002	B
Class No.	338·5 Pos	
Cont. No.	✓	
PLYMOUTH LIBRARY		

Contents

Figures

Contributors

Vicky Allsopp is Principal Lecturer in Economics at Middlesex University Business School, UK

Philip Arestis is Professor of Economics, South Bank University London, UK

Roger E. Backhouse is Professor of the History and Philosophy of Economics, University of Birmingham, UK

Peter J. Buckley is Professor of International Business and Director of the Centre for International Business, University of Leeds (CIBUL), UK

Malcolm Chapman is Senior Lecturer in International Business, University of Leeds, UK

Sheila Dow is Professor of Economics, University of Stirling, UK

Paul Downward is Reader in Economics, Staffordshire University, UK

Stephen P. Dunn is Policy Advisor, Strategy Unit, Department of Health, Economic Advisor, Her Majesty's Treasury, and Senior Research Fellow in Economics, University of Staffordshire, UK

Bill Gerrard is Reader in Economics, Leeds University Business School, UK

John Hillard is Director of Taught Postgraduate Programmes, Leeds University Business School, UK

Brian J. Loasby is Emeritus Professor of Economics, University of Stirling, UK

Uskali Mäki is Professor of Philosophy, Erasmus University Rotterdam, The Netherlands

Iris Biefang-Frisancho Mariscal is Senior Lecturer in Economics, University of East London, UK

Sohei Mizuhara is Professor of Economics at Ryukoku University, Japan

Paul Ormerod is Director of Volterra Consulting Ltd, UK

G.B. Richardson is former Chief Executive of Oxford University Press and Warden of Keble College, Oxford, UK

Preface

It is both a pleasure and a privilege to write the Preface to this volume of the second Leeds conference on Keynesian matters, so ably organized by Sheila Dow and John Hillard. The conference was a wonderful occasion for me especially; I made new friends and renewed old friendships in pleasant surroundings and I heard serious, stimulating and inspiring papers and discussion. The contents of the volume show that the wide-ranging interests, example and inspiration of Keynes himself guided our discussions. Much unfinished business from Keynes's own agenda received attention: the vexed place of imperfect competition in the Keynesian system; the compromises needed to do effective systemic analysis; the roles of knowledge, information and uncertainty in economic analysis; appropriate methodologies; the place for econometric procedures in effective analysis; the usefulness of the insights of Keynes and his followers for current international issues, not least taming speculators and coping with the economic ignorance that underlies Maastricht.

Because it was a gathering of Keynes scholars we were not afraid to learn from the past, from both historical events and scholars now dead. This was not piety but the application of critical intelligence combined with perspective.

I am sure that readers of the volume will get pleasure and knowledge in equal measure from it. It only remains now for me to thank the editors and the contributors for their splendidly cooperative efforts. Please read on:

G.C. Harcourt
Cambridge, UK

Introduction

Sheila C. Dow and John Hillard

The first Keynes, Knowledge and Uncertainty conference was held in Leeds in 1993 under the aegis of the Post Keynesian Economics Study Group. The purpose of that conference was to gather together a distinguished international collection of authors to build on the impressive foundation of Keynes scholarship which had built up over the previous ten years. Not all were themselves Keynes scholars – some brought new insights from new developments in the philosophy of the physical sciences, and from post-modernism and rhetoric studies. The aim was to provide a forum for an exchange of ideas along the lines of taking forward the insights of Keynes, which were now better understood, in the development of methodology, theory and policy for the 1990s and beyond. The proceedings of this conference were published by Edward Elgar in 1995, under the title of *Keynes, Knowledge and Uncertainty*.

The second Keynes, Knowledge and Uncertainty conference took place in Leeds in 1996, again under the aegis of the Post Keynesian Economics Study Group. Its aim was to build on the work of the first conference, taking ideas forward still. This theme is encapsulated in the title for the conference volumes, *Beyond Keynes*. The majority of chapters in the *Keynes, Knowledge and Uncertainty* volume had focused on the methodological implications of Keynes's philosophy, spelling out in particular the implications of adopting a non-dualistic, open-system mode of theorizing. But two chapters in particular (by Skidelsky and Fitzgibbons) reminded us of the ultimate goal, which is to provide useful policy advice. In the present volumes, the emphasis has shifted on from methodology. While some chapters still focus on methodology, they are tied into wider discussions in other chapters about developments in theory, empirical work and policy questions.

Post Keynesian economics is most developed at the macroeconomic level, yet the orthodox agenda has brought to the fore a concern with understanding macroeconomic outcomes in terms of individual behaviour. The theoretical chapters in both volumes deal, in one way or another, with microfoundations. In the first volume, the theoretical chapters focus on specifying the form that microeconomics should take when account is taken of the knowledge requirements of firms in a competitive environment and the requirements for markets to function. The motivation is realist, in the sense that the microeconomics incorporates those features of behaviour and convention without which markets could not function. This is the parallel, within the theory of the firm, of Post Keynesian macroeconomics, which emphasizes money on the grounds that capitalist economies could not function without it.

Uncertain knowledge raises particular methodological questions about the nature and role of econometrics. All address the role for, and scope of, econometrics, which is controversial from a realist perspective. There is a consensus that econometrics is a useful descriptive tool for identifying stylized facts on which theory may focus (more than a tool for discriminating between theories). But differences of opinion are evident on the relative merits of particular approaches to econometrics, and the extent of its usefulness.

The theoretical chapters in the second volume focus on the relationship between the microeconomic and macroeconomic levels. Again the motivation is realist. Some of the chapters carry forward the analysis of uncertainty and its implications for individual behaviour as it underpins macroeconomic behaviour, building on Keynes's philosophy. Other chapters extend the application further by applying Post Keynesian theory to policy questions, notably in the international arena.

In what follows we consider the chapters in Volume I in greater detail. The chapters in the first part of this volume focus on issues of knowledge, with an emphasis on microeconomic application. *Brian Loasby* makes apparent the parallel between the knowledge of the economist and knowledge in the economy. In the first chapter, he considers issues of market coordination in terms of the division and coordination of knowledge. In particular, he concludes that dispersed and incomplete knowledge is necessary for, and the outcome of, the growth of knowledge. *G.B. Richardson* focuses on knowledge acquisition (in the form of developing capabilities) as the basis for investment. Inter-firm cooperation and intra-firm planning are necessary, along with pure market transactions to underpin the process of innovation, which in turn increases competition. But he argues, echoing Keynes, that the process is held back by uncertainty about the outcome of investment.

Uskali Mäki steps back from this analysis in order to examine the foundations of knowledge for Richardson and for Coase. He identifies a common rejection of the 'unrealisticness' of neoclassical economics. In particular, neoclassical economics is seen as isolating analysis from essential features of what Richardson and Coase both see as the way the world works. This emphasis on the 'ontic' indispensability of the missing elements of institutions, information questions and so on makes their position compatible with realism. *Peter Buckley* and *Malcolm Chapman* focus on the issue to which Coase had drawn attention as explaining the existence of non-market processes, that is, of firms: transaction costs. Taking a longitudinal approach to studying transaction costs in particular firms raises issues concerning the anthropology of firms. They conclude that such costs are impossible to quantify; their internalization in firms rests on matters of judgment, and organizational questions, regarding the potential for trust within the firm to outweigh the risks of internalization. *Stephen Dunn* broadens the discussion again to consider the theory of the firm. He too emphasizes uncertainty, and the role of money which in Post Keynesian macroeconomics is understood as acting as a buffer against uncertainty. He questions the traditional dichotomization between markets and hierarchies, combining Post Keynesian theory on knowledge with Cowling and Sugden's theory of organization within firms.

Vicky Allsopp's chapter pursues further the notion of including in theory what is regarded as essential to real economic processes, by focusing on the issue of trust. After explaining the different meanings of the term, she explains its absence from neoclassical theory by its reference to interpersonal relations and its location in irreversible time. Because trust evolves, too, it is unwise to presume a continued presence of trust which can safely be ignored. Nor is it merely a rational response to transactions costs. The meaning and significance of three categories of trust are explored: personal, institutional and providential trust. *Sohei Mizuhara* rounds off this section, which has put so much emphasis on uncertainty, by providing an account of Keynesian thinking on uncertainty, in terms of evidence, comparing the treatment in the *Treatise on Probability* with that in the *General Theory*. He explains the concept of weight, and the distinction between uncertainty due to lack of relevant evidence and that due to lack of knowledge of relevance.

The second section of this volume considers econometrics as a source of knowledge in economics. While Keynes had been notable in expressing doubts about the scope for econometric analysis, *Bill Gerrard* argues that recent developments address many of Keynes's concerns. The traditional, 'AER', approach to econometrics sought empirical confirmation of theory based on a different set of essentials from those identified, as above, with Coase and Richardson. Subsequent, supposedly atheoretical, time-series analysis is shown also to have theoretical priors. In contrast, Gerrard argues that the LSE Hendry approach attempts to identify the model from the data; thus diagnostic tests are designed to identify problems with the model rather than the data (as was the case with the AER approach). Paul Ormerod, however, finds the Hendry approach also as not being successful in addressing the sheer complexity of economic processes relative to the available data, and the prevalence of relationships identified with variables which themselves are highly unpredictable. The solution he suggests lies with first identifying stable periods within which there is some chance that stable relationships might be identified. This is an argument for identifying periods within which there is scope for identifying some sort of closure.

Paul Downward addresses explicitly the critical realist critique of econometrics which rests on the importance of ontology (how the world works) and how far reality can be approximated to a stable, closed system. He explains the distinction between open and closed systems, and explains accordingly why econometrics cannot discriminate conclusively between theories; he uses pricing theory as a case study. Nevertheless, he argues that, where the use of econometrics is justified in the particular context, its results may add weight to arguments. This view of econometrics as one of a range of methods used to build up (non-demonstrative) knowledge is supported also by *Sheila Dow*'s chapter. Given the technical advance in mathematical modelling and econometrics since Keynes's day, she addresses the question of the modern relevance of Keynes's philosophy and methodology. She argues that modern orthodox methodology is quite different from that put forward by Keynes, so that the question is one of comparing methodologies, rather than methods. The specific question of the role of formalism is one of scope, with Keynes (and Post Keynesians) seeing that scope as much narrower than modern neoclassical economics.

Whatever the merits of econometrics, *Roger Backhouse* argues that macroeconomic textbooks make only limited reference to econometric results. Taking Blanchard and Fischer's *Lectures on Macroeconomics* and Philip Arestis's *The Post Keynesian Approach to Economics* as examples of leading textbooks in mainstream and non-mainstream macroeconomics, he finds that empirical evidence is mainly used to establish 'facts' and in a falsificationist exercise to undermine competing theories. While Blanchard and Fischer see economics as the art of identifying which elements of reality are crucial, their more general notion of cruciality contrasts with Arestis's greater emphasis on institutional, context-specific assumptions. A good case study of this latter approach is found in the following chapter, where *Philip Arestis* and *Iris Biefang-Frisancho Mariscal* set out and test empirically a model of wage and unemployment determination in the UK. The model incorporates elements stemming from the Post Keynesian understanding of what is crucial to the reality of the labour market: the importance of socioeconomic determinants of labour productivity, struggle over income shares, and the particular history and concept of social justice which workers bring to the wage bargain. The empirical results confirm the model and raise doubts accordingly about more market-based analyses of wage and unemployment determination.

Before launching into these chapters we would like to express our sincere appreciation for the support given to the conference and the production of these volumes by Edward Elgar Publishing Ltd, and in particular for the patience and understanding of Dymphna Evans.

1. The division and coordination of knowledge

Brian J. Loasby

I THE INSUFFICIENCY OF REASON

'The economic analyst . . . assumes that men pursue their interests by applying reason to their circumstances. And he does not ask *how they know* what those circumstances are.' George Shackle (1972, Preface) here raises a fundamental issue, not only of economic analysis, but of human behaviour. Keynes, having examined in his *Treatise on Probability* the logical connections between supposedly established knowledge and the further knowledge that might be inferred from it, later emphasized 'the extreme precariousness of the basis of the knowledge on which our estimates of prospective yield have to be made' (Keynes, GT: 149); and Hayek (1937: 45), speaking to the London Economic Club a few months after the publication of the *General Theory*, declared that 'if we want to make the assertion that under certain conditions people will approach that state [of equilibrium] we must explain by what process they will acquire the necessary knowledge'.

Hayek (1931) had already sought to explain the business cycle by a failure to acquire a crucial piece of knowledge, and in doing so had anticipated two key features of Keynes's theory (though in other important respects the theories were very different). First, both Hayek and Keynes identified the locus of coordination failure in a disparity between investment and full-employment savings, though Hayek feared an excess of investment and Keynes an insufficiency; and second, the reason why this disparity is not eliminated by the price mechanism is that the relevant price – the rate of interest – is determined in the wrong market. Keynes's analysis is no less dependent on problems which are peculiar to money than is Hayek's; both appear to believe that in an economy without money – what Keynes at one stage in the development of the *General Theory* called a cooperative economy – the price system works well. Indeed, Keynes (GT: 378–9) declares that 'there is no objection to be raised against the classical analysis' of resource allocation and sees 'no reason to suppose that the existing system seriously misemploys the factors of production which are in use'. Not all Post Keynesians would agree with either the positive or the normative judgment here made by Keynes. I would like here to focus on the positive judgment, and in so doing to follow the later Hayek in doubting whether orthodox micro theory provides an adequate account of economic coordination.

As Leijonhufvud (1969: 30) observed, the Walrasian story requires all economic agents to be presented with a set of prices which are guaranteed both to be the best available and to allow all agents to carry out as many transactions as they wish at those prices. The coordination game is therefore rigged before it starts; no-one needs to acquire any knowledge at all. And it has to be rigged because, as George Richardson (1960) pointed out, a perfectly competitive Walrasian economy is incapable of generating the knowledge that agents would need in order to make the decisions which would bring the economy to an equilibrium. As Hayek increasingly came to realize, coordination depends upon institutions which provide stability and reassurance. The apparently perfect flexibility of a perfectly competitive world is an illusion, since if everything is flexible, nothing can be relied on. Should we not then start by analysing the problem of coordinating those activities which seemed to Keynes, as to most economists, to be reasonably well coordinated? That is what I propose to do; and I shall begin by examining precisely why coordination might be difficult.

Hayek (1937: 49) identified the source of the difficulty in the division of knowledge, which he described as 'the really central problem of economics as a social science'. This problem, as he saw it, is how to achieve – and not merely to calculate – an efficient allocation when the relevant data about goods, resources and technologies are not universally available but dispersed among the economic agents. He does not ask why the data are dispersed in the particular way that they are; and I was once scolded – quite courteously – by Roger Garrison (1982: 136–7) for suggesting that this was a question worth asking. I still think that it is worth asking; and the answer that I give is that this dispersion is an inevitable consequence of the division of labour.

If there were no division of labour, but each individual were completely self-sufficient, then coordination problems would be strictly personal. Each individual would still have to coordinate a sequence of activities in the light of highly imperfect knowledge, as Wiseman and Littlechild (1990) entertainingly demonstrate in their analysis of Crusoe's Kingdom; but there would be no economics as a social science. Why, then, do we create so many difficulties for ourselves, from incurring entirely avoidable transaction costs to large-scale unemployment, which could be avoided by self-sufficiency? Differences of initial endowment do not provide an adequate answer, for they are insufficient to support continuing exchange.

The fundamental explanation was supplied by Adam Smith: the division of labour is the predominant source of increased productivity. But we have forgotten Smith's (1976b: 28) reasoning. He declared that the division of labour is less important as a more efficient means of using varied skills than as a means of developing them; thus the division of knowledge is not, as Hayek declared, analogous to the division of labour but its direct product. Knowledge is divided because that is the way to increase it. Smith (1976b: 20–21) illustrates this theme by identifying three distinct sources of inventions: the detailed knowledge of workers within a particular trade; the differently focused knowledge of specialist machine makers, an example that can stand for all kinds of complementary trades; and the 'philosophers or men of speculation' who 'are often capable of combining together the power of the most distant and dissimilar objects'. Within each category people have their own distinctive ways of thinking about problems, and their own distinctive capabilities; thus they tend to produce different kinds of machinery – or, to generalize, different kinds of improvement. The division of labour thus produces different kinds of knowledge, and it does so by producing different processes for knowledge generation.

II   KNOWLEDGE AND COGNITION

It will be helpful to examine briefly these different kinds of knowledge and knowledge generation. Economists typically think of knowledge as information, which may then be subjected to logical processing in order to produce further information. Shackle, Keynes and Hayek, in the passages cited earlier, are questioning the availability of information; and they have reason to question it, because it is crucial to any theory that relies on rational choice. However, intelligent action requires more than rational choice; these choices must be executed. But, as Ryle (1949) pointed out, the execution of choices does not depend on 'knowledge that', but on skills in performance, or 'knowledge how'. Now these two kinds of knowledge are at best loosely connected; and it is as well that they are only loosely connected, for it is not clear how evolution could have got started if plants, let alone animals, had to understand the fundamental laws of physics, chemistry and biology in order to differentiate and coordinate cells and organize adequate nutrition. Intellectual operations are latecomers in the history of evolution, and they have not replaced the cognitive processes which deliver effective performance.

The architecture of the human brain is the product of pre-intellectual evolution, and has proved sufficient for the formation of neural networks which not only permit the collection of sensory perceptions into orderly groups but also the collection of such groups into patterns which directly link complex sensory inputs with complex physical actions. Association, rather than deduction, seems to be the operating principle which is embodied in this physical structure. The development of logical reasoning comes later, and is relatively expensive in its demands on time and energy. The physiological truth underlying the concept of bounded rationality is that the human capacity for serial information processing is very limited, and therefore we must usually manage without it. Much of the knowledge that is generated by the division of labour does not depend on logical sequences, for this is primarily 'knowledge how'.

Greater skill in performance typically results from the development of closer connections (hand–eye coordination, for example, is not an intellectual process, but it is the product of human intelligence) and ideas for improvement are rarely the result of purely logical operations – otherwise they could presumably be produced to order – but arise from novel connections. This is most obvious in the work of Smith's 'philosophers', but it also seems to explain why so many minor improvements are produced by those who are deeply immersed in the activities which are improved, for such people have the greatest chance of initiating a new connection. This does not imply that all such new connections signify improvements, but simply that there will be many more new connections from which a small proportion of genuine improvements may emerge; for evolutionary success depends much less on the ability to derive optima than on the generation of variety.

We should not therefore be surprised to find that skills of all kinds, including the complex skills required in many technologies, should be very difficult to transfer without practice; an understanding of the scientific principles may help, but it is not sufficient. The assumption of costless replication, on which so much analysis of research policy has been based, is almost always false. Skills are difficult to codify, not least because the coding systems that have been developed for intellectual operations correspond rather poorly to the intelligent processes by which skills are developed. But what is often forgotten is that intellectual operations require their own skills. Bounded rationality imposes the need to select and simplify, and if these are thought to be logical operations that is only because the guiding principles have been invented by non-logical means. Moreover, our intellectual difficulties arise not only from our limited capacity for information processing; as Shackle above all insisted, there is also typically a serious deficiency in the knowledge from which we start, and so, in addition to simplifying and excluding, we also have to interpret, or even invent, some of the evidence for our intellectual operations. Consequently, we can always find an objection to unwelcome results, however rigorous the logical structure from which they emerge, and a reason to doubt any forecast. Some companies, notably Shell, have sought to avoid reliance on forecasts by the development and dissemination of non-probabilistic scenarios, and the pervasiveness of interpretative ambiguity is a principal theme of Fransman's (1995) intensive study of the Japanese computer and communications industry.

Each discipline has its own institutions for the generation of knowledge, and these institutions may change over time; and each newcomer to a discipline has to learn the procedures, and not just the substance, of that discipline. That cannot be done without practice; we tell our students this, but we rarely tell them why, perhaps because we believe that practice, not being an intellectual activity, is rather inferior. The tradition of privileging intellectual activity is the principal target of Ryle's book. We certainly find it difficult to explain why the skills of our discipline are different from those of other disciplines; and we do not find it easy to resolve disagreements about method within a single discipline. But if intellectual knowledge, like practical knowledge, has to be divided in order to be developed, it is surely natural that each specialism should operate by its own rules, and that there should be variants within that specialism. What has been said about specialisms is no less true of firms. The possibility of a universal code is a denial of Adam Smith's central principle for improving productivity, in the development of science as well as in the performance of the economy.

III   COORDINATION

How, then, do we coordinate activities in an economy where the division of labour is generating increasingly differentiated knowledge? Smith (1976b: 26) clearly recognized that this was a problem for each individual to solve; every person 'stands at all times in need of the co-operation and assistance of great multitudes, while his whole life is scarce sufficient to gain the friendship of a few persons'. It has to be solved on the basis of individual knowledge and perception; no-one can have access to sufficient knowledge to construct an integrated plan. Smith understood this as well as Hayek (1952: 185), who noted that 'any apparatus of classification must possess a structure of a higher degree of complexity than is possessed by the objects which it classifies'. No human brain can have a more complex structure than a system which includes millions of human brains, as well as the multiplicity of non-human phenomena.

Smith (1976a: 116) put more weight than most economists realize on the human endowment of 'an original desire to please, and an original aversion to offend his brethren', and on the related human delight in persuasion, which Smith (1978: 352) believed was the origin of 'the propensity to truck and barter', in gaining the cooperation of those whose knowledge was not directly accessible; but both sympathy and persuasion are liable to become less effective if the objects of this sympathy and persuasion organize their knowledge in increasingly diverse ways. Messages may be wrongly interpreted, for as Lachmann (1986: 46) reminds us, 'Those who speak of the "decoding of messages" lay claim to the existence of a comprehensive codebook no mortal man ever possessed.' However, the development of localized, though never complete, coding systems is a natural consequence of the division of labour; and members of both formal and informal organizations rely on some shared codes, which may be substantially embodied in routines or institutions. Such routines or institutions serve to link individual ways of 'knowing how'; and this indirect 'knowledge how', or knowing how to get things done, to which Nelson and Winter (1982) give some prominence, is also much more the product of connections developed through practice than of formal reasoning.

As a young Fellow of St John's College, Marshall (1994) wrote a paper for a discussion group in which he sketched a model of a 'machine' which embodied some basic principles of evolutionary psychology. This machine was capable of receiving impressions and performing actions, and of forming increasingly complex connections between them, thereby creating a mechanical equivalent of a neural network which controlled the improvement of performance without conscious thought. Marshall then envisaged a second level, in which connections could be formed between ideas of impressions and ideas of performance, thus allowing trial and error to operate by anticipation as well as by experience. However, since this higher-level process was slower and required more energy, it was invoked only when the operating level encountered difficulties that it was unable to resolve, such as a cluster of impressions which gave contradictory indications, or unsatisfactory results from every action which it associated with a particular group of impressions.

Raffaelli (2001) has argued that Marshall appeared to have this early psychological model in mind when he came to consider the organization of a firm; for he there drew a distinction between operations, which generated what we now call learning by doing, and 'deliberate choice and forethought' (Marshall, 1920: 5) leading to the introduction of new products, new processes, and new patterns of organization, such as Marshall (1920: 318) included in his definition of increasing returns (or as he put it, 'return'). Since the development of operating skills depends on the particular sequence of experiences within a firm, and the deliberate introduction of change depends on the identification of a problem or opportunity at the operating level, this model naturally allows for that variation between firms in their routines and their experiments which was Marshall's most distinctive addition to Smith's theory of continuing improvement through the division of labour. This addition owes much to Darwin; but what is not Darwinian is Marshall's emphasis on the ability of firms to learn from one another, and even to combine ideas from several firms into a new idea. The process clearly requires a high degree of coordination between the frameworks of thinking used within an industry, but it also requires the preservation of sufficient differences to ensure that the detailed pattern of connections differs between firms.

His organization of 'various businesses in the same trade' thus permits a distinctive evolutionary process in human societies; but Marshall (1920: 138–9) identified another form of organization which distinguishes economic evolution, that of 'various trades relatively to one another'. This form of organization is necessary in order to realize the potential benefits of separating complementary activities. The simple but essential point, which rarely receives adequate attention in those accounts of industrial organization which rely on the imperative to minimize transaction costs, but which has been definitively explained by Richardson (1972), is that what is complementary, even closely complementary, is often not at all similar, and therefore requires a different basis for the development of knowledge. The attempt to integrate complementary activities within a single organization may therefore have the effect of retarding the growth of that organization's capabilities in some, and possibly all, of these activities. Current debate about the use of 'core competencies' as a means of defining the scope of a single business sometimes fails to distinguish between competencies which that business does, or should, directly control and competencies to which it needs ready, or even privileged, access.

Marshall (1920: 500) drew attention to 'the length of time that is necessarily occupied by each individual business in extending its internal, and still more its external organisation'. He recognized that keeping these connections outside the firm allowed each member of the network to develop specialized knowledge in a way which was likely to be different but compatible with the specialized knowledge of other members; but in accordance with his fundamental principle of progress through a combination of differentiation and integration, he was also well aware that these advantages would not be properly exploited unless there were sufficient people to fulfil, if on a more modest scale, the role of Smith's 'philosophers'. It is characteristic of Marshall that he should assign this role to the ordinary businessman. In doing so he made a substantial contribution to explaining the coordination from within which Smith saw was necessary, in the context of developing knowledge and capabilities. He also provided in advance a partial answer to the problem posed by Hayek, as was recognized by George Richardson (1960).

IV   CREATIVE DESTRUCTION

There can be no complete answer to Hayek's problem in an economy which is continuing to grow its own knowledge. This growth results from a process of trial and error, or conjecture and refutation; every addition to 'knowledge that' or to 'knowledge how' necessarily amends or displaces some part of previously accepted knowledge; and every addition to economic knowledge invalidates some part of a previous pattern of coordination. 'This fact is of course the very essence of competition', as Lachmann (1986: 5) observed. The refutation of information, explanations, practical skills, or business plans is not merely an unavoidable hazard in the process of economic evolution; it is essential to that process. All creation is destructive.

How do people respond to such refutations? No formal answer can be supplied by rational choice theory, which cannot accommodate surprises. However, it is clear that human beings do have some capacity to deal with surprises, though there are substantial differences between people in both the kind and magnitude of surprise that they can cope with, as one would expect from our understanding of the division of labour and its psychological underpinnings. Marshall's model of the two-level brain provides everyone with a personal 'research programme' which allows for some deliberate reorganization of a continuously modified core of connections; it is only because the ideas of the participants in an industry, market or academic discipline are less than perfectly coordinated that any new knowledge can arise. However, any substantial reconstruction of this core is a formidable undertaking. Indeed, the complementary structures of human capital share both the productive advantages and the inertia of those complementary structures of physical capital which non-Austrian economists too often neglect.

Hayek (1931) and Schumpeter (1934) both associated major coordination failures with the presence of inappropriate complementary structures. The essential difference between their theories is that Hayek then believed that these structures would become inappropriate only if businessmen responded to false indications of time preference, whereas Schumpeter believed that they were made inappropriate by entrepreneurship. What for Hayek was an avoidable error was for Schumpeter the symbol of successful innovation. Coordination rested on networks of efficient routines, but economic development was propelled by 'new combinations', or what Adam Smith called new 'connecting principles', which entailed the destruction of such networks. In the face of such destruction many people would simply not know what to do, or, to gloss Schumpeter's argument, if they knew what to do they would not know how to do it, for one cannot acquire new skills simply by deciding that they are necessary. As a rigorous explanation of unemployment, which may reasonably be called involuntary, this account compares well with New Classical propositions.

Keynes's (CW XXI: 385) view that the British economy in 1937 was 'in more need today of a rightly distributed demand than of a greater aggregate demand' was also an acknowledgment of the great difficulty of making radical changes in physical capital, human skills and industrial organization, but his formulation tended to divert attention from the need to encourage such changes, and may now be seen to have foreshadowed the unfortunate emphasis of regional policy after 1945 on distributing demand rather than developing new clusters of productive knowledge. The prospect of finding oneself with inappropriate structures provides the deterrent to investment in the absence of knowledge which is crucial to Keynes's theory of unemployment; Schumpeter's (1934: 85) entrepreneurs fortunately have 'the capacity to see things in a way which afterwards proves to be true', though they do require a circular flow of routinized activities to provide the reassurance that Schumpeter saw as a precondition of investment.

It is no accident that a perfectly coordinated Walrasian economy generates no knowledge, or that models of Walrasian economies do not yield very helpful theories of economic development. Coordination is important, but an insistence on coordination can damage the health of an economy, and an obsession with 'the coordination problem' can damage the health of economics. What is called 'coordination failure' is sometimes another label for an innovative system, and what is called 'market failure' is sometimes, as Richardson (1960) showed, the means by which sufficient coordination is achieved to encourage individuals and firms to make trial of their new knowledge. Both microeconomists and macroeconomists might offer more help to understanding and to policy if they recognized that dispersed and incomplete knowledge, though a barrier to the achievement – and even to the identification – of Pareto efficiency, is both a consequence and a condition of the growth of knowledge.

2. Innovation, equilibrium and welfare

G.B. Richardson

I INTRODUCTION

I should perhaps begin by justifying my choice of title. The aim of this chapter is to provide, on the basis of assumptions more realistic than those normally made, a summary analysis of the process of resource allocation within free enterprise systems. As it takes into explicit account the fact that products and processes are subject to continuous development, the chapter deals with innovation. It seeks also to adapt the notion of *equilibrium*, which economists have long since found indispensable in what has been called 'Economic Statics',[1] to a context of which innovation is a feature. I turn finally to consider whether the outcome of the process of resource allocation under consideration will exhibit allocative rationality, of the kind studied in the economics of *welfare*.

All this, it may strike the reader, is a very tall order. It may be urged that we have been able to develop a theory of the determination of prices and outputs in competitive markets on the basis of simplifying assumptions, such as that of a fixed list of goods between which consumers have given preferences. This theory has enabled us to identify equilibrium configurations towards which the actual configurations produced by the system would tend to move. Surely, it may be said, some coherent theory is better than none at all; all theories involve abstraction, but may nevertheless, like Newtonian physics, be exceedingly powerful.

I believe that we must reject this line of reasoning. The theory in question, that of perfect competition, postulates a certain market structure and associates with it a configuration, which is an equilibrium in the sense that, if realized, all consumers would be in their preferred positions and all firms would be maximizing profits. This configuration, it can also be shown, is not only an equilibrium in that sense, but also an optimum as defined by Pareto. What the theory very importantly fails to provide, however, is any reason to believe that, under the conditions postulated, the equilibrium would ever in fact be realized, other than by assuming the existence of very special, if not fanciful, contracting arrangements;[2] indeed, I have argued elsewhere (Richardson, 1960/1990) that the assumptions of the model, by denying economic agents the information needed for investment decisions, necessarily preclude the possibility of attaining equilibrium. Whatever insights the theory of perfect competition may have given us, it fails to provide either a convincing account of how free enterprise economies in fact work, or a standard by which their efficiency can be judged. And this failure results from its neglect of what we may call the *informational requirements* of any workable system, the conditions that must be realized, that is, in order that those within it can have sufficient knowledge to take investment decisions.

By abstracting from some of the circumstances of real economic life, we have, paradoxically, made it more difficult, if not impossible, to explain how the system works. I have argued elsewhere that markets generally operate not despite, but because of, some 'imperfection' of competition (see Richardson, 1960/1990, ch. 3) because of the existence, that is, of circumstances which, although excluded by definition from the perfect competition model, fulfil the informational requirements of the system by endowing the business environment with a degree of stability sufficient to make informed investment decisions possible.

Choosing to set aside, or assume away, the fact that products and processes are subject to continuous development may also make it more difficult, rather than easier, to provide a convincing model of the working of market economies. The perfect competition model has to assume that firms are operating under decreasing returns to scale, whereas we know that in reality increasing returns are very pervasive. In order to ensure the presence of many competitors within an industry, the model assumes to be true what is known to be false. If, however, we admit into our formal reasoning the reality of continuous product and process development, we no longer need to make this false assumption in order to ensure the persistence of active competition. I shall have more to say about this issue in what follows; my concern now is merely to make the point that the 'simplifications' which we hope will facilitate our theoretical analysis of market economies may sometimes in fact obstruct it.

Those who compare static equilibrium theory with Newtonian mechanics[3] may hope to give it scientific respectability. In both, it is true, we seek to predict changes by identifying states of rest towards which the system will move, self-interest being equivalent to gravitational force. But if the analogy can enlighten, it can also mislead. Any theory of the working of the economy is about the consequences of interacting decisions taken by very many different people, on the basis of knowledge which is fragmentary and uncertain. Positive economics, as distinct from that part of the subject which is a development of the pure logic of choice, must consist, as Hayek (1937) observed 60 years ago, of propositions about how people acquire knowledge, and about how the decisions they take, on the basis of what they believe, so interact as to result in an allocation of resources which appears as if it were the product of some single, overarching design.

II   THE FREE ENTERPRISE SYSTEM

I shall be concerned with what are now commonly called 'market economies'. It is important to make clear that market economies do not rely, for coordination, only on market transactions. We must recognize explicitly that, within such economies, coordination is achieved also through inter-firm cooperation and intra-firm design. The essential characteristic of the system here under consideration is economic freedom, the freedom of consumers and producers to trade as they please, within the limits of their means. Given this freedom, there will very generally, but not always, be competition; so-called 'natural monopolies' will be rare, and artificial ones usually subject to challenge. Competition will take place, most directly, between products, between firms and between alliances of firms; at the same time, however, competition will indirectly determine which managerial systems and which organizational forms will be likely to survive, and for how long.

In free enterprise economies, we have observed, the coordination of economic activity takes place within three different contexts; pure market transactions, inter-firm cooperation and intra-firm direction. And in order to understand the rationale of these three modes of coordination, we need to ask this fundamental question: how is it possible for those taking an investment decision to obtain sufficient knowledge of the circumstances upon which its profitability will depend?

Astonishing as it may seem, this question, despite its obvious prior importance, is not one that economists generally have thought it necessary to address. So-called 'pure theory', in particular, neglected this informational question and concentrated on the purely logical one; if economics is viewed as being to do with selecting the best way of applying 'given' resources to 'given' ends, it does indeed become merely an extension of the logic of choice, so that problems about how knowledge is acquired and transmitted do not appear to arise. Economists seem commonly to have featured prices as the necessary and sufficient signals guiding investment decisions and simply assumed that these are known to all concerned. But even if prices alone were to provide the information needed, their future, rather than their present, levels would be relevant and these cannot simply be assumed to be known. Economic theory, therefore, by here taking for granted what it is surely necessary to explain, has precluded us from understanding those features of the free enterprise system that have emerged, or have deliberately been developed, as ways of making the necessary knowledge available.

I have sought elsewhere (Richardson, 1960/1990) to present a full analysis of these features and am limited, in this context, to providing only a very summary account of them. We must begin by accepting that the beliefs on which businesses take decisions, as Keynes among economists so particularly appreciated, will always be uncertain, and frequently contradictory; this notwithstanding, these beliefs must be sufficiently well grounded, in the view of those who entertain them, to provide a basis for taking actions. We have to think in terms of an informational twilight, for business decisions are made neither in utter darkness nor in the clear light of day.

Some of the knowledge needed for investment decisions is embodied in the *capabilities* of those firms that take them. The capability of an organization[4] is its possession of knowledge, experience and skills such as enable it to undertake a specific range of activities related to the discovery of future wants, to research, development and design, to the execution and coordination of processes of physical transformation, the marketing of goods and so on. Its essential ingredients are, of course, the knowledge, experience and skills of individuals working within the organization, but the capability of a firm, by virtue of both its internal structure and external relationships, must be regarded as different from, and more than simply the aggregation of, its members' qualifications.

A firm committing resources to a particular investment needs the knowledge embodied in its capabilities; it needs also to form reasonably dependable expectations about the future volume and character both of products competitive with its own and of products which are necessary complements to it. This it may be able to do in either of two ways. It may depend on the general stability of its economic environment, on the fact that there is no good reason to believe that the future availability of certain goods, substitutes or complements, will differ markedly from their availability at the present. Alternatively, it may enter into arrangements specifically designed to provide predictability where this would otherwise be lacking.

Some natural stability, and therefore predictability, is given to the real world precisely by those circumstances in which it differs from the perfect competition model. The required degree of stability is associated, that is to say, with the imperfection of competition, knowledge and mobility, with the fact that not everyone knows, or can do, everything. Firms can, in the short run, undertake only those things for which they have the capabilities; these capabilities can, of course, be extended, but the process takes time. There exists, therefore, in most markets, sufficient friction or viscosity to provide a measure of the stability on which prediction, about either competing substitutes or necessary complementary inputs, may have to depend.

Where these conditions do not exist, a firm has to seek other means of securing the future. Where, for example, a firm requires inputs specifically designed for its investment, which, lacking the appropriate capability, it cannot easily make itself, it will have to seek arrangements with other firms, with which it will typically be linked in networks of cooperation and affiliation of the kind to which students of industrial organization are now prepared to give attention.[5] The rationale of these arrangements is, first, to make use of the technical knowledge, experience and skills that are distributed among different concerns, and, secondly, to reduce uncertainty (about what others will do) through reciprocal assurances.

Inter-firm cooperation can frequently give firms the predictability or assurance they need, and which would otherwise be lacking. But there are limits to the amount of coordination that it can achieve. Where a large number of activities have to be fitted together, where each has to be closely related to the others in terms of nature and timing, conscious design is required. Coordination must take place, in other words, within a firm, and economics now properly concerns itself more than hitherto with how it is promoted.

This highly summarized account may be sufficient to indicate, I hope, that informed decision taking is possible under free enterprise, partly because a firm's economic environment may be naturally stable enough to permit predictability, and partly through the mediation of inter-firm cooperation and intra-firm planning. There are particular circumstances in which each of the three forms of coordination is specially, or even uniquely, appropriate, but there are also circumstances in which they are effectively alternatives, the relative efficiency of which will be tested by competition between them. For a system based on economic freedom there is consequently no single, ideal structure, but a variety of different structures, suited to different circumstances, and adapting appropriately, in character and balance, as circumstances change over time.

III   ROUTINE INNOVATION AND INCREASING RETURNS

I shall take it for granted that, within the type of economy to be analysed, products and processes are generally subject to continuous development. In static equilibrium analysis, we assume that they remain unchanged, and seek to show how, on this basis, the system will move, in response to some change, such as an increase in the demand for a product. Within this analytical framework, the expectations of producers and consumers, in so far as they are considered at all, must, by implication, be that products and processes remain the same. The two different approaches, obviously enough, have profoundly different analytical consequences, as the investment, price and output decisions of firms that expect the continuous emergence of new products and processes will differ from those that do not.

Is it, however, reasonable to assume continuous product and process development? Industries clearly differ in respect of the rate at which development takes place, with, say, computer software at one end of the spectrum, and with salt and sugar at the other. It seems clear, however, that the rate of development has been increasing generally over the decades, to the extent that unchanging products and processes are now the exception rather than the rule. Economic theory often features an innovation as an external shock, followed by a tendency towards a new static equilibrium. In some historical periods, during which innovation came mainly in fits and starts, this may have been a justifiable approach, but scarcely at the present time. The question arises, therefore, as to whether innovation should be treated as endogenous, the level of investment in it being determined, as investment generally is determined, by the expectation of return.

Of key importance is the way in which firms and consumers themselves view the process, for upon this will depend the way they behave. In the case of computer software, for example, a firm bringing a new product to market will generally anticipate its replacement or modification within about two years; by the time it starts marketing this product, it is likely already to be working on its replacement or modification. Computer software is perhaps an extreme case, but it is easy to think of other industries in which firms take it for granted that, without continuous innovation, ground will soon be lost. (This is the case, for example, in the much older industry of book publishing, where firms must continue to bring out new titles.) In these industries, investment in a new product will be made in the expectation that it will have a limited life, and pricing policy is chosen accordingly.

We may entitle continuous product and process innovation of the kind I have been describing as *routine innovation*, thus distinguishing it from *radical innovation*, where major breakthroughs so change the industrial landscape as to permit routine product and process development to set off in new directions. The internal combustion engine represented a radical innovation, while the continuous development to which it has been subjected since its introduction may be called routine. The semiconductor was a radical innovation which opened up the way for a sustained product development in many fields. As with all distinctions of this kind, the impossibility of drawing a clear line does not invalidate the distinction.

In most industries, firms now expect routine innovation and will not expect to stay in business unless they can successfully undertake it. Innovation of this kind is a necessary, if not sufficient, condition for earning normal profits. Firms are of course aware of the possibility of radical innovations, such as that of the semiconductor mentioned above, which close avenues of development with which they are familiar, such as thermionic valve technology, while opening up totally new ones down which their own capabilities may or may not permit them to proceed. But being able to foresee neither the form that these seismic changes will assume, nor when they will occur, firms cannot take them into account in their planning. For this reason it makes sense to treat routine innovation as endogenous, when seeking to provide an explanation of how the system works, but to continue to regard radical innovations as exogenous shocks.

The act of successful innovation is commonly regarded as yielding, if only temporarily, abnormal profits. Where radical innovation is concerned, this can be so, but routine innovation of the kind I am describing is a condition, necessary if not sufficient, for earning normal profits. In static long-run equilibrium, a firm maintains its position with zero net investment, with only the level of investment, in other words, needed to ensure capital replacement. Where there is scope for continuous product and process development, the notion of replacement investment in this sense ceases to apply; irrespective of whether the demand for what it sells is rising, a firm, in order to maintain its position, will have to invest in development, this requiring expenditure on a variety of activities, such as research, consumer surveys, testing and marketing, as well as on new capital equipment.

The pressure to undertake such investment is created by the opening up of opportunities, each firm knowing that, if it does not seek to exploit them, others will. Many such opportunities depend, of course, on fundamental work done in the field of science and technology, the direction of which will be determined more by scientific curiosity than by the prospect of commercial use. There are, however, two endogenous sources worthy of note.

The first is found in the process by which, as Adam Smith explained, increased output accompanies an ever-finer division of labour, thus providing an opportunity for the development of new techniques and new products independently of any fundamental scientific advance. The second arises from complementarity between products. Consider, for example, microprocessors and software operating systems, both of which have been subject to continuous and rapid development. When the power of the former is increased, the so-called functionality of the latter – the variety of things it can do – is enhanced. The development of software applications also creates a demand for more powerful processors; and, within this area, whole networks of complementarity provide opportunities for product development.

Quite generally, a firm may be obliged to introduce a new product, not because of a change in consumer 'tastes', but because of changes that take place in other products, both substitutes and complements.

Routine innovation, it therefore seems to me, is an essential feature of modern economies and I shall take its existence for granted. I shall also assume that increasing returns are prevalent. These two features, indeed, go together, the investment in developing and testing new products and processes, largely independent of the volume of output subsequently produced, being itself one cause of increasing returns.

It is worth remarking that both Smith and Marshall accepted that, in manufacturing, increasing returns were the rule,[6] and made no use of the notion of perfect competition introduced, by Cournot and others, in the latter part of the nineteenth century. Setting questions of realism apart, these two approaches produce very different analytical consequences; within the Walrasian system, for example, an increase in the demand for a commodity will result merely in an increase in the number of firms making it, whereas, for Smith and for Marshall, a mutation in industrial structure will result.

IV   THE TENDENCY TO EQUILIBRIUM

Let us now assume that conditions for informed decision taking, such as I have discussed above, are in fact in place, and that a firm is contemplating investment. The purpose of the investment, we shall assume, will be to develop, manufacture and market a product different from those it has itself made previously and different from those available from other suppliers. Sometimes a firm may plan merely to increase the supply of a product already being produced, in the same form, by others, the incentive to do so being an expectation of increased demand, but this, however, is clearly not the general case.

We shall assume, as is again the general case, that the firm typically expects the product planned to become obsolete after a period of time, either through the development of superior substitutes, in which competing firms are investing, or through the development of complementary products to which the product has to be adapted. The firm supplying it will therefore seek to defend itself by investing in appropriate product development of its own. In this context, as we noted, routine innovation is a condition for earning profits, and investment in it will be directed where the prospect of profit seems best. Given free competition, profits are not likely for long to remain much higher in one direction than in another, although, at any time, there will be a marked spread in profitability between firms, particularly when the nature and pace of development is such that investment decisions have to be taken on the basis of very uncertain knowledge.

There exists therefore, in the circumstances which I have described, a tendency towards equilibrium, a tendency, that is, for competition to bring profits towards a uniform level, with, of course, a wide dispersion about the mean. That this is a central feature of free enterprise, and is crucial to the allocative efficiency of the system, has long been recognized. The existence of the tendency is not dependent on there being homogeneous products made by large numbers of firms, but can result from investment in product development without either of these conditions being present. The equilibrium which I have described differs both from that associated with perfect competition and from the essentially static equilibrium discussed by Chamberlin. He was concerned to show that, if postulated demand and cost conditions remained unchanged, the prices of competing, but differentiated, products would tend towards unit costs, provided the number of firms was large enough to rule out oligopolistic behaviour. The point I make is that, where products and processes are subject to continuous development, abnormal profits become eroded by virtue of the fact that firms are free to invest in this development in whatever directions seem to offer the best prospects.

This is only one way, but a most important way, in which abnormal profits will tend to be eroded. If they were occasioned by an excess of demand over the supply of a product, then an increase in its supply will reduce them. An increase in the variety of offerings, as Chamberlin pointed out, will have the same result. But a modern economy is characterized, not merely by an increasing volume and variety of products, but by their continuous development. Without such development, competition would be much less intense than it is; agreements to fix prices or limit capacity, difficult although they are to make effective, are nevertheless much easier to arrange than the limitation of investment in development. Indeed, the habit of abstracting from product development, the pace of which has been accelerating, may have led economists to view the real world as much less competitive than businessmen know it to be.

We are used in microeconomics to describing as an equilibrium the configuration to which prices and outputs will move so long as preferences and production possibilities remain the same. The tendency to equilibrium that I have sought to identify is different; it is associated with continuously changing processes and products, and to refer to its existence is a way of saying that, in competitive conditions, any return from investment in product development will tend towards a uniform level determined by the return being obtained from investment generally. There exists, I am therefore claiming, a tendency towards what we may therefore call a dynamic equilibrium, in order to distinguish it from the equilibrium normally identified in analysing the determination of prices and outputs.

V ORGANIZATION, EFFICIENCY AND WELFARE

The theory of welfare economics aims to help us judge the efficiency of economic organizations by providing criteria for the rationality of the resource allocation they will tend to produce. Essentially, it is a development of the logic of choice, the assumption being that resources, wants and production possibilities are objectively 'given'. Positive economics cannot be based on this premise; it must seek to analyse the process of resource allocation that results from the interaction of many individual decisions taken on the basis of partial, uncertain and conflicting beliefs.

Adam Smith and earlier economists argued that, under free enterprise, the pursuit of private interest, subject to some important qualifications, would promote public welfare, the distinction between positive and normative economics not at that time being explicitly drawn. A century or so later, seeking to make the analysis more rigorous, economists introduced the perfect competition model and claimed that, in its equilibrium state, resources were allocated optimally, in the sense that no-one could be made better off without someone else being made worse off. In this way, Walras, Pareto and others claimed to have identified both the criteria for efficient allocation and the type of economic organization that would produce it. This claim, I have argued, was invalid, but the need to appraise, as well as explain, the working of free enterprise systems nevertheless remains. My intention, in the rest of this chapter, is to consider how far we are able to fulfil it.

I shall assume, conventionally, that resources are used efficiently when they maximize welfare in the Paretian sense, when there is no reallocation, that is to say, which could make someone better off without making someone else worse off. I propose to leave out of account so-called externalities, positive or negative, which make a *prima facie* case for governmental intervention. These can create important divergences between private profit and public interest, but the analysis of this chapter does not add to our understanding of them. Our specific concern is with how far, if at all, the principles of formal welfare economics are applicable once we admit the realities of imperfect knowledge, innovation and increasing returns. The question, it can scarcely be doubted, is an important one; our normative theory is of little or no use if it cannot be applied to the real world, and positive economics loses most of its interest if we are unable to say to what extent the processes of resource allocation which it studies produce desirable outcomes.

Let us start with the fact that firms seeking profit take investment decisions on the basis of subjective and uncertain expectations. In seeking to appraise the efficiency of an economic organization, we have therefore to ask, first, to what extent it will enable these expectations to be adequately informed, and therefore likely to be fulfilled, and, secondly, to what extent investments which do turn out to be profitable will promote a rational allocation of resources.

The first of these questions has already been partially addressed. We noted that investment decisions must be based on some information about what other relevant parties in the system were likely to do, and we observed that its acquisition was facilitated, within a free enterprise economy, by the stability provided by natural 'frictions', by networks of inter-firm cooperation and by the consolidation within a firm of activities which could not be coordinated otherwise. There will, however, be a limit to the kind and quantity of information provided in this way, so that decisions will inevitably still be taken on the basis of uncertain and conflicting beliefs. As a result, some projects will fail, and others succeed. The failures represent a misallocation, or waste, of resources, viewed *ex post facto*; but the process itself cannot be regarded as wasteful, if it is impossible *ex ante* to know which projects will prove profitable.

An efficient organization will therefore permit some *ex ante* inconsistency between investment decisions, the important issue being the terms on which it does so. Essentially, in a regime of economic freedom, the authority to take these decisions depends on the resources and credit that a firm can command, and will therefore be augmented by success and curtailed by failure. A plurality of decision-taking centres is a feature of the system, but so are the competitive forces that, by regulating the resources at a firm's disposal, determine where the authority to take decisions will lie. Variety of approach, accompanied by a process of natural selection, is an appropriate social strategy in the face of uncertainty, and an efficient organization must be able to provide for it.

The efficiency of an economic organization, I have suggested, depends, first, on making it possible for investment decisions to be informed, and, secondly, on whether these decisions, taken for profit, will promote the public interest. It is to this second issue that I now turn.

The coincidence of private and public interest, subject to important qualifications which are not our present concern, was seen, by Adam Smith and others, to depend on the profits earned in different trades tending towards a uniform level. It was perceived, albeit broadly, that if the profits in one line exceeded those in another, the satisfaction of consumers, as measured by what they were prepared to pay, would be increased by a transfer of resources.

The tendency for a uniform rate of profit to be established (with differences attributable to differential risk) depends on the prevalence of effective competition, but by no means on the conditions of perfect competition. We observed earlier how routine innovation, in a regime of economic freedom, acts to undermine established positions and abnormal profits associated with them. Both the differentiation and the continuous development of products create a powerful tendency towards an equilibrium in which profit rates are uniform, however marked the dispersion of rates at any particular time. They also make it possible, as we earlier observed, for effective competition to be compatible with increasing returns to scale.

The key question, therefore, assuming a system which adequately fulfils the informational requirements, is whether the existence of a tendency for profits towards uniformity promotes a rational allocation of resources. That there is a broad presumption in favour of this conclusion I do not doubt, but a strict demonstration of its truth seems impossible.

The major problem is not created by abandoning the assumption of a fixed list of goods and accepting the reality of routine innovation; the profit motive will induce firms to balance the gain from product development, in terms of a better price, against its cost, their decisions thus taking account of the strength of consumer preference for novelty or improvement. The profit motive will also ensure that investment in innovation will be directed, just as investment in capacity, in accordance with consumers' demands. It is right to point out how much of economic activity within a market economy can be described as knowledge seeking, but right also to recognize that knowledge seeking itself takes place within a framework of competitively determined prices that reflect the scarcity of resources and the strength of consumer demands. The reality of continuous product development, therefore, does not seem to me to invalidate the proposition that, subject of course to other reservations, the profit motive will lead to a rational allocation of resources.

Considerably more difficulty is presented by the prevalence of increasing returns. We have already observed that this condition is compatible with effective competition and its consequent tendency towards an equilibrium in which profit rates, adjusted to compensate for different degrees of risk, will be uniform. But, in this situation, unlike the general equilibrium associated with perfect competition, the prices of products will not equal their marginal costs, for the reason that, under increasing returns, marginal cost will be less than average cost. It is therefore not possible to say, as in the case of perfect competition, that the associated equilibrium configuration is also an optimal one. The criteria for a rational allocation of resources, developed on the assumption of decreasing returns, appear no longer to apply.

These criteria, we must remember, are associated with the stationary state in which, production possibilities and preferences remaining unchanged, the production of each good continues at the same rate indefinitely. Optimal allocation, in so far as final output is concerned, is then specified in terms of what these rates should be. Within the more realistic context which we have assumed, where products will after a time be superseded, this is not the issue; we have to be chiefly concerned with how much of a good should be produced in total, and of course, with whether it should be produced at all.

If a firm invests successfully, the total receipts from the sale of the product will exceed the development, production and marketing costs incurred. Consumers will have been willing to part with a sum equal to these total receipts in order to obtain the product, which, we can therefore presume, was worth more to them than the cost of the resources used to produce it. This may be accepted as providing at least some indication that welfare has been increased by the production of the good. Nevertheless, we cannot conclude that resources have been allocated optimally; although competition creates a tendency for prices to equal average costs, prices will exceed marginal costs, and to an extent that will generally differ from one product to another.

A free enterprise system, therefore, on the face of it, will not result in an optimal allocation of resources, the presumption being, to put the matter at its simplest, that there will be underinvestment in the directions where increasing returns are most marked, and the difference between average and marginal costs is therefore greatest. Given this circumstance, it seems possible, at least in principle, to improve matters by a reallocation of resources, such as might be promoted, say, by taxing industries subject to decreasing returns in order to subsidize those subject to increasing returns.[7]

In interpreting this conclusion, however, the informational issue is crucial. So long as we think solely of the pure logic of choice, of the dispositions to be made by some omniscient, central authority, the resource allocation produced under free enterprise will indeed seem inferior to that which such an authority could make, although it is fair to say that even the *logic* of efficient allocation in such circumstances is hardly well developed. The case against free enterprise, however, becomes much less than compelling once we accept that, as there does not exist, never will exist, and never could exist, such an omniscient authority, the task of economic organization is to make the best of the uncertain and distributed knowledge at society's disposal.

Under free enterprise, the goods produced will be those which firms expect to be profitable, and there are unlikely to exist better estimates of profitability than those made by the investing firms, given that they best have the knowledge, as well as the incentive, to get it right. Even if profitability is an imperfect indicator of whether a good should be produced, it is hard to see what other could, in general, be put in its place. Within the free enterprise system, moreover, firms will seek to adapt their pricing strategies to increasing returns. The publisher of a new title, for example, knows that his unit costs will fall with the volume of output planned, and will seek, as far as is practicable, to maximize revenue by differential pricing. Following dear hardback editions, at an interval, with cheap paperback ones is a common enough device of this kind. Where price discrimination is practised, in one way or another, total receipts will be influenced by the extent of consumer surplus generated by a product, so that profitability is probably made a better test of whether, and on what scale, it should be produced.

We should also recognize that, although government, seeking to take account of the differing incidence of increasing or decreasing cost, will lack the knowledge systematically to apply a system of taxes and subsidies across the whole of industry, it may have the information to justify a subsidy in a particular case. It may be possible to make a reliable estimate that the cost of building a bridge could be met from toll charges, thus justifying its existence; having done so, and recognizing that the marginal cost of using the bridge is virtually zero, it may be best not to charge, costs being met out of taxation. In the case of competing software programs, on the other hand, such a strategy would not be appropriate, even although their use would likewise incur virtually zero marginal cost. No-one is likely to be able to know in advance which of them will be most successful and it is therefore better to put their profitability to the test.

Let us now turn our attention to one further circumstance which weakens the presumption that a firm, in pursuit of profit, will promote an optimal allocation of resources, namely, the fact that the return from an investment may be highly uncertain, particularly if it is to be long deferred. Firms are likely to discriminate against investments, on account of their risk, and, from society's point of view, it is right that they should do so. It is by no means obvious, however, that the degree to which they discount the return from an investment, on account of its uncertainty, will be that which is socially appropriate. I have endeavoured to address this complex issue elsewhere (Richardson, 1960/1990, Pt III), but its proper consideration must lie outside the scope of this chapter. One recalls Keynes's famous observation that 'our basis of knowledge for estimating the yield ten years hence of a railway, a copper mine, a textile factory, the goodwill of a patent medicine, an Atlantic liner, a building in the City of London amounts to little and sometimes to nothing; or even five years hence', and his resultant conclusion that investment may often be sustained only by 'animal spirits' (GT: 149–50).

Considerations of this kind point up the limitations of formal economic theory, whether positive or normative. Uncertainty has to do with attitudes as well as evidence, and the attitudes, habits and psychology of the members of a community will not be independent of the type of economic system in which they live currently, or have lived in the past. I have suggested that normative theory, in appraising the efficiency of an economic system, should take account of informational considerations that have generally been neglected, but there are yet other relevant considerations which cannot be brought into formal analysis. Economic theory is an indispensable instrument of analysis, but effective only when we are aware of its limitations.

NOTES

1. The distinction between economic statics and economic dynamics is usefully discussed by Sir John Hicks in his *Methods of Dynamic Economics* (1985). He is concerned with the issues with which I shall be dealing, but follows an approach different from my own.
2. I have in mind, of course, Walras's *prix criés au hazard*, Edgeworth's recontracting, and the sophisticated developments of these devices proposed by Arrow and Debreu.
3. As Walras (1954: 374) notes:

    > The law of supply and demand regulates all these exchanges of commodities just as the law of universal gravitation regulates the movements of all celestial bodies. Thus the system of the economic universe reveals itself, at last, in all its grandeur and complexity; a system at once vast and simple, which, for sheer beauty, resembles the astronomic universe.

4. There is now an extensive literature on this subject. Professor Edith Penrose, in *The Theory of the Growth of the Firm* (1955/1995) must have been one of the first contributors and Professor Brian Loasby has since notably defined and developed the idea. I discussed it in an article 'The Organisation of Industry' (1972), reprinted as an annex to the second edition of my *Information and Investment*.
5. I originally drew attention to, and sought to explain this phenomenon in 'The Organisation of Industry' referred to above.
6. This observation has to be interpreted with care. Increasing returns characterize processes and lead, not necessarily to larger firms, but to specialization. It is in this connection that Adam Smith states that 'the Division of Labour is limited by the Extent of the Market', and offers us, in effect, a theory of endogenous growth. This is discussed in my essay 'Adam Smith on Competition and Increasing Returns' (1975).
7. All this, of course, is in Marshall (1920: ch. 13), in which he considers whether the benefits of subsidizing goods produced under conditions of increasing returns would offset the 'indirect evils of artificial arrangements for this purpose'.

3. On the issue of realism in the economics of institutions and organizations: themes from Coase and Richardson

Uskali Mäki

I INTRODUCTION

As suggested on an earlier occasion, the new economics of institutions and organizations deserves special attention by those who are interested in methodological issues in economics (Mäki, 1993b). There appears to be an opportunity for mutual benefit from a closer contact between economic methodology and this broad and varied field of economics. On the one hand, like many other young and burgeoning fields, the new economics of institutions abounds with intriguing methodological issues awaiting the touch of methodologists equipped with sophisticated tools of meta-analysis. Contributions to the resolution of these open methodological issues may turn out to be contributions towards the resolution of some of the more substantive issues in the field at large. On the other hand, economic methodology as a semi-autonomous subfield of study is in need of reorientation, and for this it needs to develop more intimate forms of interaction between methodological theory and the substance of economics. One way of accomplishing this is to acquire empirical evidence pertaining to economics by looking more closely at what economists in this thriving field are doing, what their theories are like, and how they themselves perceive the nature of their endeavour.

Most practitioners in the economics of institutions and organizations share a concern for realisticness of theories. This chapter suggests steps towards an analysis of this concern by examining the ideas of two modern classics in the field, Ronald Coase and George Richardson. There is much that these economists share. First, both have been in the periphery rather than in the very core of the mainstream of economics, at least in regard to the reception of their work as well as their perception of the orientation of the discipline they recommend. Some of Coase's ideas have been acknowledged, albeit with quite some delay, on a broad enough basis to win him the Nobel Prize. Richardson's ideas are celebrated by many, but their full recognition is still to come.[1] Second, both are critical of textbook neoclassicism, the model of perfect competition in particular, as well as related trends in orientation or approach in research. Third, both believe that the study of institutions and organizations is not only indispensable but also one of the key tasks of economics. Fourth, both are methodologically reflective upon what is good and what is bad in economics. They agree that economics has to be more realistic than what is provided by textbook neoclassicism. They even agree on some major forms of 'realisticness' that they find as virtues of theories.

Even though Coase and Richardson share at least this much, they do not share an economic theory.[2] This is an indication of the possibility of agreement on what makes an economic theory good, on the one hand, and disagreement on which theories are good theories, on the other. The criteria of goodness do not uniquely determine the choice of theory (see Mäki, 1994).

The chapter will focus on what the two economists share. Both Coase and Richardson believe that conventional economics is too narrow, in that it excludes factors that should not be excluded. In this sense they hold that conventional theory is 'unrealistic' and that theory should be made more 'realistic' by incorporating some of the excluded factors. This will be conceptualized as the issue of isolation and de-isolation. Coase and Richardson also share a stronger idea, namely what appears to be an *abstract ontological constraint* on theorizing. This is the idea that it is the task of economics to inform us about 'the way the world works'. This serves as a constraint on the choices concerning the theoretical isolations and de-isolations adopted by economists.

II   THE QUEST FOR REALISTICNESS

The quest for realistic theories has been a recurrent theme in Coase's methodological pronouncements. This seems to have been one of his major concerns from the beginning of his career:

> My article ['The nature of the firm'] starts by making a methodological point: it is desirable that the assumptions we make in economics should be realistic. Most readers will pass over these opening sentences . . . and others will excuse what they read as a youthful mistake, believing, as so many modern economists do, that we should choose our theories on the basis of the accuracy of their predictions, the realism of their assumptions being utterly irrelevant. I did not believe this in the 1930s and, as it happens, I still do not. (Coase, 1993b: 52)

Richardson agrees on the need to construe theories with assumptions that are realistic or more realistic than in conventional neoclassical theorising. The second sentence of his chapter in the present volume states: 'The aim of this paper is to provide, on the basis of assumptions more realistic than those normally made, a theoretical analysis of the process of resource allocation within free enterprise systems' (Richardson, in this volume). Now, given the ambiguity of the attributes 'realistic' and 'unrealistic' (see, for example, Mäki, 1989, 1994, 1998c), we cannot yet pretend to understand what Coase and Richardson have in mind when they argue for realistic assumptions. This implies that we cannot yet decide whether they are making the same claim, that is, whether both of them want assumptions to be realistic in the same sense. They share the idea in the abstract, but to see whether they share the idea when it is specified in more concrete terms, we need to examine what they mean by 'realistic'. I will follow a major line of thought that the two authors pursue.

Before proceeding to the main body of the discussion, let me mention one form of unrealisticness which seems to be shared by the two economists. Coase's notion of what he calls 'blackboard economics'[3] is somewhat ambiguous, but there is at least one meaning that we can also find in Richardson. Here is one of Coase's formulations: in his characterization of marginal cost pricing, he says that this policy 'is largely without merit', and asks:

> 'How then can one explain the widespread support that it has enjoyed in the economics profession? I believe it is the result of economists using an approach which I have termed 'blackboard economics'. The policy under consideration is one which is implemented on the blackboard. All the information needed is assumed to be available and the teacher plays all the parts. He fixes prices, imposes taxes, and distributes subsidies (on the blackboard) to promote the general welfare. But there is no counterpart to the teacher within the real economic system. There is no one who is entrusted with the task that is performed on the blackboard . . . Blackboard economics . . . misdirects our attention when thinking about economic policy. (Coase, 1988b: 19–20)

Richardson is talking about the same phenomenon when referring to the 'confusion' which

> we might term a confusion of perspective, to denote the failure to distinguish clearly enough between the point of vision of the model-builder himself and that of his creatures within the model. For the creator there is no problem of knowledge, for the objective facts about the system appear as postulated data from which could be deduced (or so it was believed) the equilibrium configuration. Was it always appreciated that information about these 'determinants', that 'perfect knowledge', in this sense, would have been of no use to the members of the system even if they could ever have been assumed to possess it? (Richardson, 1960: 40)

Thus it seems that Coase and Richardson share a concern about the pitfalls of a mismatch between the informational considerations on the blackboard or in the model, on the one hand, and those in the real world of agents, on the other. Our focus in what follows will be on a somewhat different, yet related, form of unrealisticness.

III BROADENING THE THEORY

There is one obvious and common form of 'unrealisticness' that is shared by Coase and Richardson: a theory is unrealistic if it is 'unjustifiably' narrow' – that is, if it excludes from consideration factors that are deemed important. Both think that standard neoclassical theory is unrealistic in this sense: it excludes factors that should be included in the theory. To put it in other words, conventional neoclassical theory isolates from factors that should be explicitly theorized; thus, the theory should be de-isolated so as to incorporate these factors (see Mäki, 1992a, 1993a).

However, and this is where Coase and Richardson part company, they do not share the idea of where to start de-isolating the theory, that is, what precisely to include that was excluded from consideration. Any theory excludes an enormous number of elements in reality. From this set of excluded elements, one may then only choose for inclusion a small subset comprising those that are found most important. Coase and Richardson choose somewhat differently. For Coase, the most important element to be included is transaction costs; for Richardson, it is the process of information acquisition that will ensure the satisfaction of what he calls the 'informational requirements'. Both also mention other excluded factors that they think should be included.

For Coase, the incorporation of positive transaction costs required the relaxation of the assumption of zero transaction costs, which 'is, of course, a very unrealistic assumption' (Coase, 1960: 15). With the relaxation of this assumption, the theory could be broadened by way of theoretical de-isolation. The item thereby incorporated is what he calls 'the missing element' in economic theory (Coase, 1993c: 62). This is not the only missing item, however: 'No doubt other factors should also be added'(Coase, 1988b: 30).

Richardson, at the very end of his contribution to the present volume, stresses his main theme by saying that economists 'should take account of informational considerations that have generally been neglected' and then goes on to suggest that 'there are yet other relevant considerations which cannot be brought into formal analysis'. There is a lot that has been neglected, but not all of these factors can be incorporated into formal theory. 'Economic theory is an indispensable instrument of analysis, but effective only when we are aware of its limitations' (ibid.). Yet much that has been excluded can and should be included. Among them are product and process innovations. Richardson blames standard theory for '[c]hoosing to set aside, or assume away, the fact that products and processes are subject to continuous development' (1997: 11). This is not an innocent exclusion, since 'the habit of abstracting from product development, the pace of which has been accelerating, may have led economists to view the real world as much less competitive than businessmen know it to be' (1997: 18).

Coase is explicit that some of the excluded factors are those that characterize the internal organization of the business firm, thus leading to a notion of the firm as a black box:[4]

> The concentration on the determination of prices has led to a narrowing of focus which has had as a result the neglect of other aspects of the economic system. . . . What happens in between the purchase of the factors of production and the sale of the goods that are produced by these factors is largely ignored. . . . The firm in mainstream economic theory has often been described as a 'black box'. And so it is. This is very extraordinary given that most resources in a modern economic system are employed within firms, with how these resources are used dependent on administrative decisions and not directly on the operation of a market. Consequently, the efficiency of the economic system depends to a very considerable extent on how these organisations conduct their affairs, particularly, of course, the modern corporation. Even more surprising, given their interest in the pricing system, is the neglect of the market or more specifically the institutional arrangements which govern the process of exchange. (Coase, 1993[1992]: 229)[5]

Richardson shares the belief that price theory gives an overly narrow, if not distorted, picture of economic reality; he also thinks that its prominence may be based on the mechanical analogy borrowed from physics:

> if we are led to study the informational aspects of social systems only in terms of a rigid conceptual framework borrowed from physics, we shall certainly obtain a distorted picture. Prices, for example, and particularly the current values of prices, assume from this point of view an undeserved prominence, because it is in terms of them that a quasi-physical signalling mechanism can be elaborated and given mathematical expression. (Richardson, 1960: 41)

Coase puts some of the blame on the conception of economics as a theory of choice which has contributed to the exclusion of the human and institutional 'substance' of the economy from theoretical consideration:

> This preoccupation of economists with the logic of choice . . . has nonetheless had, in my view, serious adverse effects on economics itself. One result of this

divorce of the theory from its subject matter has been that the entities whose decisions economists are engaged in analysing have not been made the subject of study and in consequence lack any substance. The consumer is not a human being but a consistent set of preferences. The firm to an economist . . . is effectively defined as a cost curve and a demand curve . . . Exchange takes place without any specification of its institutional setting. We have consumers without humanity, firms without organisation, and even exchange without markets. (Coase, 1988b: 3)

Now economists have an amazing variety of grounds for thinking of a given theory as unrealistic, but a major one is certainly the perception of the theory as excessively narrow, or partial, or isolative. As the above quotations indicate, this is also one of Coase's and Richardson's critical perceptions of standard neoclassical theory. Their quest for realisticness here takes on the form of insisting on the de-isolation of the theoretical picture of the economy by incorporating neglected elements into the theory. Thus the relevant meaning of 'making economic theory more realistic' here is 'broadening economic theory', or, in other words, 'de-isolating economic theory'.[6]

IV THE WAY THE WORLD WORKS

I have shown that Coase and Richardson share the belief that the conventional picture of the organization of the economy misses some items. The task, they think, is to include those factors, to de-isolate the theory by incorporating them into the theory. Of course, not everything is to be included. Both Coase and Richardson are aware of the triviality that complete 'unrealisticness' is neither possible nor desirable. Coase says that

our assumptions should not be completely realistic. There are factors we leave out because we do not know how to handle them. There are others we exclude because we do not feel the benefits of a more complete theory would be worth the costs involved in including them . . . Again, assumptions about other factors do not need to be realistic because they are completely irrelevant. (Coase, 1988c: 66)

In other words, Coase is comfortable with a theory being isolative in general, provided there are good reasons for this, such as the ones he cites above.[7] The opening page of Richardson's *Information and Investment* hints at this possibility in the case of the perfect competition model: 'The conditions which define it, as everyone knows, are rarely, if ever, characteristic of the real world, but it can be argued that this divergence represents no more than the normal degree of abstraction associated with general theoretical models' (Richardson, 1960: 1). However, there are limits to unrealisticness, including narrowness or isolativeness; some items simply cannot be excluded. This is the fundamental message shared by Coase and Richardson. They also share an idea of what determines these limits. These limits, they believe, are determined by our conception of *the way the world works*.

Coase and Richardson believe not only that the conventional picture is narrow – every theory is, strictly speaking, narrow – but that it is narrow in unduly excluding important factors. The next question is to ask, what is it that makes those factors *important*? Why are they claimed to be *unduly* excluded? Why should *precisely they*, and not some other factors, be included? In order to answer these questions, something else is needed. I suggest that, in the case of Coase and Richardson, this something else amounts to the invocation of the notion of *the way the world works*. Indeed, Coase and Richardson share the important idea that it is the task of economics to give an account of the way the world works. Plenty of documentation can be provided in support of this suggestion.

Let us first look at Richardson. It is no accident that the subtitle of Richardson's main work, *Information and Investment*, is *A Study in the Working of the Competitive Economy*. Indeed, it is a recurring theme of the book that it is the task of economics to give an account of how the economy 'works'. Richardson's persistent critique of the perfect competition model is telling. The second page of *Information and Investment* summarizes his critique of the model precisely for failing to account for the world's workings: 'Perfect competition, I shall affirm, represents a system in which entrepreneurs would be unable to obtain the minimum necessary information; for this reason, it cannot serve as a model of the working of actual competitive economies' (Richardson, 1960: 2). Here is the claim put in more specific terms:

> I feel convinced that one of the essential elements of any adequate account of the attainment of equilibrium has not been provided; for the most part, indeed, the need for it has been ignored. No explanation has been given of how, in the conditions which define the perfectly competitive model, entrepreneurs could obtain the information on which their expectations, and therefore the investment plans required for equilibrium, would have to be based. (Ibid.: 23–4)

Note that Richardson says that considerations of information are supposed to be 'one of the essential elements' involved in the process of 'the attainment of equilibrium' and that the model under criticism fails to incorporate this essential element. In his contribution to the present volume, Richardson puts the idea explicitly in terms of the working of the world:

Whatever insights the theory of perfect competition may have given us, it fails to provide . . . a convincing account of how free enterprise economies in fact work . . . And this failure results from its neglect of what we may call the *informational requirements* of any workable system, the conditions that must be realized, that is, in order that those within it can have sufficient knowledge to take investment decisions. (Richardson, this volume: 16 original emphasis)

He goes on to explain why he thinks the model of perfect competition fails in accounting for the way the system works:

By abstracting from some of the circumstances of real economic life, we have, paradoxically, made it more difficult, if not impossible, to explain how the system works. I have argued elsewhere that markets generally operate not despite, but because of, some 'imperfection' of competition, because of the existence, that is, of circumstances which, although excluded by definition from the perfect competition model, fulfil the informational requirements of the system by endowing the business environment with a high degree of stability sufficient to make informed investment decisions possible. (Ibid.)

The 'imperfections' that Richardson refers to are precisely the kind of institutional features of economies the study of which has preoccupied the economics of institutions recently, including forms of information sharing such as signalling, price agreements and vertical integration, as well as reputation and trust. Such 'imperfections' reduce the cost of information and constitute commitments, and thereby facilitate the coordination of competitive and complementary investments. The 'imperfections' are among the core elements in the way the world works. To understand the workings of the economic world one has to understand such institutional features. Such understanding is not provided by the model of perfect competition:

Perfect competition earned its reputation as an ideal market structure because of the belief that, to the extent that the conditions defining it were realised, resources would be allocated so as to exhaust all profit opportunities. No one, in my view, ever provided a fully satisfactory explanation of how this was to come about . . . the conditions favourable to successful adjustment are not those laid down in the perfectly competitive model. (Richardson, 1964: 160,161)

Richardson's thought is that the process of adjustment is part of the way the world works. If an account of this process is not incorporated into one's economic theory, then the theory is seriously defective precisely in failing to grasp the world's workings (see Mäki, 1992b).

To understand (even the possibility of) successful adjustment, Richardson argues that we need to incorporate institutional features in the economy. This happens as a consequence of relaxing assumptions such as those of perfect information, atomistic firms and homogeneous goods, and of paying attention to the ways in which the 'informational requirement' is met. In the imperfect information world, institutions matter. There is a parallel logical structure in Coase's account. By relaxing the zero transaction cost assumption, that is by incorporating positive transaction costs into his account, Coase was not only able, but also was forced, to incorporate institutional features that were previously neglected in systematic analysis. In the positive transaction cost world, institutions matter.

We cannot yet pretend to fully understand the notion of the world's working as it appears in Richardson and Coase. What does it mean, precisely? Why does one theory fail and why does another theory succeed in representing the way the world works? A complete account would be impossible to pursue here, but one observation can be provided. An element of ontic necessity – necessity *de re* rather than just *de dicto* – appears to be involved. Let us look at Richardson, who is more explicit about this. He puts the idea variously, including references to 'conceivable' systems and to some elements being 'essential' or 'necessary' for the functioning of the system. Here is an example:

> Irreducible uncertainty, as a factor in any *conceivable* economic system, owes its existence, in part, to incomplete information about preferences and production functions. In much of economic theory, this incompleteness is ignored . . . But where the object is to study the working of a competitive economy, the question of the availability of information *cannot* thus be pushed aside. (1960: 81; emphases added)

He also says that 'some market imperfections may be *essential* to the process of successful economic adjustment' (1960: 38; emphasis added) and that 'the conditions which define the system of perfect competition are not such as would *permit* the economic adjustments required' (1960: 10; emphasis added). As Loasby puts it, Richardson's 'conclusion is that in perfecting the model of perfectly competitive equilibrium, economists have refined away the essential mechanism' (Loasby, 1986: 152). Here is yet another way of formulating the idea: 'By assuming, overtly or tacitly, that [the optimum strength for these restraints] is zero, and therefore by neglecting the whole problem of information, the perfect competition model condemns itself not only to unrealism but to *inadequacy even as a hypothetical system.*' (Richardson, 1960: 69; emphasis added). The following may be taken as an explanation of what Richardson means by 'inadequacy even as a hypothetical system':

> It is no defence to appeal, moreover, to the analogy of mechanical statics which, though neglecting friction, can still identify the equilibrium position of a system of forces, for we cannot demonstrate that economic systems have such positions

of rest without reference to expectations and information which *could not* be presumed to be available in the absence of restraints. (1960: 69; emphasis added)

Thus 'inadequacy even as a hypothetical system' can be taken to mean something like 'ontic impossibility'. This can then be taken to imply that there are some ontically *necessary* features that a system has to possess to count as *adequate* 'even as a hypothetical system'.

To sum up, there seem to be two ontically necessary connections envisaged by Richardson. One is that information is necessary for successful adjustment. The other is that 'restraints' are necessary for information. And since these restraints appear in the form of institutions – 'customs, conventions, and the laws' (1960: 69) – this implies that a theory about the working of the competitive economy has to incorporate institutions. This is a theoretical necessity suggested by the two ontic necessities. I think it is fair to say that this conception has an essentialist leaning to it.

Let us then briefly discuss Coase's version of the idea of the world's workings. We have already cited Coase's complaint about economics which theorizes 'consumers without humanity, firms without organisation, and even exchange without markets' (Coase, 1988b: 3). Let us try to see what grounds Coase has for this complaint. Such grounds are far from intuitively obvious provided we have any respect for scientific theories that study planets without extension, planes without friction, and molecules without colour. Coase explains that it took him a long time to realize that 'the whole of economic theory would be transformed by incorporating transaction costs into the analysis' (Coase, 1993c: 62). The somewhat revolutionary tone in this judgment can only be understood as reflecting the idea that transaction costs constitute a major factor in economic reality and that its inclusion in theory has major consequences for economics. But what does 'major' mean here? It does not just designate the idea that here we have another 'factor' which has a large impact on economic phenomena and therefore had better be included in explanation. More is involved than just causal relevance, namely what we might call *ontic indispensability*. The introduction of positive transaction costs in the theory brings with it new kinds of entities, namely institutions, such as legal rules and contractual structures. If it is held that such institutions play an *indispensable* and *powerful* role in the functioning of the economy, it would be inexcusable to exclude them from the analysis.

This suggestion is based on a central idea that occurs frequently in Coase's writings, namely that it is the task of economic theory to provide 'insight into how the system works' (Coase, 1988c: 64). He argues that 'realism [that is realisticness] of assumptions is needed if our theories are ever to help us understand why the system works in the way it does' (ibid.: 65). Of course, by this he must mean realisticness subject to the ontic constraint – and this leaves room for plenty of legitimate unrealisticness.

The idea that there is a way in which 'the economic system works' suggests that the complaint about a 'missing element' in theory is in effect a complaint about an indispensable *missing link* in the working of the real system; without this link, the system would not function as it does – or would not function at all. Therefore this link has to be theorized in order to understand how the system works. There is an essentialist flavour in Coase's view, too, amounting to the suggestion that some sort of necessity is involved: 'The solution was to realise that there were costs of making transactions in a market economy and that it was *necessary* to incorporate them in the analysis' (Coase, 1993a: 46; emphasis added). He says that the point of theorizing is 'to get to the essence of what [is] going on in the economic system' (Coase, 1988c: 68).

V REALISM

I have pointed out that Coase and Richardson think not only that economic theory has to be broadened by incorporating some missing items, but also that the required theoretical isolations and de-isolations are constrained by our conception of how the world works. It may be said that both economists argue for increased realisticness as a property of economic theory. What precisely does this have to do with realism as a philosophical theory of theories?

As we know, the notion of realism is ambiguous in many ways. The term 'realism' is used by economists to designate ideas about some properties of theories and their constituent parts, such as assumptions and concepts. This may be misleading, since it may be taken to suggest that those who advocate more 'realism' in theories also hold realism as a theory of theories. It is important to keep in mind that realism is a family of philosophical doctrines, while realisticness is a family of properties of theories and their constituent elements. Both families are large and, in many cases, their members do not mesh easily. That is, the advocacy of realisticness does not always imply the advocacy of realism, nor is it always – that is, in all senses of 'realistic' – a necessary condition of realism. But sometimes they do go together. In the case of Coase and Richardson they do. Note that, while it can be argued that Friedman, even if *opposing* realistic assumptions, is a realist (Mäki, 1992b), it can be argued that Coase and Richardson, who *endorse* realistic assumptions and theories, are also advocates of realism.

The underlying presupposition here is that there is, as an objective fact in economic reality, such a thing as 'the way the world works'. This is in line with ontological realism. The requirement that it be the task of theory to capture the way the world works amounts to a quest for realisticness: the theory should be a true representation of the workings of the world. This is in line with semantic realism. The idea is that there is a fact of the matter about the functioning of the economic system, and that it is the task of theorizing to represent this objective circumstance as truly as possible. Ontologically, Coase and Richardson might think that reality is objectively organized into systems and that there is a characteristic way in which the systems function. Implying the modal idea of necessity *de re*, they may think that the presence of certain elements is necessary for the functioning of a given system, while some others are not. In theorizing, it is permissible and advisable to leave out the latter, but it would be inexcusable not to be realistic about the former. As cited above, Coase believes that the point of theorizing is 'to get to the essence of what [is] going on in the economic system' (Coase, 1988c: 68). The realist interpretation of this idea presupposes that 'the essence' of how the economic system works is something objectively real rather than created by our theoretical endeavours.

It is illuminating to contrast this idea with the view that Richard Posner expressed in the context of his critique of Coase's views. Posner put forth what may be characterized, without much hesitation, as an instrumentalist claim, namely that

> a model can be a useful tool of discovery even if it is unrealistic, just as Ptolemy's astronomical theory was a useful tool of navigation . . . even though its basic premise was false . . . We should be pragmatic about theory. It is a tool, rather than a glimpse of ultimate truth, and the criterion of a tool is its utility. (Posner, 1993: 77)

In other words, Posner is comfortable with an astronomical theory which represents the structure of the solar system as being diametrically opposite to what we have every reason to believe it in fact is. It is obvious that such a theory cannot tell us how the solar system works, even though it may, in some circumstances, be useful for predictive purposes. Given Coase's interest in how the system under study functions, he would not be content with Ptolemaic theory. He would prefer Copernican heliocentrism to the false geocentrism, even if the Copernican theory has many minor details wrong and may therefore fail in predictions. As Coase says, 'Faced with a choice between a theory which predicts well but gives us little insight into how the system works and one which gives us this insight but predicts badly, I would choose the latter' (Coase, 1988c: 64).[8]

Coase may think that, just as it is part of the essence of the solar system that the planets revolve around the sun and not vice versa, it is part of the essence of the economic system that institutions are there to reduce transaction costs. Without having these essential core ideas right in one's theories, no understanding of how the respective systems work is forthcoming. The 'essentialist' ingredient in this view is that such missing elements in Ptolemaic and conventional neoclassical theories are essential elements. The realist ingredient is that such elements and the systems they constitute are objectively real, unconstituted by the respective theories. A similar argument might be applied to Richardson's views.[9]

VI   CONCLUSION

Coase and Richardson admit that all theories are bound to be unrealistic in the trivial sense of excluding much, in being isolative. But they also think that there are limits to narrowness. The appropriate isolations have to meet an ontological constraint provided by a well grounded conception of the way the economic system works. They further believe that the model of perfect competition does not meet the constraint, and therefore cannot be taken as an adequate representation of the core or essence of the competitive economy – not even as a hypothetical possibility. The need for de-isolation, for incorporating institutional 'imperfections', is ontologically grounded. The idea is not the simple one that these 'imperfections' are really causally significant, and therefore should be included, but rather that they play an essential role in the working of the world, and that therefore they play an indispensable role in theory.

A meta-methodological remark of self-characterization may conclude this exercise. The approach followed in the foregoing discussion is not a top-down one, purporting to impose on some part of economics a ready-made philosophical system adopted, perhaps in an authoritarian manner, from a more or less profound philosopher. It is rather a bottom-up approach, trying to extract a meta-theoretical lesson from the substantive economics and meta-theoretical remarks of two important economists.

NOTES

1.   It took three decades for Coase's 'The nature of the firm' (1937) to make a major impact on the theory of the firm, while 'The problem of social cost' (1960) was recognized almost immediately, launching a new research field, law and economics. Richardson's main work, *Information and Investment* (1st edn 1960; 2nd edn, 1990) is being rediscovered by an increasing number of economists studying the institutional organization of the economy.
2.   In a footnote to his 1972 article, Richardson explains what appears to be a fairly small difference between his view of the market–firm boundary and that of Coase:

The explanation that I have provided is not inconsistent with his but might be taken as giving content to the notion of this relative cost [of the coordination by firm and market, respectively] by specifying the factors that affect it. My own approach differs also in that I distinguish explicitly between inter-firm cooperation and market transactions as modes of coordination. (Richardson, 1972: 896n)

3. For a fairly detailed analysis of the concept of 'blackboard economics' in Coase, see Mäki (1998a).
4. The exclusion of internal characteristics of the objects under study (such as the internal organization of business firms) amounts to what may be called 'internal isolation' in contrast to 'external isolation' which is a matter of excluding characteristics of the system surrounding the object (such as other markets in partial equilibrium analysis); see Mäki, 1992a, for details.
5. Given statements like this, it is not surprising that Coase is critical of what he finds as the dominance of price theory in microeconomics. Note that it may be somewhat misleading to say that standard microeconomic theory is characterized by 'the concentration on the determination of prices'. Standard price theory, of course, never provided an account of the *determination* of relative prices, in the sense of the process whereby prices are formed; of course, this is not the unique meaning of 'determination', which is an ambiguous expression. This is relevant from the point of view of the idea of the world's working that I will suggest plays a central role in both Coase and Richardson.
6. More precisely, we are here talking about what I have elsewhere (Mäki, 1993a) termed 'horizontal de-isolation': de-isolation at a given level of abstraction or vertical isolation. Note that there seems to be a more general form in which the insistence on horizontal de-isolation appears in Coase. He is worried about the practice amongst economists of examining economic problems in separation from the complex context in which they are embedded. 'Any actual situation is complex and a single economic problem does not exist in isolation. Consequently, confusion is liable to result because economists dealing with an actual situation are attempting to solve several problems at once' (Coase, 1988[1946]: 77). In contrast to Coase's quest for horizontal de-isolation, he also insists on vertical de-isolation, that is, lowering the level of abstraction by engaging oneself in empirical case studies (see Mäki, 1998a).
7. For arguments that show why an economist espousing realism as a theory of theories is entitled or even required to use unrealistic assumptions, see Mäki (1992b, 1993a, 1994).
8. Coase is quite unambiguous in his rejection of the instrumentalist conception of theories: 'But a theory is not like an airline or bus timetable. We are not interested simply in the accuracy of its predictions. A theory also serves as a base of thinking. It helps us to understand what is going on' (Coase, 1988c: 64). Coase's point is, quite obviously, that, while bus timetables may help us predict the behaviour of buses and thus to serve as 'inference tickets', they fail to give us any idea about the mechanisms and processes that keep buses running as they do. For a critique of Posner's critique of Coase, see Mäki (1998b).
9. For a related, detailed argument that links realism to a specific version of the idea of 'how the system works', namely a causal theory of the market process, see Mäki (1992c, 1998d and chapters in Mäki, 2001).

4. Transactions costs and uncertainty: theory and practice

Peter J. Buckley and Malcolm Chapman[1]

I LONGITUDINAL AND COMPARATIVE RESEARCH ON TRANSACTIONS COSTS

Transactions costs exist in prospect, in retrospect and in process. Their analysis requires a many-faceted approach and poses a challenge for economics. Transaction costs have been described (by Williamson amongst others) as a bridge to other disciplines from economics, but it is essential to realize that bridges are often two-way conduits and that, through the analysis of transaction costs, economics opens itself up to alien influences.

Transactions cost-based decisions are non-routine. They cannot be covered by a management philosophy predicated on routine operations. Such decisions are analogous to innovation (for an analysis of the management of innovation see Buckley and Casson, 1992). The decisions involved are idiosyncratic and dynamic.

The dynamic nature of transaction costs opens up problem areas for traditional theory. Standard transaction costs analysis, based on a comparative static framework, runs the risk of justifying the (any) status quo, and has difficulty in specifying the conditions which shift the world from one state (a firm/market configuration, for example) to another. The elusive nature of transaction costs and their relationship to other types of cost are also in need of clarification.

There are essentially three ways of tackling this problem. The first is to adopt a *prospective* method, specifying a model by setting out the initial conditions, the key forces driving events and the mechanisms by which these independent variables affect the dependent variable. This is the economic methodology utilized by modellers, exemplified by Vernon's Product Cycle Model (1966), and by Buckley and Casson (1981, 1996) in examining the market servicing strategy of multinational firms.

The second approach is *retrospective*. Retrospective research methods take a point in time (the present) and look backward over a given time period to discover how the system arrived at its end point. This is the most usual method employed heretofore by internationalization researchers. It is the method used by the Uppsala School in producing their 'stages models' (Johanson and Wiedersheim-Paul, 1975; Johanson and Vahlne, 1977) and by one of the present authors in the Bradford studies of the internationalization of smaller firms (Newbould, Buckley and Thurwell, 1978; Buckley, Berkova and Newbould, 1983).

The third approach is *longitudinal* research. This method attempts to examine processes as they happen in real time by observation which is as close to the ethnographic method as possible. In practice this means repeated interviews with the protagonists as events unfold. To some degree this was the method attempted by Aharoni (1966), who tried to gain an understanding of the foreign investment *process*. This was only imperfectly realized and, like most studies, there is reliance on retrospective restructuring of material. In Buckley and Chapman (1998) we attempted to track decisions in prospect, at the time they are made, and in retrospect. Interviews are conducted with an open agenda in an attempt to allow managers to use the concepts with which they feel most comfortable – the categories of the observed, rather than the observer. This method also has a built-in check on veracity and on the retrospective rewriting of history, in that the manager being interviewed knows that the interviewers will return at some future date and will revisit the issues from the perspective of the then current time. Thus anticipation, failed strategies, chance events and changes in decision making can be more accurately pinpointed by a genuinely longitudinal method (Buckley and Chapman, 1996a, 1996b).

This chapter addresses a specific problem: what theoretical toolkit is necessary to conduct a longitudinal (or ethnographic) study of a firm? To undertake a social anthropological study of a corporation, using participant observation as classically understood, a researcher would need to work for the company for several years. Various problems arise, different from those facing the anthropologist working on a coral island.

Disclosure

Anthropologists traditionally came back from exotic fieldwork with a total conviction that the world of their research (coral island, tropical jungle, mountain village) was totally separate from the world of the academic publication. The classic anthropological monograph was about illiterate people speaking another language on the other side of the world. An anthropologist could say what he or she pleased, without any thoughts of confidentiality, libel, ethics, lawsuits and the like. An anthropologist could publish photographs of the naked savages, without any fear that the savages or their children or grandchildren, would turn up demanding reparation and apology. Anthropologists today are almost morbidly sensitive about this kind of problem. This sensitivity is of relatively recent date, however, and until the early 1960s no problem was perceived.

A company, unlike a primitive society, is potentially a highly sensitive and litigious organization. The researcher can have no illusions that the published findings will be confined, in their readership, to a small scholarly audience, or that the company in question will have no access to, no interest in, and no ability to read, the results. The information, moreover, is not just morally sensitive, but potentially commercially sensitive as well. This is not an issue with which social anthropologists have commonly had to deal.

Access

In many societies, there are no formal barriers to an anthropologist. Most anthropologists have not needed 'permission' to go and do their study. They have simply moved in with their tent, or rented their flat, and begun making local contacts. Company research is not like that. We can readily suppose that if an anthropologist wandered vaguely into the executive dining room, sat down and announced an intention of learning the local language and living there for three years, the security men would move in rather rapidly. The fact that all work must be done *by permission* somewhat changes the nature of the enquiry, and the possible results. As noted above, however, responsibility to the 'objects' of study is increasing everywhere in the anthropological universe, and to some extent the increase in problems of disclosure *everywhere* reduces the difference arising from the access problems as between corporate and non-corporate research.

Scope

Anthropologists tend to attempt to study the entirety of societies. This leaning towards holism has been important, since it helped to confirm the important break with atomistic positivism. It meant, however, for various reasons, that anthropologists had some difficulty bringing their methods back to 'complex' societies. If we are to follow the classical model, a social anthropologist studying (say) a pharmaceutical company is not just studying the company, but everything about the lives of everybody concerned, which leads out into all the other specialisms of modern academia: economics, demography, politics, religion, consumption, tourism, and so on. A manager's thought and actions *within* a company cannot be divorced from his or her thought and actions *outside* the company. This problem, within anthropology, has been extensively discussed; there is no space here for summary, but one might say that the characteristic solution so far has been to muddle through: 'holism', in some form, remains a potent idea, and one which anthropologists are reluctant to abandon, however complex the social reality.

Of crucial importance to the comparative method in research is choosing the right comparator. There are three basic possibilities (Buckley *et al.*, 1988: 195). First, there is the historical comparison – the situation relative to a different point of time. Second, there is the spatial comparison – relative to a different locational, national, cultural or regional point. Third, there is the counterfactual comparison – what might have been, had not a particular action been taken or event occurred (this method has been used to good effect by cliometricians). Of great importance in this type of research method is to ensure that as many factors as possible are held constant other than the research object which is being comparatively analysed.

If we see quantitative studies and longitudinal case studies as irreconcilable opposites, and used exclusively by different groups of researchers, this is no doubt to take too black-and-white a view of the matter. The most open-minded researchers, of course, use both. They may, however, as a result, find it difficult to accommodate their findings within a clear theoretical framework. It may be suggested that statistics collected primarily for other purposes and over large samples are (a) more objective in comparison with the 'subjectivity' of interviews, and (b) more readily generalizable across a wide population. However, there are great difficulties in using data collected for other purposes: definitions may not be congruent, particularly where cross-cultural comparisons are being made (see Buckley and Chapman, 1998). Good compromises are often made by business historians, who have proved successful in combining aggregative data and archival material in focusing on key research issues.

International business lends itself to this type of analysis and it is relatively well developed. Analyses of firms and nations over time are well established. National comparisons are the stock-in-trade of the international business research community which often takes advantage of the uniqueness of the multinational enterprise: the *same* firm operating in different national environments. Paired groups of firms (for example of different national ownerships within the same market) are also utilized. Counterfactual comparisons are also frequent, particularly in the analysis of foreign direct investment outcomes. The actual situation is often contrasted with 'the alternative position' – what would have happened if the investment under scrutiny had not taken place. The difficulty, of course, lies in specifying the feasible (or most likely) alternative position.

II THE MEASUREMENT OF TRANSACTION COSTS

This difficulty leads us to the heart of the issue of how transactions cost-reducing configurations come about. It is a fact that there is very little extant research in which transaction costs have been successfully measured. Buckley and Casson (1991: xiii) argued that: 'Problems in the definition and measurement of transaction costs have not yet been fully resolved; in particular the magnitude of these costs in relation to production, transport, marketing and distribution – as well as their spatial configuration – remains to be specified in detail.'

Similarly, Williamson (1975: 249) noted that 'recent efforts to introduce transaction costs into mathematical models of markets are as yet tentative and exploratory' and we can probably say the same again in 1996 (although see Williamson on this point, 1993: 456, n. 25). Innumerable analyses exist in which transaction costs are analysed and discussed in a context which is redolent of mensuration. In virtually all cases, however, we find that we are dealing with a comparative algebra of modelled transaction costs, not an empirically based mathematics; the terms of the argument are letters from the Greek and English alphabets, joined by $<$ and $=$ and $>$. Casson provides some rigorous and keenly interesting examples (see, for example, Casson, 1991: 48–51); at one point, however, we get a glimpse of the gulf between modelling of this kind and real-world enumeration, when Casson, slipping into another language, tells us that 'the amount of guilt, $g > 0$, is commensurate with output and effort, in terms of some *numéraire*' (Casson, 1991: 31).

An interesting, if oblique, light has been shed on transaction costs in a study of foreign licensing by Australian companies (Welch, 1993). Licensing has proved a most interesting test case, standing as it does as the market alternative to the internal absorption of technology (Buckley and Casson, 1976). Welch shows that fully 44.7 per cent of total establishment costs of licensing were represented by 'communication between involved parties' and 22.8 per cent in search costs for suitable licences. In addition, 9.7 per cent of total maintenance costs were 'audit of the licensee'. If all of these costs were transaction costs, then around 36 per cent of the total costs of licensing overseas could be considered as transaction costs. In addition, several of the other categories of cost could be taken to include transaction cost elements (see Welch, 1993: 88, table 8). Were this study to be redesigned to test the empirical importance of transaction costs directly, it would, of course, run into difficulties of precise definition and into the key issue that production and transaction costs interact and are not simply additive.

In a fully specified and ideally mensurable world, we might imagine that we could look, for example, at a single two-outcome decision, with implied future transaction costs, and put figures to these costs. The two outcomes are *A* and *B*. Their associated transaction costs are *X* and *Y*. We have measured *X* and *Y*, and we make a rational decision:

$$\text{If } X > Y, \text{ then } B$$
$$\text{If } X < Y, \text{ then } A$$

This makes textbook sense, and we can construct models within which transaction costs can be measured in advance and compared, just as can production costs or interest rate costs. From a strictly objective point of view, however, it is clear that we can never have access to both terms, *X* and *Y*, of the above equations, since only one outcome ever arises, after the decision is made. We can observe, in some way, one of the outcomes and its associated transaction costs; perhaps we can even make mensurational approaches to these. The other outcome, however, the one that did not happen, remains forever in the world of the imagination. Empirical comparison based upon actual observation is not available, either to a company or to a research worker. Even at its most optimistically objective and empirical, then, research or prediction in this area must of necessity stray well into the domain of the imaginary. The problem is graver still for those wedded to objectivism and enumeration. Transaction costs, one can generally say, are made up of elements which are exceptionally difficult to quantify; it is perhaps not an exaggeration to say that in many respects they are often outside the domain of quantification altogether. They are also, crucially, intertwined with costs normally enumerated as production costs.

This is not to say that the managers involved are making ill-considered, irrational, or unjustified decisions. Far from it; they are prepared to engage in long and thoughtful justifications of their activities and decisions. They always consider that they have valuable insight into the industry around them, which informs their decisions in a positive manner. They are almost without exception unaware of the existence of the theoretical discourse of Transaction Cost Economics, but they are necessarily engaged in decisions where transaction cost issues are paramount, and their discussions of these issues are often sophisticated. In no case, however, is enumeration brought to the issues. If costs are discussed, these are costs of production, selling or finance. A manager, for example, discussing the issue of whether to make or buy a component, in a situation where both were possible options, discusses the relative costs of in-house production versus the external price. The important issues of reliability of supply, trust, control, motivation and the like, however, are subject to an entirely different discourse, one whose terms are not numerical, but verbal: the mechanisms of decision are construed in terms of (for example) 'judgment', 'gut-feeling', 'intuition', 'experience', 'knowledge'. This proves true for a wide range of transaction cost problems. Managers, if offered the idea that there might exist an objective answer to the problems they face, typically laugh. 'Everybody knows the world is not like that!', or words to that effect, is a common riposte.

This, although not altogether surprising, has some major implications for our outlook upon research in these areas. We have argued that we are not, in retrospect, in any strong position to distinguish, empirically, between transaction cost outcomes based upon calculation and prescience, and transaction cost outcomes based upon random events and selection. When we come to attempts to tackle transaction cost issues in prospect, we find that, theoretically, a fully objective study is in any case not logically available. Managers who are actually engaged in decisions where transaction costs are at issue usually have no doubt in their own minds that they are making informed and intelligent decisions; but the material that they use to construct these decisions is not in any simple sense objective. Their choices are not random; that is very clear. But nor are their choices computationally rational, in the sense that the alternatives facing them can be fully costed and compared.

In such an environment, it is perhaps not helpful to continue to pretend that all the relevant transaction costs are really there to be measured, if only someone would take the trouble. The transaction costs that are really there, in the sense that they determine the outcome, are those transaction costs that are perceived by the manager (or managers) who make the decisions. Both sets of perceived transaction costs have social existence in advance of the decision, and can be compared, which is theoretically satisfactory. If a manager perceives the future costs of buying the small supplier to be less than the future costs of continued cooperation with this supplier, then (assuming he is in a position to do so) he will decide to buy the supplier; the outcome is transaction cost-minimizing, in this very important sense – that transaction costs as perceived by the decision makers are minimized.

Having taken this position, we have clearly put ourselves in the perceptual realm. This is not a realm which business and management studies have commonly occupied, since these disciplines have been, predominantly, positivist. 'Perception' of reality has tended to be understood as a marginal problem, one perhaps relevant in certain areas of consumer behaviour, but not relevant to the major positivist fields of economics, finance, production and the like. Social anthropologists, by contrast, have long been content with the notion that all reality is, in important senses, 'perceived reality' – that the world we live in is socially constructed, and the material is subordinate to the cognitive. Something like this admission is sometimes made in business analysis, even occasionally in rather unlikely places, but the position is far from being dominant. Peppard and Rowland (1995: 81), for example, say 'perception is everything and never more so than in service delivery'; we might note, primly, that 'everything' does not strictly speaking allow of comparative augmentation, and still go on to echo their formulation: 'perception is everything, and never more so than in transaction costs'.

All transaction costs are, in an important sense, 'perceptual' matters. One advantage of taking this viewpoint is that it allows us to restore some formal rigour to the internal dynamics of the original theoretical tautology. If we take 'perceived transaction costs', then we can argue that we have a rich tautology to which we can turn our empirical attention: 'perceived transaction costs are always minimized'. We then have a formidable research agenda as well: to look at the structures of understanding and perception which, upon the rolling frontier between past and future, generate the present in which we exist. Such a research agenda cannot be other than longitudinal. And it cannot be other than interdisciplinary.

III CAN MANAGERIAL PERCEPTIONS SAFELY BE IGNORED?

An example (taken from Douma and Scheider, 1991) illustrates this position. It concerns baseball umpires, and their calling of 'balls' and 'strikes'. Three positions are represented: (1) I call them as they are, (2) I call them as I see them, (3) They are nothing until I call them. The first umpire assumes that there are balls and strikes 'out there', and he sorts them correctly. The second acknowledges that his perception is crucial. The third is existentially correct in that, in the final analysis, it is only his judgment that counts. Thus the best view is represented by a combination of umpires 2 and 3. There are transaction costs 'out there', some of which managers can recognize and which determine the structures and boundaries of firms. But the crucial issue is the way that individual managers perceive, weigh and judge these costs. Different managerial judgments determine different outcomes, and this explains, in part at least, the consistent differences observed between firms.

A second level of argument may be to accept the position, but to argue, on similar lines to Friedman's critique of cost plus pricing (Hall and Hitch, 1951; Friedman, 1953b), that firms can be assumed to behave 'as if' they were setting price equal to marginal cost (thus managerial perceptions can be assumed away). Perhaps the issue here is one of the level of the analysis. At what level should we abstract from the detail of the decision making process and retreat to the 'black box' outcome analysis?

. One issue is clear – organizations equip managers to make choices when decisions are made about balancing transaction costs versus agency costs. We can observe the outcome, but the input to the managers' mind-set is a much more difficult process to observe.

It is clear that there remains a rich research agenda. Such an agenda requires an interdisciplinary perspective. Our contribution has been to draw on the perspective of social anthropology, to illuminate problems arising from the more traditional literature. From this perspective, we have focused attention upon the social actors, and upon their perception and definition of reality; we have focused attention on the linguistic (not numerical) expression of transaction cost issues by managers who are grappling with such costs. There is much virtue in widening this agenda to encompass social processes and systems (for example, Vromen, 1995: 216; Teubner, 1993). This agenda goes beyond the traditional economic calculus, but should enrich economic explanation, and in the process make such explanation more useful to practising managers.

IV   CAN TRANSACTION COST ECONOMICS ACCOMMODATE THESE ISSUES?

Meanwhile, microeconomists such as Kenneth Arrow and Gerard Debreu have pursued the elaboration of the traditional Walrasian model. Using a subjective concept of probability, they showed that uncertainty could be accommodated in the Walrasian model by extending the notion of a product to encompass a claim to a product which was valid only under specific circumstances (Debreu, 1959). This generalized concept of a product was analogous to an insurance policy in which payment is due only when a specific event occurs. This was a brilliant example of how to do the seemingly impossible by a simple redefinition of terms.

For an Arrow–Debreu economy to achieve full efficiency, a complete set of these claims must be traded. It is obvious that in practice many of the relevant markets do not exist. These missing markets create 'externality' problems – in particular, people are underinsured against risk. A simple reason why many of these markets are missing is that it is difficult to check the validity of the claims when they depend on events that it is hard for outsiders to observe. Once people have been insured, moreover, they may take risks that they would otherwise avoid. Furthermore, high-risk types of people may pretend to be low-risk types in order to get insurance at favourable rates. These problems of 'moral hazard' and 'adverse selection' are specific instances of the way transaction costs inhibit the operation of markets.

There is an obvious connection here with the 'new institutional economics' pioneered by Ronald Coase (1937) and redefined by Oliver Williamson (1975). Transaction costs in inter-firm trades can be avoided by vertical integration. Transaction costs in inter-firm collusion can be avoided by horizontal integration. But integration generates transaction costs of its own (often called agency costs) in the relation between shareholders and salaried managers, and between superiors and subordinates within the management team. The boundaries of the firm —and indeed of any institution — are set where the gains from reducing inter-organization transaction costs are just offset by higher intraorganizational transaction costs (agency costs).

Arguing from this by analogy, costs, including transaction costs, are subjective. These costs are only revealed when one option is specifically chosen, so we can imagine an array of costs incorporating a premium for the risk that the chosen configuration is not the least-cost option. Transaction costs attached to different strategy choices can thus be considered as an array of options. When one option within this array is chosen, how is it possible to check the validity of this costs estimate? The notion of moral hazard (not knowing subjective probabilities) and adverse selection suggest that the (impossible) job of monitoring outcomes will be important. This suggests several propositions (testable hypotheses): (a) transaction cost decisions will be subject to higher monitoring than other types of decision, (b) managers making transaction costs–sensitive decisions will be subject to more job insecurity and firing than other managers, and (c) the rewards to these managers, similarly, will be higher than the norm.

It is obvious that there is a close connection between the notion of transaction costs and that of trust. Situations of trust have been described as 'a subclass of those involving risk. They are situations in which the risk one takes depends on the performance of another actor' (Coleman, 1990: 91). Thus trust is warranted when the expected gain from placing oneself at risk to another is positive, but not otherwise (Williamson, 1993: 463). That this (estimation of) risk may be more positive when the second actor is part of the same institution (firm) is a basic reason for trade being organized internally.

As mentioned above, internalization removes the costs of using the market, but it implies increased agency costs (shareholders versus salaried managers, supervisors versus inferiors). The firm provides an institution in which repeated trades take place between its members (employees). This fosters mutual forbearance (Buckley and Casson, 1988) and shared goals and should lead to improved motivation, sharing of information and enhanced coordination (Buckley and Carter, 1996, 1997). We can envisage a 'sense of agency' which provides organic solidarity amongst the membership of firms (perhaps this is analogous to Williamson's notion of 'atmosphere'). This shared sense of agency may be reduced when the boundaries of the firm (its scope) increase or it becomes more complex. A sense of agency may be shared within a section of the firm: a good example of this occurred in the Buckley and Chapman study (1996–7) where research (R & D) managers felt happier in dealing amongst themselves (even across the boundaries of firms) rather than with managers from other functions of the firm.

V   LANGUAGE, INFORMATION AND MANAGERIAL JUDGMENT

To paraphrase a comment by Carrier (1997) on Buckley and Chapman (1997) the decisions that transaction costs seek to explain exist in the realm of subjective assessment and judgment. This is the realm of perceived costs, of assessments based on intuition, experience and argument, rather than the direct comparison of monetary costs. All transactions costs are thus perceptual matters and we can return to our earlier tautology: 'perceived transaction costs are always minimized'. The research agenda is to examine the structures and processes of managerial perception and understanding.

Williamson (1975: 9, following Simon, 1957), distinguishes between 'neurophysiological limits to computation capacity' and 'language limitation'. However, the Buckley and Chapman research suggests that this is an unnecessary distinction. Transaction costs, in our view, are the result of generating alternative comparative choices among options which minimize perceived transaction costs, as long as the managers know, or think they know, the *relative* size of the quantities. The process which leads to comparison finds its expression in language rather than in computation.

In assessing the array of options presented by transaction costs-weighted choices, managers have a further strategy, the collection of information to help elucidate their decision. Key areas of uncertainty can be reduced by information-gathering activities (Aharoni, 1966). The difficulty of putting information on a single, quantitative scale is well expressed by Arrow (1974a: 38):

> The definition of information is qualitative . . . The Quantitative definition which appears in information theory is probably of only limited value for economic analysis, for reasons pointed out by Marschak: different bits of information, equal from the viewpoint of information theory, will usually have very different benefits or costs.

Thus the multidimensional nature of information often permits of only qualitative expression in terms of language-embodied comparatives.

A dictum of Keynes may be useful here. 'It is better to be roughly right than precisely wrong.' It can be argued that measurement is only classification (comparatives) carried out with great precision. How far should the firm invest in precision? Is the dichotomy ('different discourses') simply a view of opposite ends of a spectrum (as in Figure 4.1)? Some decisions need careful enumeration, others do not.

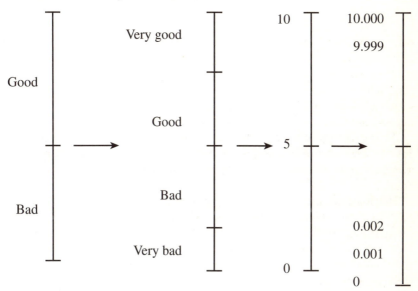

Figure 4.1   Precision in decision making

It is in collective decision making that views are taken on whether it is worthwhile to make precise calculations. The participant observation sessions in the Buckley and Chapman project suggest that the process of refinement occurs in collective 'hammering out' of transaction cost magnitudes. These meetings help to define the logic of business process design (Buckley and Carter, 1996, 1997). This echoes work on managerial roles which has 'repeatedly shown that managerial activity has a high oral communication content' (Gowler and Legge, 1983). The sheer amount of time which managers spend on verbal activity illustrates the importance of language and face-to-face communication (Mintzberg, 1973).

We can attempt to reconcile the above issues by separating two elements. First, what decisions (on foreign-market-servicing strategy, on outsourcing versus in-house production) are actually made? Second, how are these decisions made? These are distinct, but related, questions. It is possible to regard these issues as subject to entirely different fields of explanation (call the first 'economics' and the second 'ethnography', for instance), but here we are attempting to suggest that both can be encompassed in a broader approach.

VI   UNCERTAINTY

To return to Williamson (1981), there are three critical dimensions which drive transaction costs. These are (a) frequency of transacting, (b) uncertainty, and (c) the degree to which the transactions are supported by specific investments (asset specificity). It is notable that it is only asset specificity which is usually supported by numerical evidence. However, Casson (1981) also shows the relationship between frequency of transacting and the likelihood of internalization.

We are thus led into the minefield of uncertainty. As Keynes (CW VII: 150) tells us, 'Businessmen play a mixed game of skill and chance, the average results of which to the players are not known by those who take a hand.'

The issue of uncertainty is best handled by considering transaction costs as a set of contingent contracts or contracts in contingent commodities (Arrow, 1974a: 34). Managers do not have access to the full range of costed contingent contracts and therefore describe magnitudes in terms of language-embodied comparatives. External observers cannot distinguish between genuine risks due to exogenous circumstances and failures to optimize in the choice of one of these contracts, which becomes the actual, because the information to evaluate outcomes is simply not available. Thus the criterion used to explain the choice between alternative modes is the purely instrumental one of economizing in transaction costs. In practice, alternative methods of management control over transaction cost-based decisions are hierarchical monitoring and the diffusion of a company approach (or culture). Both will take into account the frequency and asset-specificity of the decision. Most companies use a mixture of these methods.

A major advance of transaction cost economics is that it allows us to go inside the 'black' box of the firm. It is possible that it allows us simply to construct black boxes of smaller dimensions: the research and development unit, the production function, the marketing function, finance and so on. It does not allow us to go into the black box of the manager's mind.

It is precisely into the managers' minds we must go to deal with a further connected issue, that of entrepreneurship. It is a mistake to anthropomorphize here – entrepreneurship is a function, not an individual. Managers and entrepreneurs must exercise judgment. Judgment is the process of forming estimates of future events in situations in which there is no agreement on (or no basis at all for assuming) the probability of events occurring (Foss, 1996). Profit accrues as a return to this process of judgment – to the process of commercial experimentation.

Incomplete contracts have positive functions for the exercise of entrepreneurship: they allow sequential adaptation to changing circumstances in an uncertain world and they allow for collective learning in the firm (this is the basis for Frank Knight's (1921) theory of the firm: see Foss, 1996). The firm is thus the agency by which the entrepreneur (whose services are the most difficult to measure/evaluate) combines his assets (knowledge/judgment within the entrepreneur's head) with physical assets. The entrepreneur's assets are non-contractable and therefore the entrepreneur hires the physical assets, rather than the other way around. The firm, further, and perhaps even more importantly, enables previously segmented areas of judgment/skills to be melded together; thus individual entrepreneurship becomes managerial hierarchy. Individuals with entrepreneurial judgment coalesce and combine their skills. Because of the non-contractibility (or rather the difficulties and costs of contracting) of these skills, this coalition becomes embedded into the firm, thus giving a rationale for 'competencies' residing in certain companies. Sticky capabilities thus emerge (Prahalad and Hamel, 1990, Dosi *et al.*, 1992, Langlois, 1992). As Foss puts it: 'In the capabilities perspective, firms are emphatically not seen only as contractual entities, held together by the thin glue of transaction cost minimisation' (1996: 10). Thus Frank Knight's perspective is not only *not* a substitute for Coase's approach, it is a complement to it.

Transaction costs are of such a nature that it is difficult to impute these costs precisely to a single entrepreneurial decision. These costs may be more in the form of a central overhead (a subset of organization costs). Some of these costs will take the form of training, acculturation and indoctrination costs for managers, so then, when a decision issue arises, there is no need to examine costs directly and monitor the decision. There is a consultative process, a memory-sharing exercise and a reaffirmation of (the company's) values and objectives. Information on the likely impact of a given transaction cost type is thus a joint output of the firm which is synthesized and stored for future use and re-use. Firms can thus be seen as repositories of collective knowledge on transaction cost configurations. Managers can step into this knowledge base and reshape it as an interactive process – through conversation and refining of the company's own language.

These notions of shared knowledge on the incidence of transaction costs may explain why calculations at the level of the individual decision are never made but transaction cost issues remain such a key determinant of strategy.

VII   CONCLUSION

The firm is best seen as a system of relationships. Relationships within the firm are likely to be sharply differentiated from extra-firm relationships. Organizations have an economic logic to their design (Buckley and Carter, 1996). Several justifications can be given for this assertion:

- The contractual nature of the firm, through the employment contract, differentiates 'firm' from 'non-firm' activity.
- Repeated interaction occurs more within the firm than outside it and so 'the shadow of the future' is more likely to figure in human relationships within the firm than outside it, leading to increased levels of reciprocity, mutual forbearance and altruistic actions. The corollary of this is that rights of exclusion may be applied by insiders to those outside the firm.
- There is a straight pecuniary argument that there exist joint rewards within the firm which stop at its boundaries. This can be extended by arguing that psychic rewards reinforce this pattern and create a sense of community within the firm.
- Reputation effects are likely to accrue to the firm rather than individuals within it. Sometimes individuals can appropriate these effects but, more often, they reside with the firm and constitute a collective asset that can be capitalized to reinforce the pecuniary rewards argument above (brand names are an example).
- The firm, as an institution, allows the non-contractable judgment skills of entrepreneurship to be combined with physical assets.

Because transaction costs define the boundaries of the firm, analysis of their impact is vital. It is necessary to extend the conventional domain of economics to encompass the key issues. Buckley and Casson (1993: 1051) said 'all economics does is to infer from observed behaviour the nature of the preferences and beliefs that underlie it'. However, the Buckley and Chapman study suggests that we need to go beyond 'behaviour' and look not just at what people (managers) are doing, but also at the meaning of their activity, which generates preferences and beliefs. The meaning of the activity will depend upon context; that is, the firm in which they operate and what managers do, and what they think they are doing, are intimately affected by the organizational context. Views of external transactions costs versus internal agency costs are generated by a collective good within the company which arises out of the company's internal discourse. This collective asset can be drawn on for decision making support, checked and monitored as outcomes become known. It is also subject to revision over time under internal managerial pressure and external market forces. Transactions costs may be outside the domain of precise quantification except in limited, comparative instances, but they are central in explaining management activities.

A longitudinal study of managerial decision making in a company thus needs to adopt a pluralistic approach to underlying theoretical concepts. Transactions costs are a crucial part of such a study. So, too, are concepts of entrepreneurship, involving judgment under conditions of uncertainty. Firms are contractual entities but they are also coalitions of competences, the theoretical rationale for which also lies in the non-contractibility of entrepreneurial skills. Thus a coherent and tight theoretical framework is emerging to tackle longitudinal issues.

NOTE

1. We would like to thank Mark Casson, Martin Carter, Stephen Dunn and participants at The Management School, University of Lancaster, for comments on an earlier draft. Some of the early parts of this chapter are derived from Buckley and Chapman (1996a, 1996b, 1997).

5. A Post Keynesian approach to the theory of the firm

Stephen P. Dunn[1]

I INTRODUCTION

> Its [the firm's] existence in the world is a direct result of the fact of uncertainty. (Knight, 1921: 271)

> With uncertainty entirely absent, every individual being in possession of perfect knowledge of the situation, there would be no occasion for anything of the nature of responsible management or control of productive activity. (Knight, 1921: 267)

> When uncertainty is present and the task of deciding what to do and how to do it takes ascendancy over that of execution, the internal organisation of the productive group is no longer a matter of indifference or mechanical detail. (Knight, 1921: 268)

> A firm is likely therefore to emerge in those cases where a very *short-term* contract would be unsatisfactory . . . It seems improbable that a firm would emerge without the existence of uncertainty. (Coase, 1937: 337–8)

> Uncertainty is inherent in production. (Shackle, 1955: 82)

> There is a second economic role with which we are concerned, distinct from the bearing of uncertainty about the outcome of a course of action once that course has been embarked on; this second role is the actual deciding upon one course of action out of many that are open and whose respective consequences are, in strictness, unknown. (Shackle, 1955: 82)

In the first half of the twentieth century both Knight and Coase suggested that without uncertainty there would be little need for the firm or for that matter the strategic control of production. However, Coase largely dismissed Knight's account of entrepreneurship and the firm and a major opportunity to integrate the study of uncertainty into the theory of the firm was lost. More recently, Cowling and Sugden (1987, 1993, 1998) have returned to the notion of strategy while reflecting on developments in the theory of the firm stemming from Coase. They have concentrated on Coase's original starting point, the notion of economic planning, and provide an alternative approach and definition of the firm, as a 'means of co-ordinating production from one centre of strategic decision making'. However, they fail to appreciate the key insight recognized by Knight and Shackle that 'uncertainty is inherent in production' and to examine the implications for coordinating decision making.

This chapter proposes an extension to the definition of the firm advanced by Cowling and Sugden by arguing that centres of strategic decision makers coordinating production operate under conditions of fundamental uncertainty or non-ergodicity. This extension reinforces many of Cowling and Sugden's central conclusions and, more importantly, extends and clarifies their notion of strategic decision making. Cowling and Sugden's approach also implicitly suggests a focus on the role of money in production given that 'In the strategic decision-making approach what others have referred to as market exchanges falling outside the ambit of the firm, notably subcontracting relationships, are incorporated inside the firm' (Cowling and Sugden, 1998: 60–61). From a Post Keynesian perspective, we argue that this link should be made explicit and that by embedding Cowling and Sugden's discussion in terms of uncertainty we underscore the fact that market exchanges are conducted in terms of money-denominated contracts as a planning response to an unknowable future (Galbraith, 1967; Davidson, 1972; Dunn, 2001b; forthcoming).

The definition of the firm advanced in this chapter also has implications for Post Keynesianism. We suggest that our extension to Cowling and Sugden offers a way of integrating Post Keynesian monetary economics, which is largely Keynesian, more fully with its analysis of the firm, which is broadly Kaleckian, by making explicit the contractual nature of the firm and its nexus to strategic nodes of power, uncertainty and money. This promotes further coherence across the different Post Keynesian traditions and provides a good example of open systems theorizing (see also Arestis et al., 1999a, 1999b; Dunn, 2000a; Downward, 2000).

The chapter begins by outlining the transaction cost approach to the theory of the firm that descends from the seminal contribution of Coase (1937). We then consider the essence of 'transaction costs', noting that it primarily refers to informational problems and some radical conceptualization thereof. The next section considers the recent critique of the transaction cost approach by Cowling and Sugden (1987, 1993, 1998). We then extend Cowling and Sugden's contribution to the theory of the firm to account for fundamental uncertainty (nonergodicity). Finally, it is argued that this extended definition might provide a basis for a further integration of the broad 'Keynesian' and 'Kaleckian' strands of Post Keynesianism.

II   THE CONTRACTUAL APPROACH TO THE THEORY OF THE FIRM

Coase (1937) attempted to provide a definition of the firm that permitted its nature to be more fully understood. According to Coase, markets and firms are alternative means of coordination. Firms represent the internal supersession of the market mechanism by command. As markets and firms are alternative mechanisms for resource allocation, a choice is offered. The allocation of resources by planning or command as opposed to movements in the structure of relative prices is conditional on the fact that the use of the price mechanism is costly. In finding what are the relevant prices, undergoing a process of negotiation and in engaging in contractual behaviour, resources are consumed. Command, with one party obeying the direction of another, reduces the need for costly continual renegotiation and reformulation of contracts. Economic institutions such as the firm economize on, but do not eliminate, contracting costs that arise when using the market. Firms succeed where markets fail; that is, 'in the beginning there were markets'.

Williamson (1975, 1979, 1981, 1985, 1987) has labelled such contracting costs as transaction costs. Williamson (1981) highlights five core methodological elements associated with the transaction cost approach:

1. The basic unit of analysis is the transaction (that is, exchange).
2. Agents exhibit bounded rationality and act opportunistically.
3. The critical dimensions for describing transactions are (a) the frequency with which they occur, (b) the uncertainty to which they are subject, and (c) the degree to which transactions are supported by specific investments.
4. The criterion employed to explain the choice between alternative modes of contracting is a purely instrumental one of economizing on transaction costs.
5. The assessment of differences in transaction costs is a comparative institutional undertaking.

A transaction occurs 'when a good or service is transferred across a technologically separable interface' (Williamson, 1981: 1544). These transaction costs refer to three sequential aspects of the exchange process, namely search and information costs, bargaining and decision costs, and policing and enforcement costs (Dahlman, 1979).

Williamson employs two principal behavioural assumptions, bounded rationality and opportunism. The notion of bounded rationality, as developed by Herbert Simon (1957, 1959, 1976), refers to conduct that is 'intendedly rational behaviour but limitedly so' owing to knowledge and computational constraints on individual economic agents. As a result, all complex contracts are inevitably incomplete and future states of the world cannot be fully specified (Radner, 1968; cf. Dunn, 1997, 1999). Opportunism refers to 'self-interest seeking with guile'. The import of this assumption is that agents can be selective in their information disclosure and can distort information in such a way that contracts-as-promises lacking credible assurances are ultimately naive. For Williamson, such considerations suggest that transactions should be contrived so as to economize on bounded rationality and protect the transaction from the hazards of opportunism; that is, to reduce the behavioural uncertainties that surround transactions.

In terms of the critical dimensions that describe a transaction, transaction specific investments or asset specificity is seen as the most important and distinctive. Asset specificity refers to the extent to which an asset can be redeployed to alternative uses without a reduction in its productive value. Asset specificity is critical in that, once an investment has been undertaken, the buyer and seller become locked into a transaction for a considerable period thereafter, a situation of *ex post* bilateral dependence. Such dependence is exacerbated by problems of information impactedness that arise in light of the complexity and opportunism that surround a transaction-specific investment. The asset specificity principle transforms the exchange relation 'from a large-numbers to a small-numbers condition during the course of contract execution' (Williamson, 1981: 1547).

The situation whereby market transaction costs are greater than those incurred by superseding the market arises as a result of the coexistence of asset specificity, bounded rationality and opportunism. The market is superseded by the firm by virtue of its ability to reduce or economize on market transaction costs arising from these constituent elements. The coexistence of these three factors represents a necessary condition for hierarchical modes of organization (firms) to be economically viable and for the study of economic institutions to be meaningful. In situations where bounded rationality, opportunism and asset specificity are pervasive, then, hierarchies replace markets. As Pitelis (1991: 12) notes 'the advantages of internal organisation are that they facilitate adaptive, sequential decision making in circumstances where complex, contingent claim contracts are not feasible and sequential spot markets are hazardous'.

The presence of an authority relation represents the capacity to stop protracted disputes and, as well, the potential to promote cohesion: members of a hierarchy might identify with the objectives of an organization, thus reducing the desire to engage in opportunistic behaviour.

However, as the problems of asymmetric information cannot be solved fully by the employment relation, the firm has to provide an incentive structure to induce worker cooperation. This yields the replacement of the external labour market by an internal labour market. The bargaining costs associated with asset specificity can be reduced via use of an authority relation and by assigning a wage for a position or job as opposed to an individual. In internal labour markets a wage is attached to a position and not an individual worker. [2] Although workers accept a loss of freedom in the acceptance of an authority relation and monitoring framework, they still retain the right of exit. This provides a check on employers indulging in opportunistic behaviour. *Employers'* opportunism is further attenuated for reputation reasons and by the monitoring of employers by employee organizations such as trade unions.

The transaction costs or markets versus hierarchies framework provides an *ex post* rationalization of various institutional structures such as the 'employment relation', the degree of vertical integration, the evolution of multidivisional (M-form) corporate structure and transnational corporations. It permits an opening up of the previously closed neoclassical 'black box' view of production and suggests a focus upon the institutions of corporate governance. Pitelis (1991) notes, however, the primacy of the 'employment relation', in that only it can explain the emergence of hierarchy from markets. Other institutional arrangements presuppose the existence of firms: the choice is then one of hierarchies versus hierarchies: firms vertically integrate up to the point where it is equally costly not to. So how does the transaction cost framework address the principal question raised in Marglin (1974): why did the authority-based factory system succeed the putting out system?

For Williamson the emergence of the factory system is an example of efficient transaction cost economizing. Williamson's principal claim is that employees have tacit skills which in conjunction with opportunism and bounded rationality give rise to high market-based transaction costs; that is, the result would be protracted haggling. In terms of an explanation of the emergence of firms, it is evident that, from an employer–merchants perspective, some of the problems of the putting out system could be resolved by installing an authority relation (Pitelis, 1991). It may be the case that monitoring did result in enhanced productivity and that such a movement from a market to a hierarchy does (superficially) appear to be in line with efficiency arguments. Yet before we critically evaluate this *ex post* transaction cost rationalization, we must attempt to clarify more fully the essence of transaction costs.

III CLARIFYING TRANSACTION COSTS

It has been noted that in Williamson's discussion of transaction costs he has failed to provide a precise definition of what the term is to constitute (Hodgson, 1988). Dahlman (1979: 148), as noted above, in attempting to apply some precision to the concept of transaction costs, has related them to three sequential aspects of the exchange process: search and information costs, bargaining and decision costs, and policing and enforcement costs. These three aspects of transaction costs denote more simply a resource loss due to *information inadequacies*.

But what is the nature of these informational inadequacies? Following Stigler (1961; see also Hodgson, 1988, 1999), can we not ask whether it is not the case that such informational problems could be accommodated within the standard 'marginal apparatus', given that they can be characterized by a probability distribution? Why should we treat information as distinct from other commodities? Why would agents not collect information until the marginal benefit of such information is equated to its marginal cost? And thus, if information can be conceptually treated as being just like any other commodity, why should we view firms as distinct from other modes of organization? Even the assertion that there are substantial informational economies of scale will not help. 'If informational economies of scale are substantial, why is it that such syndicates of independent producers should not arise to minimise the information costs that they would each face on their own, and thus obviate the need for the firm?' (Hodgson, 1999: 205).

The intuitive response to such 'Stiglerian posturing' may be put quite simply: if we lack a piece of relevant information, how can we assess its marginal return? 'The very fact that information is lacking means at most such expectations are hazy and ill-defined' (Hodgson, 1999: 205). This response suggests some radical conceptualization of the informational problems faced by agents (see Dunn, 1997, 1999, 2000b). A lack of information, associated with a probabilistic framework, is not a necessary prerequisite for us to rationalize salient institutions such as firms or money (Loasby, 1976; Davidson, 1977):

> There is no need for a theory for non-market forms of organisation in the general equilibrium model. Even the probabilistic version of general equilibrium theory, which implies informational problems of a stylised and limited kind, provides no reason why firms, as such, should exist. (Hodgson, 1999: 206)

Recognition of such considerations focuses our attention more fully on the nature of information problems faced by economic agents such as the firm.[3] Langlois (1984) suggests that it is instructive to distinguish between (probabilistic) risk and (fundamental) uncertainty by introducing the concepts 'parametric' and 'structural' uncertainty (see also Hodgson, 1988, 1999). However, the concepts of 'parametric' and 'structural' uncertainty are vague and imprecise. This has meant that, when the importance of uncertainty to the study of the firm has been recognized (see, for example, Loasby, 1976; Langlois, 1984, 1988; Langlois and Everett, 1992; Hodgson, 1988, 1999; Kay, 1984), the salience and distinctiveness of the concept of fundamental uncertainty has not always been fully appreciated – not least its ability to explain the existence of long-run transaction costs (Dunn, 1996, 1997, 1999).

Post Keynesians technically differentiate situations of (probabilistic) risk and (fundamental) uncertainty by drawing upon distinction between ergodic and non-ergodic processes, with the latter providing a radical conceptualization of uncertainty (see Davidson, 1982–3, 1988, 1991). This distinction is instructive in providing a precise technical delineation of the nature of the informational problems confronted by economics agents. Ergodic processes ensure that 'the probability distribution of the relevant variables calculated from any past realisation tends to converge with the probability function governing the current events and with the probability function that will govern future economic outcomes' (Davidson, 1988: 331). Under a situation of non-ergodicity, such convergence does not exist; statistical distributions of the past provide no guide to the course of future events. Uncertainty prevails.

The source of transaction costs and thus the *raison d'être* for firms and contractual behaviour must be embedded in some non-probabilistic concept of uncertainty (see Dunn, 1999, 2000b).[4] This echoes Post Keynesian claims that the institution of money as a distinct economic category can only be understood in the context of a non-ergodic environment; that is, under conditions of fundamental uncertainty.[5] As Hodgson (1999: 207) notes, 'there is a *prima facie* case for seeing the concept of uncertainty as a necessary – but not sufficient – concept to explain the existence of any kind of firm'. We now turn to Cowling and Sugden, who attempt to address the sufficient conditions that characterize the firm as a distinct economic category.

IV   A RADICAL CRITIQUE: COWLING AND SUGDEN

In his approach to the theory of the firm, 'Williamson poses two basic questions: (a) why markets versus hierarchies, i.e. why carry out a transaction in a hierarchy rather than in a market? (b) what organisational form within a hierarchy, i.e. why carry out a transaction in a hierarchy in one way rather than in another?' (Cowling and Sugden, 1998: 72). Williamson's answer, to both questions, concentrates on the transaction costs (and their alleged causes; see above) associated with using either markets or hierarchies. When transacting in a market is more costly than in a firm, hierarchies efficiently replace markets.

However, this contractual approach to the theory of the firm exhibits an excessive concern with markets and exchange, to the neglect of the main activity of firms, the organization, and the execution, of production (Coase, 1993c; Simon, 1991; Cowling and Sugden, 1993, 1998; Fourie, 1993). The focus in the contractual approach still resides on exchange; that is, 'in the beginning there were markets'. As Fourie (1993) notes, without prior production, that is firms, there can be no market transactions.[6] This distinction directs attention to the different focus of firms (production) and markets (exchange), with the emphasis on the primacy and the salience of the former conceptually.[7] Is it not preferable, as Cowling and Sugden suggest, that rather than view the firm as being incorporated into the market, 'we may see the modern corporation as incorporating more of the market into the organisation'.[8]

The notion that the firm is an alternative mechanism for resource allocation may initially appear attractive. Yet such a dichotomy between market and non-market activity may be unwarranted and misleading. We would follow Cowling and Sugden (1998: 62) and 'question at the outset the focus on market versus non-market activity'. Focusing on type of transaction used in production, be it market, non-market or some composite form, precludes consideration of the nature of the transaction.

For Cowling and Sugden, contemplation of the nature of the transaction directs analysis to the nature of control, that is the power and ability to make strategic decisions and to take a firm in a direction that may or may not be in the interests of others. This does not entail that production is solely determined by strategic decisions; rather, they constrain operational and working decisions (and vice versa). Those that undertake the strategic decisions represent the apex of the hierarchical system of decision making and give rise to a firm's broad direction (see Pitelis and Sugden, 1986). The actual outcome of production, however, results from the interaction of the three tiers of decision making: strategic, operational and working levels.

One could suggest that there are no strategic decisions to be made: that competitive product markets force firms into a line of action consistent with loss avoidance. Cowling and Sugden (1998: 66) argue, however, that 'mainstream industrial economics rejects this characterisation', that product markets are typically not competitive and as a result this is an empirically invalid objection.[9] To summarize, Cowling and Sugden suggest that the characteristic of a transaction within a firm is that it is subject to strategic decision making from one centre.[10] In their view, the essence of the firm is not to do with a set of transactions, but with strategic decision making. This, Cowling and Sugden (1998: 61) suggest, returns the focus of the firm to Coase's real starting point, the notion of planning, and this 'concern with planning points to the particular relevance of strategic decision-making in today's large corporations'. In light of this, Cowling and Sugden propose a definition of the firm that highlights its essence as a 'means of coordinating production from one centre of strategic decision making'.

There are several implications of this definition worth dwelling on. In the contractual approach to the theory of the firm, it is presumed that inter-firm contact comes under the ambit of the market mechanism and is competitive. Yet, as Sawyer (1993) notes, firms may engage with others in non-competitive activities such as tacit collusion. The salience of Cowling and Sugden's definition is the implication that a firm incorporates all market and non-market transactions coordinated from one centre of strategic decision making; that is, subcontracting relationships fall within the scope of a single firm. Arguably, the markets versus hierarchies dichotomy is misleading. Intra-firm transactions may be conceived as being constituted as either a market or non-market transaction, given that production is coordinated from one centre of strategic decision making. Inter-firm transactions represent market transactions, although different in character to intra-firm market transactions. Inter-firm (market) transactions take place between two centres of strategic decision makers. Intra-firm (market) transactions emanate from one centre of strategic decision makers. Consequently, Cowling and Sugden ask, not why 'markets versus hierarchy', but 'why are some activities coordinated from one centre of decision making and some others not?'

The implications are striking. By focusing on the type of transaction, market or non-market, one may fail to appreciate fully the scope of a firm's production and the subsequent extent of concentration within an economy. Such a definition of the firm shifts the analytical focus away from an excessive concern for property rights to one where power and distributional considerations are centre stage.

The response to Williamson's second question, 'What organisational form within a hierarchy?', will depend ultimately on the objectives of those making strategic decisions. A key aspect of Cowling and Sugden's definition is that capitalist firms disallow Pareto efficiency. The firm is not viewed as an optimal outcome from a collective choice process as typified in the contractual approach (cf. Fitzroy and Mueller, 1984). Strategic decision makers may effect decisions that yield advantages, that is distributional gains, at the expense of others through the exercise of power. This contradicts the conventional wisdom that firms emerge as an efficient response to transactional market failure. Given that efficiency may be sacrificed for distributional gains, interference with the degree of discretion exerted by strategic decision makers may augment economic efficiency as well as alter the distribution of wealth. 'How else can one explain why unionisation, a most significant form of constraint on managerial prerogative, can actually increase productivity as well as wages?' (Fitzroy and Mueller, 1984: 75; see also Freeman and Medoff, 1984; Belman, 1992). Transaction cost theorists typically employ 'evolutionary' arguments to explain the replacement process of markets by firms as a 'comparative static' one of efficiency calculus. According to Cowling and Sugden, and most Post Keynesians, it would be more appropriate to view competition as a process that culminates in monopoly and a wasteful use of resources (Marx, 1976; Baran and Sweezy, 1966; Cowling and Sugden, 1987; Rutherford, 1989).

Exploring these points, Cowling and Sugden focus on the movement from the putting out system to a factory-based system in the English textile industry during the Industrial Revolution. They suggest that this can be seen as contradicting the Pareto criterion, in that the move from one organizational form to another is made at the expense of one group (workers) for the benefit of another (strategic decision makers, such as capitalists). Transaction costs remain important in the study of 'what organisational form within a hierarchy?', but as a delineation of the essence of the firm it does not go far enough (Cowling and Sugden, 1998: 73–4). For Cowling and Sugden, such a movement is efficient in the distributional sense in that it enhanced the gain of the decision makers at the expense of workers. It is not, however, necessarily Pareto-efficient. According to Cowling and Sugden, hierarchy emerged for power-distributional reasons and not narrow efficiency reasons (Marglin, 1974).[11] The focus on the role of strategic decision makers suggests that the choice of organizational form will be one that suits strategic decision makers. The benefit to strategic decision makers is thus the critical factor.

This discussion, however, points to a confusion evident in Cowling and Sugden. As noted above, they explicitly relate their concept of strategy to non-competitive product markets. Yet in demonstrating how their (strategic) decision-making approach to the firm disallows Pareto efficiency, they refer to Marglin's (1974) discussion of the movement from the putting out to the factory system. 'According to the strategic decision-making (but unlike the pure Coasian) approach this was a change in the organisational form within a firm' (Cowling and Sugden, 1998: 73). Now the movement from the putting out to the factory system occurred in an environment that is widely considered to have been in some sense competitive. This creates many new questions. Are all (capitalist) contexts non-competitive or, if they are not, why did the firm succeed the factory system succeed the putting out system? Moreover, is power synonymous with strategy?[12] Such conundrums are avoided in the Post Keynesian framework proposed below (see Dunn, 2001a, for a further discussion).

V   A POST KEYNESIAN CONTRIBUTION TO THE THEORY OF THE FIRM

Cowling and Sugden, in emphasizing the overriding importance of the role of strategic decision making, fail to enquire as to the source and essence of transaction costs. As a result, the implications of a non-ergodic environment in the context of the firm are little explored. The discussion above suggests that a theory of the firm would do well to note the role played by both strategic decision makers, uncertainty and transaction costs in addition to pure production costs in the context of production (see also Dunn, 1999). We propose here to extend Cowling and Sugden's contribution by defining the firm as a means of coordinating production from one centre of strategic decision making in a non-ergodic environment. As we shall see, this extension reinforces several of Cowling and Sugden's central conclusions and it facilitates a better understanding of the role of money in production.

Although Cowling and Sugden propose a historically specific analysis, an appreciation of the nature of a non-ergodic environment in which decisions, strategic or otherwise, are made, represents a significant extension and refinement of their concept of strategic decision making. In an uncertain world, decisions have to be made. The past cannot be relied upon as a guide to the future, a fundamental feature of ergodic environments.

> If . . . the concept of uncertainty involves important non-ergodic circumstances, then there currently does not exist information (complete, incomplete, distorted or otherwise) that will aid human beings to discover the future. Instead human beings will have to invent or create the future by themselves by their actions within evolving and existing organisations.(Davidson and Davidson, 1984: 329–30)

Strategy according to this perspective refers to the process by which those at the pinnacle of a hierarchical decision-making process attempt to mitigate the impact of this uncertainty by attempting to control for as many factors as possible that impinge on the process of production. The practice of strategic decision making is the practice of dealing with uncertainty. The concept of strategy employed here is linked to the nature of the environment, of time, and not to 'market structure' (see also Dunn, 2000b, 2001b; forthcoming).

In emphasizing the fact that strategic choices have to be made, and consequently emphasising the coordinating role of strategic decision makers in production, Cowling and Sugden are somewhat forced, given their definition of the firm, to limit their contribution to situations in which product markets are not typically competitive:

> For some economists the idea of making strategic decisions would not be meaningful: a typical view is that firms operate in a more or less perfectly competitive environment, which if true implies that strategic decision makers would be forced into the only course of action enabling a firm to avoid losses and stay in business. (Cowling and Sugden, 1998: 66)

Following mainstream industrial economics, Cowling and Sugden reject this characterization, suggesting that in reality product markets are not typically competitive. Their notion of strategy is thus linked to the structure of the market and the resultant discretion permitted in the conduct of firms and the objectives of strategic decision makers. Cowling and Sugden, by refusing to focus on the type of transaction used in production, propose an unnecessarily restrictive concern with non-competitive product markets. However, as noted above, strategy is an inevitable consequence of a non-ergodic environment. Market structures may indeed reflect the responses of strategic decision makers to an uncertain environment, given that size (both absolute and relative) helps to reduce the impact of uncertainty on the firm (see Galbraith, 1967; Rothschild, 1947; Dunn, 2001b; forthcoming). But competitive markets do not remove the need for strategy. As Knight (1921: 226–7) notes, in even what we may consider to be a competitive context,

> The business man himself not merely forms the best estimate he can of the outcome of his actions, but he is likely also to estimate the probability that his estimate is correct. The 'degree' of certainty or of confidence felt in this conclusion after it is reached cannot be ignored, for it is of the greatest practical significance. The action which follows upon an opinion depends as much upon the amount of confidence in that opinion as it does the favourableness of the opinion itself.

Competition, structural or behavioural, in an uncertain environment cannot force a course of action, a strategic decision, to be made, that *ex post* is consistent with loss avoidance or the maximization of any from a range of objective functions we may wish to choose for that matter (Robinson and Eatwell, 1973: 236). If we do not know what the future will bring or is likely to bring, that is, in a non-ergodic environment, history, be it subjective or objective, will not tell us what to do. However, the environment in which an agent operates is not unimportant. The reverse is true. The social context acquires a heightened relevance. The psychology of the business environment will affect the nature of strategic decisions.[13]

At this point parallels could be drawn to modes of behaviour invoked by Herbert Simon's (1957, 1959, 1976) notion of 'satisficing', proposed in light of his introduction of the concept of bounded rationality. We wish to clarify, however, that Simon's concept of bounded rationality and the subsequent decision-making process has come to be identified with the informational processing capacities of economic agents. It is the complexity of an environment, regardless of whether it be ergodic or non-ergodic, that requires agents to make procedurally rational choices (see Simon, 1976). Strategy here is identified with the informational processing abilities of agents. This is in contrast to the stress placed here on the uncertain or non-ergodic nature of the environment within which agents operate (Dunn, 1999). For example, Cowling and Sugden are concerned with non-competitive product markets because in an ergodic environment competitive product markets will force substantively rational agents into a course of action consistent with avoiding losses and remaining in business. There will be no room for strategic choices to be made. In a non-ergodic environment, substantively rational agents will still have to make (strategic) decisions for reasons outlined above. In a non-ergodic environment, the processing capacities of agents will affect the nature of choice, but not the fact of choice. Our notion of strategic decision making need not therefore be tied to any conception of the processing abilities of agents, although we may wish to link it with other approaches in a realistic description of decision making.

Emphasizing that strategic decisions need to be made, whatever the nature of product markets, reinforces Cowling and Sugden's suggestion that firms disallow Pareto efficiency, not to mention other modes of efficiency. Situations of strategic decision making under conditions of non-ergodicity make it impossible to assess the impact *ex ante* of price and non-price forms of competition, such as research and development, advertising, product and production innovation, that consume resources[14] in the market process.[15] With a focus on the effects of history and path dependence, that is in the face of a non-ergodic environment, the assessment of transaction costs by strategic decision makers becomes an evolutionary dynamic assessment as opposed to a comparative static assessment. As Langlois (1984: 38) notes, 'we need to be especially careful in judging organisational efficiency in terms of the environment at any moment in time – for if that environment is likely to change, an organisational mode adapted to the environment of the moment may well be maladapted in some larger sense'.

Hodgson (1988, 1999) makes a similar point, arguing that the assessment of transaction costs should be an evolutionary assessment rather than a comparative static assessment that is typical of the orthodox approach. The basis for such a diagnosis is Hodgson's suggestion that Simon's concept of bounded rationality is inconsistent with Williamson's (1981: 1544) desire to make '[t]he study of transaction-cost economising . . . a comparative institutional undertaking'. Especially as, for Williamson (1985: 32), 'Economising on transaction costs essentially reduces to economising on bounded rationality'. As Hodgson (1999: 207) notes:

> Simon's argument, of course, is that a complete or global rational calculation is ruled out, and thus rationality is 'bounded'; agents do not maximise but attempt to attain acceptable minima instead. But it is important to note that this 'satisficing' behaviour does not arise simply because of inadequate information, but also because it would be too difficult to perform the calculations even if the relevant information was available . . . Contrary to [the orthodox] 'cost minimisation' interpretation [of Simon's work], the recognition of bounded rationality refers primarily to the matter of computational capacity and not to additional 'costs'.

However, to reject the 'comparative static, efficiency calculus assessment of organisational forms' framework employed by Williamson and the like, we do not require Herbert Simon's concept of bounded rationality. Williamson's use of the concept may indeed be inconsistent with Simon's proposed use of the concept, but to suggest that the assessment of transaction costs is a dynamic evolutionary exercise requires no behavioural assumptions about the informational processing capacities of agents. The fact that the assessment of transaction costs is a dynamic evolutionary exercise is an inevitable consequence of a non-ergodic environment. As noted above, the informational processing ability of economic agents is irrelevant to situations where there is insufficient information to process, when the past cannot be relied upon as a guide to the future, when 'there is no scientific basis on which to form any calculable probability whatever' of the relevant outcomes (Keynes, 1937, XIV: 114).

Furthermore, in an uncertain environment, the centrality of control and power is given renewed importance. The necessity of planning and acquiring control of strategic cost factors is essential in mitigating the impact of an uncertain environment (see Rothschild, 1947; Galbraith, 1967; Dunn, 2001b; forthcoming). Control represents the means to achieve survival. As Lavoie (1992b: 99–100) notes:

> power is the ultimate objective of the firm: power over its environment, whether it be economic, social or political . . . The firm wants power over its suppliers of materials, over its customers, over the government, over the kind of technology

to be put in use. The firm whether it be a megacorp or a small family firm, would like to have control over future events, its financial requirements, the quality of its labour force, the prices of the industry and the possibility of take-overs. 'The firm is viewed as being able to exercise a degree of control over its environment through R&D, market development, interfirm co-operation, entry deterrence' (Davies and Lee, 1988, 21). In a world without [fundamental] uncertainty, the notion of power dissolves and loses much of its importance. In such a world, for instance, firms always have access to all of the financial capital that they require provided their investment project is expected to be profitable. The source of financing is immaterial.

This is related to the point made above. If, as Malcolmson (1984) suggests, firms acquire monopoly power by 'economizing' on market transaction costs then it follows that the notions of market power, transaction costs and uncertainty are inseparable. Market (and firm) structure must be viewed as the evolutionary response of strategic decision makers to a non-ergodic environment. This is the logical consequence of the above discussion as to the source of transactions costs. Moreover, the Post Keynesian approach has much to offer to the study of such processes. In the Kaleckian and Eichnerian approaches to the firm, the role and relation of strategic decision makers to the external environment, that is, in the context of price determination, investment behaviour and the links to the macroeconomy, are well understood (Sawyer, 1993, 1994a).

This leads us, however, to the most important contribution from a Post Keynesian perspective. That is the focus, role and *raison d'être* given to money in terms of production in a non-ergodic environment (Davidson, 1972, 1977, 1988). In their delineation of the firm as a distinct economic category, Cowling and Sugden fail to allow for a substantive role for money in the process of production. Although they note that, in their strategic decision-making approach, what others have referred to as market exchanges falling outside the ambit of the firm, notably subcontracting relationships, are incorporated inside the firm (given that they are coordinated from one centre of strategic decision making), they still do not explicitly introduce money and its analytical properties into their theoretical schema.[16] In fact, this criticism generalizes for most contractual treatments of the firm (Davidson and Davidson, 1984: 333). This is symptomatic of the markets versus hierarchies dichotomy, a dichotomy Cowling and Sugden are keen to avoid, whereby money is viewed as crucial to market behaviour, and firms represent islands in which monetary or market exchanges are excluded.

Money is essential in the conduct of market exchange and plays a significant role in the contracting that allows the formation of the hierarchical relation. Money is essential because it economizes on the transaction costs associated with barter:

The use of money in exchange transactions presupposes a certain degree of organisation of trading activity. Such organisation is socially beneficial because it enables individuals to channel into production or leisure labour and resources that would otherwise be devoted to search and bargaining activity. Barter would always be possible in a world with organised markets, but it would never in any circumstances be efficient as long as organised markets continued to function ... [G]oods buy money and money buys goods – but goods do not buy goods in any organised market. (Clower, 1969: 13–14)

As Davidson (1972) makes explicitly clear, it is only in monetary economy that an extended system of production and a highly specialized division of labour can evolve. As a result, the primacy of production as opposed to exchange, both historically and theoretically, is emphasized, with its nexus to money and money contracts. To reiterate, insufficient attention is paid to the role of money in the context of production. The circuit of money or capital is integral to any understanding of the firm and the nature of production. We may recall Keynes's (CW XXIX: 81) recognition of Marx's 'pregnant observation' that:

the nature of production in the actual world is not, as economists seem often to suppose, a case of C − M − C′, i.e. of exchanging commodity (or effort) for money in order to obtain another commodity (or effort). That may be the standpoint of the private consumer. But it is not the attitude of business, which is a case of M − C − M′, i.e. of parting with money for commodity (or effort) in order to obtain more money.

By focusing on the role of money in production, we note that, in the circulation of finance, money represents and expresses the power relationship contained in production. It is the existence of money contracts in a non-ergodic environment that creates the possibility of conflict, *ex post* to contract formation, a situation not generally acknowledged in neoclassical and Williamson-type approaches (Davidson and Davidson, 1984). Moreover, having made explicit the role of money in production, we must contemplate its nexus to the strategic decision makers and how it relates to their objectives (growth maximization, the role of profits, prestige, psychological love of money). Despite Cowling and Sugden's emphasis on the role of power within the firm, which they suggest has been ignored in the mainstream literature, they fail to highlight money's nexus to hierarchy. We may recall Marx's insight that money is the symbolic representation of the underlying antagonistic structure of social relations that govern production.

However, consideration of the 'essential properties of money', the reasons for money's 'moneyness', and the fact that the existence of money as a human institution can only be rationalized in the context of a non-ergodic environment directs us to liquidity considerations as they bear down and impinge on production (Davidson, 1972, 1977).[17] That is to say, money's nexus to production derives from the fact that

> In all modern market-orientated production economies, production is organised on a forward money-contracting basis . . . Since production takes time, the hiring of factor inputs and the purchase of materials to be used in any productive activity must precede the date when the finished product will be at hand. These hiring and material-purchase transactions will therefore require forward contracting if the production process is to be efficiently planned. The financing of such forward production-cost commitments . . . requires entrepreneurs [or strategic decision makers] to have money available to discharge these contractual liabilities at one or more future dates before the product is sold and delivered, payment received, and the position liquidated. (Davidson, 1981: 165)

The salience of such considerations seems little understood, especially as it impinges upon the theory of the firm. For example, in the contractual approach to the firm, there is little regard for the way liquidity constraints affect the scope of the firm (cf. Coase, 1937: 340). In noting that certain market transactions are costly and thus noting the cost advantages of internal organization, what factors limit the expansion of the firms? The typical reply is to suggest that we may list

> three main factors which would limit the expansion of a firm.
>   Economies of scale in the production of an input . . . [that is] when the production of an input is subject to economies of scale, but the users of the input make small use of the input (relative to the minimum efficient scale).
>   A loss of control by the mangers of the firm as the firm expands, particularly as that expansion involves not only increased size but also a larger range of activities.
>   The comparative advantage held by specialist firms and a reluctance of those firms to be taken over. (Sawyer, 1985: 200)

However, as opposed to mainstream analysis, we suggest this can be explained by the non-ergodicity of the competitive process and the creative crucial decisions of strategic decision makers and thus need not find its origins in the bounded rationality of agents and the fact that they indulge in opportunistic behaviour. This is due to the integrated Post Keynesian approach that links a micro strategic conceptualization of the firm to the macroeconomy. Post Keynesians have been willing to go beyond the typically partial analysis of industrial economics in examining the link between the way the macroeconomy affects firms and vice versa (see Sawyer, 1994b). However, such insights have not generally been explicitly embedded in a contractual approach to the firm.

VI THE THEORY OF THE FIRM AS A CONTRIBUTION TO POST KEYNESIANISM: A SYNTHESIS

It should be recognized that the definition of the firm advanced here contains the notion that some organizational forms are more costly than others. However, as opposed to mainstream analysis, we see this as a result of the non-ergodicity of the environment and the decisions of strategic decision makers, not as a result of the fact that agents are subject to bounded rationality or indulge in opportunistic behaviour. We may, however, retain the notion of asset specificity, given that it has links to, and is suggestive of, the Post Keynesian emphasis on the irreversibility of time, that is non-ergodicity; differentials in productive efficiency as a result of different vintages of capital investment; the capital controversies; and notions of learning by doing and cumulative causation.[18]

Moreover, the definition of the firm advanced above, by focusing on fundamental uncertainty and power, provides a link between the Post Keynesian theories of income distribution and industrial structure and the macroeconomics of a monetary economy. That is, our definition of the firm suggests a focus on the important decisions made by strategic decision makers: investment behaviour, under conditions of non-ergodicity (cf. Keynes, 1936: ch. 12; 1937). It allows a marriage of the key themes of reproducibility and liquidity in a microeconomic context of accumulation and non-ergodicity. The Post Keynesian 'black box' of production may be opened up and an explicit focus can be given to the fact that firms operate under conditions of uncertainty, a point not generally theorized upon. Post Keynesian contributions on the theory of the firm focus on the role and power of strategic decision makers with the implications for firm objectives, pricing behaviour, levels of investment and savings and their consequences for the distribution of income, level of growth and the level of aggregate demand in the macroeconomy. These contributions, as Davidson (1992) notes, leave an underdeveloped role for the monetary sector.

However, for Post Keynesian monetary theorists, money enters in an essential and peculiar manner as a result of its essential properties in contemplation of a non-ergodic environment (see Davidson, 1972, 1977). As production takes time and planning, money-denominated contracts represent the means by which uncertainties about the future may be mitigated and money enables the discharge of such contractual arrangements. Contractual behaviour, internal organizational change, institutional development and money and financial innovation allow the constraints imposed by an uncertain environment to be reduced. That is, attempts will be made to remove and mitigate constraints or barriers to accumulation and reproducibility that bear down on strategic decision makers: uncertainty. Moreover, it is the institution of money that will be pivotal to such developments.

By focusing on a definition of the firm that encompasses the notion that strategic decision makers are coordinating production under non-ergodic conditions, we are provided with a link between the way in which we can account for institutional organizations (and their internal structure), such as firms, and how we can account for money and its distinctiveness. In recognizing the role that strategic decision makers have in eliciting the response of institutional organizations such as firms, we avoid the reduction of all choices as ones solely concerned with uncertainty, and the associated problems of such reductionism.

Additionally, the focus and development of a contractual theory of the firm may provide a more rigorous theoretical explanation of the postulate of a preference for internal as opposed to external finance by Post Keynesian theorists of the firm. Here the transaction costs of using external finance become a prime consideration (Sawyer, 1989: 184). Post Keynesians generally recognize the links between uncertainty, power, decision making and financing arrangements, but fail to enquire systematically what this means for a firm's organizational structure; its pricing procedures, its relationship to labour, its investment procedures, its attitude towards inter-firm cooperation, and the motivation of its owners and so on. Lavoie (1992b: 100) is typical when he suggests that it is only 'in a world where fundamental uncertainty prevails, [that] firms must find means to guarantee access to financial capital, all of their material inputs, or critical information'. However, he subsequently presents a technical 'black box' approach to the firm under conditions of certainty equivalence largely derived from the Kaleckian tradition.

Similarly, in all Davidson's discussion of the role of money in a non-ergodic world, in which production takes time and is conducted in terms of money-denominated contracts, he fails to examine the implications for the theory of the firm; that is, that its contractual nature and modes of internal organization should be addressed more fully. Thus, while Post Keynesians have opened up the orthodox 'black box' approach to price determination as contained in Walrasian and neoclassical models, they have generally been happy to leave the 'black box' approach to production relatively closed. In a nutshell, Post Keynesian theorizing on the internal organization of the firm is ad hoc at best and non-existent generally. That is not to say that Post Keynesians reject a focus on the 'firm as an organisation' (Sawyer, 1994a: 10, 19); rather that they have yet to theorize about it. Focusing on the informational problems faced by (strategic) decision-making agents within firms facilitates the further opening up of this 'black box' and provides a bridge between the Keynesian and Kaleckian strands of Post Keynesianism which will further allow it to refute accusations of incoherence (cf. Walters and Young, 1997, 1999; Arestis *et al.*, 1999a, 1999b).

VII CONCLUDING COMMENTS

In this chapter we have advanced an extension to the definition of the firm proposed by Cowling and Sugden that accounts for the fact that strategic decision makers engaged in the coordination of production operate under conditions of 'fundamental uncertainty'. We have argued that theorists of the firm should account for the fact that uncertainty bears down upon those strategic decision makers engaged in the production of commodities and that such decision makers will respond to the nature of the environment they face in their choice of organizational form. Moreover, as we have seen, the import of this extension is threefold. Firstly, such considerations *reinforce* Cowling and Sugden's main conclusions while making explicit the *informational* basis of the firm and the need for strategy. Secondly, it facilitates a more adequate treatment of the role of money in production, a feature underdeveloped in the literature on the theory of the firm. Thirdly, by directing the focus onto uncertainty, money and power in production, our definition of the firm brings together central themes from the Keynesian and Kaleckian traditions of Post Keynesianism and further promotes steps towards coherence. This amounts to a positive contribution to both the theory of the firm and Post Keynesianism, providing a new agenda for future research.

NOTES

1. I would like to thank Professor Malcolm Sawyer, Dr Bill Gerrard, Dr Neil Kay, Dr Fred Lee and Dr Mike Oliver for several insightful comments on earlier versions of this work. The paper was presented at the first Annual Post Keynesian Study Group, postgraduate economist workshop in Leeds on 1 November 1996. I would like to thank the participants for their comments. The usual disclaimer applies.
2. This represents an important critique of the marginal productivity theory of income distribution, but its implications as such have generally been ignored by transaction cost theorists.
3. Langlois (1984: 28) notes that 'having collapsed all such costs into the lack-of-information category, we now need to make new distinctions within this category if we are to explain internal organization modes'.
4. However, there are important caveats to such a strict conclusion (cf. Langlois, 1984: 30).
5. 'Money matters only in a world without ergodic processes' (Davidson, 1982–3: 190).
6. This argument rests on the assumption that we may treat 'production' and 'firms' as synonymous. Here we note the essence of this point, the primacy of production. As Hodgson suggests (1999: 79–81), we may wish to clarify more precisely what we mean by the firm, especially in the context of differentiating between several modes of production, such as feudalism, capitalism and so on. Although important, this clarification does not alter the argument here.

7. Pitelis (1991) suggests that it is not even clear that, historically, markets predate hier-
    archies.
8. Because of the focusing on the primacy of transaction costs associated with market
    exchange, the features associated with production, that is planning, innovation, the man-
    agement of technical change and so on, are lost, along with the associated time scales
    that are involved. Such considerations suggest a wider range of functions that firms
    provide (see Sawyer, 1993; Hodgson, 1999).
9. 'For example Tirole (1988: 3) refers to "most real markets" being imperfectly competi-
    tive, and he expresses the view that "analyses that rely on models of perfect competition
    may be quite unsatisfactory from a positive and normative perspective"' (Cowling and
    Sugden, 1998: 8).
10. This view has some 'similarities to Coase (1937), given the latter's focus on *hierarchical*
    direction . . . However our concern with strategic decision-making as against a hierarchy
    which (according to Coase) "includes . . . management . . . foremen and . . . workmen"
    is arguably a discriminating focus on the *prime* determinants of a firm's activity'
    (Cowling and Sugden, 1998: 10).
11. Even it can be demonstratively proved that both groups gain financially we still must
    assess the psychic or utilitarian costs that are incurred in such a transition, a point under-
    developed in the literature (see Sugden, 1983).
12. On this latter question, Marxists presumably would reply 'maybe not'. Marx examines
    the nature of exploitation in a competitive environment. Capitalists by their nature
    possess power, the ability to extract a surplus from the workers, but it is the competitive
    environment that *compels them* to exercise this power to the full. Individual capitalists
    have no alternative but to accede to the demands of accumulation.
13. One is reminded of Keynes's (1937, XIV: 114) observation that 'Knowing that our own
    individual judgement is worthless we endeavour to fall back on the judgement of the rest
    of the world which is better informed. That is we endeavour to conform with the beha-
    viour of the majority or the average.'
14. We suggest here that the Walrasian fiction that allows the costless movement along
    demand and cost curves due to the price setting function of the auctioneer is irrelevant
    to *any* Post Keynesian conception of the firm. See Dutt (1992) and Chick (1992) on the
    small firm under uncertainty.
15. 'An efficient analysis of organizational forms is thus a kind of *ex post* reconstruction. It
    is an attempt to demonstrate the rationale for what exists by superimposing after the fact
    an axiomatic framework on a structure that could not have been predicted *ex ante* from
    such a framework . . . This does not mean . . . that we can ever portray an organizational
    mode as optimal, except in a very narrow sense of the term' (Langlois, 1984: 37).
16. There are no references to money as it affects the firm and production in Cowling and
    Sugden (1998).
17. Money's essential properties are that it possesses a zero (or negligible) elasticity of pro-
    duction and a zero (or negligible) elasticity of substitution, along with low (or negligible)
    carrying costs (see Keynes, 1936: 230–31).
18. 'Investment in firm-specific human capital makes both labour and management depen-
    dant on each other. Asset specificity makes less palatable those alternatives, which would
    involve both parties in capital-asset valuation losses. Opportunism is therefore discou-
    raged and co-operation encouraged, as the existence of firm-specific assets makes both
    parties aware that their opposite is similarly constrained . . . Bargaining situations where
    one or both parties cannot be credibly constrained are unstable, because there are
    no assets uniquely specified to them that can be lost if either side withdraws from co-
    operative activity. Asset specificity can therefore play a useful role in creating an environ-
    ment for contractual agreements in a non-ergodic world . . . Without clearly realising it,
    Williamson has located one of the Achilles' heels of neoclassical economics and its effi-
    ciency approach – namely, the implicit assumption that all assets are *not* agent specific.
    Neoclassical theory always presumes that all assets are liquid and readily resaleable for
    use by others. In a neoclassical world, capital is liquidity fungible if not malleable'
    (Davidson and Davidson, 1984: 331–2).

6.   Trust, time and uncertainty

Vicky Allsopp[1]

I   INTRODUCTION

This chapter aims to examine the nature and significance of trust in economic relationships, whether in market or non-market transactions – indeed, in brief or protracted economic encounters. Here an emphasis is placed on the relevance of different conceptual treatments of time, and the related ideas of knowledge, ignorance and uncertainty for emphasizing and explaining the importance of trust.

Trust has not featured conspicuously on the conventional economic agenda. Whilst Adam Smith (1776) recognized trust as a valuable asset and had no qualms about highlighting the role of trust in determining wage differentials, many economists completely overlook trust. Smith (1776: 66) clearly stated that, in settling the wages of a principal clerk, 'some regard is had commonly, not only to his labour and skill, but to the trust which is reposed in him'. Trust had an important function. Although trust has been afforded a notable place in game theory, and wider discussions of trust have developed amongst economists in recent years (with contributions, for example, from Casson, 1991, 1995; Williamson, 1993; Fukuyama, 1995), economists, by and large, have ignored the concept. This is a significant omission, particularly as it can be argued that trust, or its absence, is important for explaining economic behaviour, economic outcomes and the effectiveness of economic policy. Indeed, whether the claim is that '[t]rust is central to all transactions' (Dasgupta, 1988: 49) or simply that there is a component of trust in every transaction, in this account trust is underlined as a valuable human feeling, with significant and wide-ranging economic repercussions. Trust has 'real, practical, economic value' (Arrow, 1974: 23).

Trust is a diffuse term embodying quite different nuances, depending on the context and the emphasis given. Historical time and place have a bearing on trust; diverse perceptions matter. People in different circumstances may trust their own judgment, place trust in other individuals and groups, or trust institutions, like the value of money and the rule of law. *In extremis*, they may simply trust to luck. Trust can be offered, rejected or accepted and may be shared in a mutual relationship, where, over the passage of real time, reciprocity may breed intensifying degrees of trust. Trust underpins and facilitates cooperation, but whether the economist focuses on competition, cooperation or conflict, all human economic encounters require trust.

Often trust is not defined, its meaning is taken as self-evident. However, there are exceptions: social scientists in general and economists in particular have sought to define trust in different contexts. For Luhmann (1979: 4) trust means 'in the broadest sense [having] confidence in one's expectations'. S. Herbert Frankel's (1977: 36) work on money, sees 'trust and faith . . . as the assured reliance on some person or thing: as a confident dependence on the character, ability, strength or truth of someone or something'. More recently, Cruise O'Brien, examining employee–management relationships in a corporate context, defines trust as: '*an expectation about the positive actions of other people, without being able to influence or monitor the outcome*. It is an anticipation of positive behaviour regarding actions of importance' (Cruise O'Brien, 1995: 40; original emphasis).

Often the terms 'trust', 'faith' and 'confidence' are used interchangeably, although Cruise O'Brien differentiates, for example, between confidence and trust. Trust can be considered to be more enduring than confidence, a firmer feeling, based on surer ground. Cruise O'Brien sees confidence as more volatile and less permanent – and carrying a lower risk (ibid.: 47). Confidence may grow over the passage of time until the more permanent trust is established: trust on an unbroken basis. But writers usually conflate trust, faith and confidence, although in some situations it may be useful to distinguish between these concepts.

The term 'trust' may be used in circumstances where positive actions and outcomes are not firmly expected or where there is, in fact, distrust. 'Well, trust them!': a comment on the announcements of large percentage increases in the salaries of the chief executives of newly privatized industries. Trust can be employed ironically, to indicate that a negative outcome could have been predicted before the event. A person or group could have been reliably expected not to meet their obligations, not to act with fairness, or in accordance with the group's goals, or to have any consideration for another party's interest or well-being. The term 'trust' can be used in many ways.

While trust may be present in a relationship, this does not guarantee that the ends and means are desirable, either of the trusted party or of the party who trusts. Elements of trust are arguably an important feature in the workings of criminal enterprise, although such activities are illegal and often reprehensible. Moreover, trust, in whatever circumstance, can be misplaced or abused; acts of trust secure no guaranteed final outcome.

In analysing trust it is instructive to ask: why and how has trust largely been ignored in mainstream economic debate? Specifically, what role can different conceptions of time play in explaining this and in understanding the general nature and importance of trust? How can trust be categorized? What are the processes which develop or destroy trust? What happens when trust breaks down?

II SIDE-STEPPING TRUST

Trust, in the sense of a human sentiment, is not a word readily associated with economics. Even where there are, relatively speaking, significant discussions of trust, as in Hutton (1994), this does not guarantee that trust will gain prominence as a subheading or for that matter warrant an inclusion in the index. Questions of trust may often be fundamental, but they are not highly visible in economic literature. In fact, when the term 'trust' is actually employed in economics it is usually with other meanings, for example in the context of trust-busting legislation – the breaking up of monopolies – or in the legal sense where money or property are vested with an individual or a group to administer in the interests of others; in questions of legal guardianship. Trust features in the titles of different organizations: for example, investment trusts and charitable trusts. These are quite distinct legal forms, for organizations with different objectives and agendas, operating in very different circumstances and facing distinct constraints. Yet despite significant variation they all bear a reassuring 'trust' label; one which is designed to signal integrity and reliability.

Whatever the claims for the economic significance of trust, much conventional debate ignores trust and its converse, distrust. Albeit implicitly, basic neoclassical models affirm that trust is a human feeling which rational economic man can do without. At the same time, the notable antithesis of trust, distrust, is also safely dispelled. Why should this be?

Conventional theory, on the whole, abstains from the use of such 'imprecise', diffuse words; they do not fit in with the Cartesian view of science (Dow, 1985, 1995; Chick, 1995) where scientific concepts are precise in the sense of being 'susceptible to mathematical expression' and scientific terms have fixed meanings. Trust, like love or fear, defies precise definition and mathematical measurement. Joan Robinson (1964a: 25) reminds us: 'Economics is not only a branch of theology. All along it has been striving to escape from sentiment and to win for itself the status of a science.'

Now, trust smacks of sentiment. Perhaps such expressions of feeling unsettle the neat conventional perspective. Certainly, the mainstream emphasis on mathematical formalism and closed systems does not provide a fertile ground for the wider discussion of trust. Obvious expressions of subjective feelings and moral sentiments, if not completely expunged, have been relegated to the margin. They are not at the core of modern economics (Nelson, 1996). Concepts with intuitive, emotional and feminine connotations are on the fringe, if not beyond.

However, not all such terms are 'inadmissible'. Compare 'trust' and 'satisfaction'. While 'trust' is a standard, familiar word which may indicate a 'warm' and positive human feeling, like satisfaction, it is not one for which a central economic synonym, like utility, can be customarily supplied. Whilst satisfaction or utility cannot be measured acceptably in cardinal units, this concept lies at the core of neoclassical economics – the maximand for rational individuals. Satisfaction is treated as individualistic, private. In contrast, trust applies more obviously to human relationships. Not surprisingly, in what is seen as rigorous, objective and detached analysis, the material, tangible underpinning of utility is emphasized; the emotional intangible elements, conveniently, are ignored or played down. Economists are very comfortable with the notions of satisfaction and utility – good things – albeit as metaphysical concepts. Economic man maximizes utility on a market stage, 'and set out in a diagram, [utility] looks just like a measurable quantity' (Robinson, 1964a: 49).

Analogously, trust cannot be measured precisely. There is no agreed objective standard of measurement. Just as in the case of utility or satisfaction, interpersonal comparisons of trust cannot be made. Yet that does not render either utility, satisfaction or trust unimportant. However, unlike utility, trust does not face the glare of analytical probing; discussions of cardinal or ordinal trust do not feature in mainstream modelling. Methodological individualism might exclude trust. Nevertheless, that does not mean that trust should be dismissed as an illogical sentiment.

Not all economists ignore trust, although they may award it differential importance. Mainstream formal game-theoretic treatments have made reference to trust, usually in situations where the economic actors are involved in abstract sequential repeated games, where people consider only their own self-interest and rational calculation rules, as for example in the Prisoner's Dilemma and the Assurance Game.[2]

Williamson (1993) focuses on trust, in particular the concept of 'calculative trust'. He argues that the very use of the term 'trust' is misleading in a commercial context, where he assumes that behaviour is based on self-interest and opportunism. For him, 'trust is irrelevant to commercial exchange' – essentially deceptive in a money-making context. Indeed, he argues that 'invoking trust merely muddies the (clear) waters of calculativeness'(Williamson, 1993: 471). Williamson would banish the term 'trust' to non-commercial confines, for 'trust, if it obtains at all, is reserved for the very special relations between family, friends, and lovers' (ibid.: 484). For

Williamson, the term 'calculative trust' is not 'trust' as such. 'Calculative trust' is designing, self-interested and opportunistic:

> Not only is 'calculated trust' a contradiction in terms, but user-friendly terms, of which 'trust' is one, have an additional cost. The world of commerce is reorganized in favour of the cynics, as against the innocents, when social scientists employ user-friendly language that is not descriptively accurate – since only the innocents are taken in. (Ibid.: 485)

Williamson perceives trust as 'a diffuse and disappointing concept', a term with mixed meanings to be avoided. Given this perspective, it seems that trust is a factor for the 'hard-headed', 'objective', scientific economist to shut out – to dismiss to the realms of the household and affective relationships. There is a neat and clear divide between commercial and personal relations. Trust is subtly linked with the naive.[3]

Perhaps a rationale, in part, for this 'trust antipathy', for the association of trust with a soft, 'cuddly feeling',[4] lies in the question of vulnerability. Trust may imply dependence within the bonds of family or in a principal–agent situation. Such dependence may threaten masculine autonomy and, moreover, be associated with affective relationships. In a principal–agent situation, the principal, for example a shareholder or patient, is in a weaker position *vis-à-vis* the agent, respectively the manager or the doctor, given information asymmetries and the sheer impossibility of gaining appropriate knowledge and expertise. In the scheme of things, some notable matters have to be taken on trust. Smith (1776: 122) recognized this:

> We trust our health to the physician; our fortune and sometimes our life and reputation to the lawyer and attorney. Such confidence could not safely be reposed in people of a very mean or low condition. Their reward must be such, therefore, as may give them that rank in the society which so important a trust requires.

Their remuneration, in part, would reflect this. Moreover, the principal clerk had to be left to work without close supervision; such a relationship between employer and employee required trust, not merely the taking of a calculable risk.

Whilst there are those who place trust on the economic agenda, in the main, economists have avoided the consideration of trust; some, like Williamson, are essentially dismissive, or discuss trust within the confines of a mathematical game. Indeed, trust is perceived as an Achilles heel, to be kept hidden; as a symbol of human fallibility, tainting the reputation of the cool, rational, calculating, independent economic actor; as an embarrassing human emotion to suppress as a concept with feminine associations, to be denied.

III   THE IMPORTANCE OF TIME

The argument here is that trust matters. How can conventional economic modelling readily ignore it? An examination of the different conceptual treatments of time is informative. Trust can be overlooked with impunity in the safe, small world of basic neoclassical economics focused on market exchanges; here trust has no purpose. For the use of an abstract time model, the analytical (Winston, 1988), mechanical and timeless time (Shackle, 1958, 1961; Carvalho, 1983–4) of the mainstream model simply absolves individuals from the experiencing of events and renders trust irrelevant. Rational economic people are assumed to be autonomous: self-reliant, operating in a world of perfect information. Perfectly specified inputs, outputs, technologies and utilities rule in this hypothetical time mode. Production and consumption do not require the passage of real time. Events are taken out of the time which people experience and are merely categorized as occurring 'before, after or simultaneously'. Vitally, time can be reversed; all things put back exactly as before: an impeccable action-replay facility enabling different experiments with different departure points. The outcomes of what would be, in reality, mutually exclusive events can be juxtaposed at one and the same point in analytical time. Moreover, time can be fast forwarded, moved on – a useful means for analysing and theorizing – to sort out patterns, causes and consequences (Winston, 1988). Yet such modelling of time dispenses with the human need to trust. It displays individuals in a very simple world, where it is possible for them to show a high degree of rationality. A calculating, narrow prudence rules.

Take the Ricardian trade model, applied to exchange between two individuals, as an illustrative example of the use of the analytical time mode (Allsopp, 1995: 34–44). In this 'person to person' case, each trader is assumed to maximize self-interest. Moreover, the production and trade options – the transformation curves – facing each individual are precisely delineated. The analytical time mode enables the theorist to abstract from real world complexity, to make an uncluttered explanation of the laws of comparative and absolute advantage, and the circumstances in which there will be private benefits from cooperation in exchange, given different price ratios and opportunity costs. The possibilities for total production and total consumption can be set out clearly in this theoretical system, a useful heuristic device.

However, the model also abstracts from all human sentiment, bar self-interest. In this scheme, fully-known production possibility boundaries with their given, constant transformation ratios are juxtaposed. From a series of potential outcomes, different equilibrium positions can be instantly achieved; these are hypothetical situations, simultaneously available in what is effectively a timeless time warp. Here, production and consumption do not require the passage of real time – the time in which people actually experience and take decisions. Rational economic people in analytical time move instantaneously or very rapidly from one equilibrium position to another as exogenous circumstances change. There are no doubts or questions, no contingencies to be met, no fears of emergency or hope of surprise, pleasant or otherwise. Trust and distrust do not feature; they have no function in a hypothetical world where perfect information prevails, where time can be turned.

In analytical time, there are no problems in forming or meeting agreements, drawing up contracts. Both parties are assumed to be willing and able to meet their production and exchange commitments; no unforeseen circumstances will render either party unable to meet such obligations in a pre-reconciled world. No-one will deviate, dither or deceive – much less worry. No-one needs to believe in and rely on the sincerity of another; no legal rules, customs or conventions are required to underpin an individual's word. Each person knows the best way of doing things, given a known technology – no learning is required; no-one has to trust his or her own judgment or have faith in the technology employed or in the quality of a product to be exchanged. No insurance is required. Indeed, it is quite irrelevant whether or not the two parties in an exchange have met in the past, or expect to meet again in the future. Their cultural milieu, their class or status, their point in historical time and place are all of no consequence. No socioeconomic clues are required to signal whether or not an individual might be trustworthy. No symbolic information is employed to make choices about which individuals or institutions can be relied upon (Gill and Butler, 1996: 82). In analytical time, the mind game is basic, essentially focused on the market exchanges of individuals.

Institutional features are not required to engender trust, to provide the backdrop or foundation for an individual's trust. The human necessity to trust can be safely and *implicitly* assumed away, along with individual differences and institutional rules, such as legal contracts or the customary conventions of trading. Rational, 'unemotional' behaviour leads to the attainment of maximum utility, the optimal, albeit hypothetical, solution in a world of 'straw men'. In analytical time, in the Ricardian trade model, there are no information asymmetries, no possibilities of adverse selection, no moral hazards or differences in what people 'know', what they perceive from information. Moreover, the likelihood of *moral uplift*, the converse of moral hazard, the possibility that an individual might do more than had been agreed, give a gift, so important for generating trust, is completely ignored. Repeated encounters over the passage of real time, where behaviour is perceived as fair and consistent, vital for building and strengthening trust, are not considered. This modelling of time elucidates and yet conceals – its insights are inevitably partial – for people do not dwell in analytical time.

Trust becomes relevant once it is recognized that human decision makers must act in real or perspective time (Winston, 1988) and have to imagine how the future will unfold (Shackle, 1958, 1961; Carvalho, 1983–4). In reality, trust is a pervasive feature. 'The question of trust hovers around every interaction' (Luhmann, 1979: 39), whether the decision maker acts in a market exchange situation – at the centre of much mainstream economic analysis – or within the internal boundaries of organizations, whether in a formal or informal socioeconomic setting. Trust, in one form or another, is important for all human action; economic behaviour is no exception. Individuals have to search for and evaluate information; the neat, fully-specified elements of the conventional model are not descriptions of reality. Moreover, no-one can say exactly what the future will bring. What lies behind trust, in whatever form trust takes, are the problems of complexity, imperfect knowledge, uncertainty and ignorance: factors of no consequence in analytical time, but the hallmarks of perspective time, where people are fallible and where time cannot be reversed or precisely previewed.

In perspective time, whether dealing with situations of risk or those char-acterized by fundamental uncertainty, godlike omniscience is lacking. When people are embedded in perspective time, trust matters. There may be insufficient time and resources available to gather and evaluate the req-uisite information – all assuming that individuals actually know what needs to be known. Some decisions have to be taken speedily and/or in an appro-priate order, a timely sequence. This makes economic life more compli-cated. Decisions are often based on limited and ill-digested information, where there is little time to mull over alternative scenarios or consider complex information. Individuals may not be able to understand the full import or the nuances of specialist knowledge. Moreover, the collection of data takes time, so it can be outdated once accumulated. Nevertheless, there are situations where too much, or conflicting, information is available. 'Knowledge overload' adds to confusion and stress. Finally, much relevant data may simply not exist; no amount of expenditure can buy certain knowledge of what is to come in the future.

There are routine decisions where much reliable information provides the basis for current action, or where probabilistic calculations can be made; where the structure of the problem is known and where actuarial and sub-jective probabilities can be assigned, where it is possible to map out a deci-sion tree of all possible outcomes and calculate an expected outcome. There is a wide variety of neoclassical models which incorporate risk, for example, in stochastic relationships and contingent equilibrium. Risk is quantifiable. Indeed, 'calculative' trust has been specified as a subset of risk

(Williamson, 1993: 463). Individuals employing 'calculative trust' actually are accepting a measurable risk. However, in reality, people frequently have to make decisions in situations of ignorance and fundamental uncertainty – they do not face neat decision trees and precise expected outcomes (see, for example, Knight, 1933, Dow and Hillard, 1995).

In perspective time, some matters have to be taken on trust because it would be impossible or too costly to glean and evaluate information. No matter how an individual or an organization searches, plans and calculates, there are always uncertainties, as distinct from probabilistic risk. As Luhmann (1979: 25) emphasizes, the knowledge which is available 'rarely occurs in terms of calculable probabilities anyway'. Despite all efforts to employ rational economic planning and to organize efficiently, it is not possible for all decisions to be based on reliable projections of their repercussions. Subjective probabilities, never mind objective probabilities, may not be available; knowledge of the structure of a problem may be hazy; and there are always 'unknown unknowns'.

By trusting, an individual is empowered to ignore some possibilities, to act without further fuss. Trust reduces transactions costs. Without the ability to trust, an individual would find the world overpoweringly complex; life would be impossible. Trust dilutes the effect of complexity; it enables Luhmann's 'leap into the unknown'. Trust gives the economic actor the ability to set aside what cannot be known, or to 'know' what would be too costly to detect. Trust enables individuals to go beyond what they know with certainty; to 'close' information gaps or provide a basis for action when they have 'no real idea' of what the consequences of that action might be. Trust is required in situations of relative ignorance, where the signposts from the past through the present to the future are either blurred, skewed or non-existent.

Trust spans the problem of the passage of real time. The complexity of what is and what may be, the risks and uncertainties based on knowledge and ignorance are *reduced* by the act of trust; particular potential difficulties are assumed away, some matters taken as read. On one level trust administers an anaesthetic, on another it gives a means to cope with and reduce complexity and uncertainty.

It is not necessary to assume that people engage in rational calculation, weighing up risks as a basis for trust. Trust can be part of routine behaviour. At times, animal spirits may prevail. Indeed, Luhmann (1979: 78) argues that the 'inner foundations of trust cannot lie in cognitive capacity'. Those who believe that trust should not be placed blindly – but only where it has been earned – transform the problem of trust into a cognitive problem. But as Luhmann emphasizes, trust has its roots squarely in inadequate cognitive capacity. Even boundedly rational calculations cannot be the only way forward; opportunistic players in the commercial world cannot exempt themselves from acts of 'non-calculative' trust; these are fundamental to the human condition. On the other hand, Hodgson (1988: 167) points to a cognitive framework which lies behind reason, where unconscious habit and routine takes the place of conscious deliberation, where trust lies in habit and convention. Tacit knowledge (Polanyi, 1967) and conventional wisdoms have a function. The uncertainties and conundrums of economic people in vulnerable transactions can be ignored by them as they act on habit – trusting in routines, although Hodgson (1988: 116) argues that trusting 'in its most meaningful sense is conscious and deliberative'.

Finally, it is important to note that the socioeconomic systems in which decision makers are actually embedded change with the passage of real time. Actual possibilities and an individual's or group's perceptions of these evolve. The world does not stand still; neither do the people who inhabit it. The degree of trust required in particular circumstances may change over time. People may perceive the same information differently, they may 'know' or 'read' something distinctive from the same data, given their own perspective; their position in historical time and place matters. Some may require greater degrees of trust than others before they can take particular actions. Tradition, habit and experience affect levels of trust and distrust. Some economies are heralded as exhibiting low or high trust cultures (Fukuyama, 1995). But, given the actuality of human encounters in real time, economic relationships would wither or die without trust. In reality, no matter at what point in historical time, *homo economicus* could not survive in a world without substantial elements of love and trust. As Bowles and Gintis (1993: 95) indicate, 'the enforcement costs of a society without trust would be monumental'. And life would be unbearable.

IV   TRUST TYPES

The explicit subdivision of trust into different categories is useful. A variety of distinct types of trust can be distinguished according to context or the way in which trust is generated. The notion of 'calculative trust' has been introduced. But, in any particular situation, from a given overall level of trust, it is possible to specify different elements of trust. Often an amalgam of constituents is involved, where non-calculative and calculative behaviour are present; where there are elements of selfishness and generosity. Different factors interact over the passage of real time. People trust in situations at one end of a spectrum, which can be classified as usual, routine/repetitive, relatively safe and familiar; in situations which carry greater measurable risk, or indeed at the other end of the spectrum, is fundamental uncertainty. Trust can be considered by broad type, in the following terms.

Personal/specific trust (see, for example, Luhmann, 1979; Zucker, 1986) occurs in the context of personal affective relationships and in non-commodity transactions; in formal economic relationships in the commercial or non-commercial environment; and it is tied to specific encounters. This type of trust usually requires the building up of specific knowledge, through socioeconomic interaction and interdependence. It can stem from repeated encounters and dealings, or from knowledge passed on by reputation. This form of trust can be built up by regular contact and cooperation over time. The family is usually the first and key locus for the development of personal trust. Within families and family networks, personal trust may be very firmly associated with love, responsibility, dependence and familiarity. Families have much knowledge about how specific individual family members will react in changing circumstances. People within family networks may not like or love each other, but trust can nevertheless be an important component. Reciprocal dependencies over the long run strengthen the trust bond.

Personal trust can be an important feature in business dealings and in non-commercial relationships. Trust in the commercial world is not of necessity 'calculative'. Consistent, reasonable and fair behaviour nourishes personal trust. Reputations are important in sustaining trust, built up on the basis of appropriate dependable behaviour. Indeed, in some instances trust may be spontaneous, given, for example, to a stranger at first meeting, on the basis of intuition – not rational calculation. Objective clues, however small, may signal whether or not trust is justified.

People also trust particular physical items. Consumers, for example, rely on the specific reputations of branded products, gained from their own experience or passed on by others.

The development and strengthening of the bonds of trust are a positive function of the passage of real time, *ceteris paribus*, provided that new knowledge reinforces expectations of future appropriate behaviour and outcomes. The social exchange process is diffuse and long-term. Luhmann points to individuals who initially have minor exchanges – like secretaries swapping small pieces of information with each other about their respective bosses until they trust each other in more significant situations. After repeated encounters (social interactions) trust may become a matter of routine, unquestioning habit. This trust, while automatic, has been assured, earned – not blindly given.

Acts of personal trust are not synchronized in real time, they are not precisely set like contractual payments, where the timing and size of a transaction may be fully specified. There may be time lapses, whether in commercial contexts or in relations of reciprocal gift giving. Love and generosity are important determinants of trust. Moral uplift engendered by the unexpected gift, such as a spontaneous act of kindness, may strengthen trust.

However, should personal/specific trust be lost, it may take much longer to regain than it did to lose; there is a time asymmetry. Contradictory, erratic, selfish behaviour can reduce trust intensity. Actions interpreted as back-stabbing, double-crossing or two-faced corrode trust. Time has to be spent erasing the ill-feeling generated by a trust betrayal and making up for lost reputation. The nature of a relationship may have been irrevocably altered; perceptions may have been indelibly changed. As real time passes, new knowledge can always cause economic actors to reappraise what they thought they knew, perhaps to dilute or strengthen the firmness of their trust or to turn trust into distrust. The unexpected adverse reaction of those trusted can make kaleidic changes in the eye of the truster. Routine or habitual trusting behaviour may be disrupted or discontinued when the weight of adverse evidence is strong.

Institutional trust, or impersonal trust (Shapiro, 1987; Zucker, 1986) and the overlapping concept of systems trust (Luhmann, 1979) are tied to formal socio/political/economic forms and societal structures. Such trust does not depend on a personal element; trust is placed in an institution or a group of institutions. This enables people to generalize beyond a particular encounter; to go beyond the personal. The concern lies with relationships which are structured and institutionalized in the form of functions and rules. People trust money, they trust in the protection of formal legislation, policing and regulatory bodies. It is automatically assumed that certain rules will be upheld, that there are appropriate controls in place, explicit processes for the reduction of uncertainty and complexity. Relevant experience gained over the passage of time will confirm trust. But inappropriate inconsistent behaviour, where rules are perceived to be applied in an unfair, erratic manner or where contradictory information is given, can undermine trust. Nevertheless, people trust the internal controls of the system to function – they do not require personal knowledge of those who provide information. Government, regulation, bureaucratic organization and professional credentialing all go to provide institutional trust. In addition, widely accepted informal rules, unwritten laws, for example, ethical codes of business conduct, also may inspire institutional trust.[5]

Providential trust occurs where there are no clear guidelines to structure action, a lack of specific/personal knowledge, and/or where appropriate institutionalized rules do not exist or have broken down. In 'uncharted waters' people may trust in gut reactions, in luck, or the stars. They may follow their 'animal spirits' (Keynes, GT). This is not irrational or illogical, but a way of coping where rational calculation is ruled out.

[H]uman decisions affecting the future, whether personal or political or economic, cannot depend on strict mathematical expectation, since the basis for making such calculations does not exist; and that it is our innate urge to activity which makes the wheels go round, our rational selves choosing between the alternatives as best we are able, calculating where we can, but often falling back for our motive on whim, or sentiment or chance. (GT: 162)

Moreover, where 'ignorance is bliss', where too much knowledge is seen as dangerous or unsettling, people may trust in God or fortune, that things will improve, or positive outcomes will occur – ignoring information to the contrary. People dispense with the uncertainty and the complexity which they cannot handle.

V   EMPHASIZING THE SIGNIFICANCE OF TRUST

The simple analytical time mode leaves no function for trust in whatever form. And yet, once people with limited knowledge and foresight act in perspective time, trust matters. There are those who argue that 'high trust' cultures are more likely to deliver higher economic growth rates than cultures which display 'low trust' (see, for example, Casson, 1991; Fukuyama, 1995). Fukuyama is clear: 'widespread distrust in a society . . . imposes a kind of tax on all forms of economic activity, a tax that high trust societies do not have to pay (1995: 27–8).

Different types of trust are vital for the functioning of individuals and their organizations. As Hodgson (1988: 166) states, 'even in a market system the degree of uncertainty and complexity means that [trust and other non-contractual values] are essential for the system to work at all'. Markets and exchange lie at the core of much mainstream debate. But the efficacy of markets and the exchange process critically depends on trust. What would happen, for example, if people lacked trust in the value of money and the role of the state as a guarantor? In the modern economy, where money is a pervasive feature, many complex market exchanges could not take place. Non-market direct money flows would be affected. Severe dislocation could occur, with individuals forced to barter or countertrade, with all the attendant difficulties. What would happen in the event of mistrust among trading partners in markets, or where very little is known of trading partners, where institutional rules are dissimilar, unclear or have broken down? Such situations may require, for example, an expensive managed simultaneity, making delivery and payment at the same point in real time. What are the implications of this in sophisticated markets? Trust and goodwill are required to make commodity trades work. When a significant number of consumers lose their specific trust in a product, markets are disrupted and can even be brought to a standstill.

The case of bovine spongiform encephalopathy (BSE) and concerns over the safety of beef is illuminating. In March 1996, after some ten years of consistently denying any link between BSE and Creutzfeldt–Jakob disease, British government ministers admitted that they could not rule out the possibility that BSE could be transmitted to humans. Scientists disagreed about the weight of evidence and some changed their minds in the light of new information. Consumers' institutional trust in impersonal government and scientists was shaken. Both cattle and beef markets were disrupted. The UK demand for and supply of beef fell. Disaggregating the retail prices index showed that the price of beef was reduced by 2.5 per cent between March and April (Bank of England, 1996: 7). European bans on British imports of cattle, beef and beef products adversely affected the overall demand for and supply of British beef. Moreover, there have been knock-on effects of the BSE scare for beef and indeed other livestock producers both at the national and international level.

Personal/specific trust enabled some consumers to continue to eat beef: for example, those who had good local knowledge of cattle rearing on the Inner Hebridean island of Islay, and those who trusted their Scottish beef and butchers, continued to demand beef. Providential trust enabled many others to continue to eat beef, for the evidence is relatively sparse and many were uncertain of its weight. Some consumers simply shut out disquieting information. Others found that the contradictory and changing information dissolved their trust in the product and reduced institutional trust. Some did not trust the word of government, regulatory authorities or specialists in this particular case. Some might be persuaded to continue to eat beef because of price reductions; others intensely distrusted the safety of beef. No price reduction could induce them knowingly to consume the product.

Trust is important for enabling and enhancing cooperation, to gain the benefits of the division of labour and specialization. At one level it reduces the need to search for and process information. Trust is important within organizations but also between them, particularly given the globalization and growing complexity of organizations and their management structures. The Barings and Daiwa cases, while complex and multifaceted, do illustrate situations where trust has been misplaced, and where trust was lacking. The individual traders were trusted and monitoring was limited. For example, information concerning Nick Leeson's trading activities were available to SIMEX but this was not passed on to the British authorities. In the Daiwa case, the home supervisor had relevant information which was not immediately shared with the host regulator. As Michael Foot, the Bank of England's Executive Director for Supervision, pointed out in his address to members of the International Swaps and Derivatives Association in March 1996 (summarized in the *Bank of England Quarterly Bulletin*, May 1996: 221), in order to identify problems at an early stage, trust and confidence are required to encourage the sharing and pooling of knowledge. This can be built up by regular contact and cooperation. Institutional and personal/specific trust interact to stimulate this. Increased international regulatory cooperation would help to increase trust and confidence, so that information available in one exchange about operating problems might come to light earlier.

Trust is essential for effective team working and partnerships, whether, for example, in home production or in the commercial world; it is important between groups and organizations. Gill and Butler (1996) in their case studies of joint ventures illustrate the crucial role of personal trust and the key importance of maintaining personal links in the development of successful joint enterprise. Certainly, given mistrust, where is the incentive to share tacit knowledge or to make new alliances? Moreover, providential trust can feature in the fashioning of new alliances. And despite all the sophistication of modern investment appraisal techniques, providential trust may often play a fundamental role in investment decision making.

In non-commercial situations different layers of trust also feature. To take one example, in the 'moral economy' of western Ireland, the relationships between farmers and non-farmers require trust bonds (Salazar, 1996). Personal/specific trust is important for the gift relationships between kin and neighbours. Gifts for strangers also require elements of trust. Where is the incentive to give to charitable organizations in the absence of trust? Personal, institutional and providential trust often interact. People trust that their donations to charity will not be misused.

Trust is a positive benefit for individuals, not simply as an economizer on search and transactions costs. Satisfaction is derived from operating in an atmosphere of trust. Distrustful atmospheres corrode the 'safe space' of organizations, encourage anxiety, reduce cooperation and efficiency and nourish conflict. All of this is not to deny that trust can be misplaced; that unwise decisions can be made on the basis of ill-founded trust; that in particular situations distrust is well founded. Moreover, whilst trust may reasonably be placed at one point in time, the future can unfold very differently from that which was expected.

Finally, over the passage of historical time with increasing socioeconomic complexity and interdependence, the relative significance of different types of trust changes. Institutional trust may feature more prominently in some areas as the workings of the system become more intricate. Nevertheless, personal/specific and providential forms of trust are also essential components; but the mix may vary in historical time and place.

VI   CONCLUSION

Questions of trust, time and uncertainty are inextricably linked. Trust may be a diffuse term reflecting a human feeling, which defies mathematical specification, and as such largely repels mainstream inquiry. However, trust is a multidimensional concept which economists handle in different ways. The argument here is that trust is material – even within a narrow focus of market exchange. Trust encompasses all faculties, a blend of distinctive elements where intuition, spontaneity and calculation have parts to play. Trust can be safely ignored, given the use of a highly simplified analytical time mode. But more realistic treatments of time underline its significance. Trust gives no guarantee of an appropriate or expected outcome; it can be misplaced or betrayed. Economic actors can be duped. Nevertheless, trust provides much more than a lubricant for human economic relationships; it is an integral part of the economic machinery. It provides a basis for action, vital for the functioning of the economic system as a whole. Trust does not simply reduce search and transactions cost; it is a positive source of utility. Whether in unconscious routine or in conscious deliberation, trust matters for economic outcomes.

NOTES

1.   I wish to thank Sheila Dow and Deirdre McCloskey for their helpful comments on a draft of this paper. The usual disclaimer applies.
2.   See, for example, Casson (1991), who uses mathematical game-theoretic models to analyse trust and the related concepts of honesty and cheating.
3.   However, this does not deter Williamson (1993) from exploring various trust concepts. He examines 'societal trust', 'institutional trust', 'hyphenated trust' and 'nearly non-calculative trust'. He argues that the developing science of organization needs common concepts and language to facilitate discussion between law, economics and organization.
4.   Meghnad Desai in his *Times Higher* review of Fukuyama's *Trust: The Social Virtues and Creation of Prosperity*, speaks of the 'cuddly feeling' given by terms such as 'trust' and 'social capital'.
5.   Informal rules, while also generating trust, may be highly specific to a particular company or situation and require individually idiosyncratic understanding (Zucker, 1986).

7. Keynes's views on information

Sohei Mizuhara[1]

I INTRODUCTION

We need a basis for judgment in order to make decisions and take action under conditions of uncertainty. John Maynard Keynes was interested in explaining behaviour under uncertainty in his works as a whole, but especially in *A Treatise on Probability* and the *General Theory*.[2] The purpose of this chapter is to explore the ways in which Keynes dealt with information in order to analyse behaviour under uncertainty, and the developmental changes in the way he dealt with the issue in the two books.[3]

The structure of this chapter is as follows. Section II sets out the basic framework for analysing behaviour under uncertainty, which Keynes developed in *A Treatise on Probability*. Section III gives an account of his approach to information in this context. Section IV explains how he treats information in the *General Theory*. Section V provides some conclusions regarding Keynes's views on information.

II AN ANALYTICAL FRAMEWORK FOR BEHAVIOUR UNDER UNCERTAINTY

Whenever people carry out any act with future consequences in the real world, they are forced to behave without any precise knowledge of these consequences. As it often takes a long time for these future consequences to ensue, it is never possible for them to be forecast accurately. The following is Keynes's explanation of this point:

> Sometimes we are not much concerned with their remoter consequences, even though time and chance may make much of them. But sometimes we are intensely concerned with them, more so, occasionally, than with the immediate consequences. Now of all human activities which are affected by this remoter preoccupation, it happens that one of the most important is economic in character, namely, wealth. (CW XIV: 113)

It is because the accumulation of wealth is a typical activity which produces most (potential) results within a comparatively long time horizon that

Keynes refers to investment behaviour. What did Keynes think of the principles of behaviour, which the need for action compels people living in an
uncertain world to adopt? In order to answer this question, it is necessary
for us to have recourse to *A Treatise on Probability*.

Keynes looked upon these principles as solving a philosophical problem
of how people manage to behave rationally when they only have vague and
uncertain knowledge of the results of their own acts. He considered the
problem of rational behaviour in the face of uncertainty to be one of logic.

It is rational to be guided by probability in action under uncertainty of
the future; in practice, people ought to depend on probability to act in such
circumstances. Therefore it is a 'guide of life' (TP: 356) for them. Keynes
exclusively concerned himself with 'the methods of reasoning [people]
actually employ' (ibid.: 135) which, he insisted, are usually not deductive
(or demonstrative) arguments but non-conclusive (albeit rational) ones.
The conclusions of the non-conclusive arguments, which are normally used
in daily life, are commonly expressed in probabilistic terms. They could be
inferred by reflecting on what Keynes called the 'probability-relation'(TP:
4). Keynes defined it as follows:

> Let our premises consist of any set of propositions h, and our conclusion
> consist of any set of propositions a, then, if a knowledge of h justifies a rational
> belief in a of degree α, we say that there is a *probability-relation* of degree α
> between a and h. [Henceforth,] [t]his will be written $a/h = \alpha$. (TP: 4 and n.1; orig-
> inal emphasis)

This passage neatly summarizes the basic analytical framework of probability in *A Treatise on Probability*. This framework shows that knowledge
of, or information on, a proposition is capable of being obtained 'indirectly, *by argument*, through perceiving the probability-relation of the
proposition, about which we seek knowledge, to other propositions' (TP:
12; original emphasis). What is known by argument is not the premises h
themselves but the propositions a which 'do not contain assertions about
probability-relations' (ibid.: 11). When primary propositions a, given the
secondary propositions which 'assert the existence of probability-relations' (ibid.: 11) which is an example of direct knowledge, are known by
argument, indirect knowledge *about* (or *of*) the conclusion a may be said
to be obtained. Thus indirect knowledge about (or of) a justifies a rational belief in a of an appropriate degree ($0 < a/h < 1$) (or that of certainty
($a/h = 1$)).

There exist two kinds of information in *A Treatise on Probability*: the
data or the evidence h which plays the role of premises in the probability-
relation q; and the probability α derived by considering a in relation to h.
The probabilities themselves may perform as the premises in other argu-

ments. The probability-relations are known by intellectual intuition. Consequently, if people do not have enough intuitive power or logical insight to detect the probability-relations, they will be unable to perceive them.

The concept of rationality is important for the consideration of the role of information in *A Treatise on Probability*. Keynes's rationality involves having good reasons:

> If a man believes something for a reason which is preposterous or for no reason at all, and what he believes turns out to be true for some reason not known to him, he cannot be said to believe it *rationally*, although he believes it and it is in fact true. (TP: 10; original emphasis)

Rational beliefs in a proposition ought be based on *reasonable* grounds. As a result, 'a man may rationally believe [the] proposition to be *probable*, [even] when it is in fact false'(TP: 10, original emphasis). Rational beliefs in propositions can be expressed in terms of degree. A *certain* (or the highest degree of) rational belief in a arises out of the certain probability-relation between a and h and truth in a;[4] 'thus *knowledge* of a proposition always corresponds to certainty of rational belief in it and at the same time to actual truth in the proposition itself' (ibid.: 11; emphasis added). On the other hand, a probable rational belief is lower than certain in degree. Keynes distinguished between rational beliefs which are certain and those which are probable:

> In order that we may have a rational belief in a proposition [a] of the degree of certainty [$a/h = 1$], it is necessary that one of two conditions should be fulfilled – (i) that we know [a] directly; or (ii) that we know a set of propositions h, and also know some secondary proposition q asserting a certainty-relation between [a] and h. In the latter case h may include secondary as well as primary propositions, but it is a necessary condition that all the propositions h should be *known*. In order that we may have rational belief in [a] of a lower degree of probability than certainty [$a/h < 1$], it is necessary that we know a set of propositions h, and also know some secondary proposition q asserting a probability-relation between [a] and h. (TP: 17; original emphasis)

We need to add to this passage that, even in the case of a rational belief of less than certainty, what is necessary for a probability to be known is still that the data or the evidence h should be either known or assumed to be true.

Keynes stated in his 1907 dissertation that a probability is always '*doubly relative*, relative to our powers [of logical insight] and relative to our information' (cited in O'Donnell, 1991: 8; emphasis added). It is important here to note that both powers of logical insight and information possess an aspect of subjectivity in Keynes's probabilistic arguments. The scantiness of the latter may completely weaken the former. This may make the probabilities unknowable, even though they may be said to exist. Thus all the *known* probabilities may be considered as information available for decision making under pervasive uncertainty, and those probabilities may in turn occupy a position of the data *h* in other probabilistic arguments.

III   AN APPROACH TO INFORMATION IN *A TREATISE ON PROBABILITY*

As we have already given a preliminary explanation of the framework, based on *A Treatise on Probability*, of the analysis of behaviour under uncertainty, let us now take account of Keynes's approach to information in the book, using this framework.

It is obvious from the second passage cited in the previous section that a probability α of an argument states a *relation* between its premises *h* and conclusion *a*. Keynes thus expressed the probability as $\alpha = a/h$ formally. This expression should not be read as 'the probability is α', such as in ordinary speech, but as 'α is the probability of *a* on hypothesis *h*' (TP: 47, n.1). Consequently, he represented the probability of the argument by $P(a/h)$. (see ibid.: 130). In this connection, it should be emphasized that this way of reading $\alpha = a/h$ seems more relevant to his idea of probability than any other. The emphasis on the *relational* aspect of probability is entirely unavoidable for the purpose of throwing light on what role Keynes allotted to information.

The very premises *h* correspond to information in his analytic framework, though he often replaced it with the terms 'data', 'evidence' or 'knowledge'. In order that Keynes might explore the role of information in probability arguments, he compared the premises to distance:

> No proposition is in itself either probable or improbable, just as no place can be intrinsically distant; and the probability of the same statement varies with the evidence presented, which is, as it were, its origin of reference. (TP: 7).

This passage suggests that the probability of any proposition cannot exist in itself without qualification: 'We mean that it [some opinion] is probable when certain considerations, implicitly or explicitly present to our minds at the moment, are taken into account' (TP: 7). Information exactly corresponds to the premises which play a role as the origin of reference in arguments. This is so because Keynes wanted to make readers of *A Treatise on Probability* take notice of the relational aspect of probability, with *a/h* as its formal expression.

What features do those premises have? Keynes referred to two essential features of them in *A Treatise on Probability*:

1. The premises of an argument, which authorize a man to entertain a degree of rational belief in its conclusion, are equal to all the information at his disposal. They consist not only of one but of many propositions and thus were called by Keynes 'a corpus of knowledge' (TP: 4). His adoption of this phraseology shows his intention of representing all the evidence available for a rational man; he packed down all the information relevant to the conclusion of non-conclusive arguments into premises.
2. The premises of an argument are either actually known or assumed to be true; they should be related to truth but should not involve any proposition known to be false.

It is not necessarily sufficient for an account of Keynes's approach to information to refer only to the premises, for he devoted Chapter 6 in *A Treatise on Probability* to exploring the concept of the weight of argument closely related to them. Keynes was somewhat diffident about how much importance to attach to the concept of weight in *A Treatise on Probability*;[5] nevertheless, he gave great importance to it in his economic writings.[6] The following paragraph affords a good understanding of the concept of weight of arguments:

> As the relevant evidence at our disposal increases, the magnitude of the probability of the argument may either decrease or increase, according as the new knowledge strengthens the unfavourable or the favourable evidence; but *something* seems to have increased in either case, – we have a more substantial basis upon which to rest our conclusion. I express this by saying that an accession of new evidence increases the *weight* of an argument. New evidence will sometimes decrease the probability of an argument, but it will always increase its 'weight'. (TP: 77; original emphasis)

The content of this quotation is perhaps best summarized in two properties of weight as follows:[7]

1. The weight and the relevant premises of an argument are correlative terms (TP: 78). This first property could be derived from the third sentence of the above extract. Every accession of relevant evidence is the same as an increase in the weight of argument: in symbolic language, $V(a/h)$ (which is a symbol of weight in *A Treatise on Probability*) is positively correlated with h.[8]
2. The weight of an argument is independent of its probability. This

second property of weight is accurately described in the first and second sentences jointly. A new piece of *relevant* evidence increases the weight of the argument, but it may increase or decrease probability according to whether it is favourable or unfavourable information: h always has a positive correlation with $V\,(a/h)$; likewise in symbolic terms, $V\,(a/h)$ may be positively or negatively correlated with h according to whether the latter is favourable or unfavourable. That is to say, '[w]eight cannot . . . be explained in terms of probability' (TP: 82).

Keynes occasionally used the words 'evidential weight'(ibid.: 77) to refer to the weight of argument. In *A Treatise on Probability*, he also employed the term 'evidential value'[9] as another expression for it. This seems to show his intention to represent the *worth*, in some sense, rather than the magnitude of arguments. Thus it is owing to the impossibility of numerical measurement of weight,[10] as in the case of probability, that he used the two expressions 'evidential value' and 'evidential weight' interchangeably.

Let us return to the paragraph cited above, where in succinct terms more relevant evidence of an argument always strengthens its weight. There is one significant sentence in which another clue can be implicitly offered for a better understanding of the role played in making decisions under uncertainty: 'we have a more substantial *basis* upon which to rest our conclusion' (emphasis added), once again quoted here. This sentence is equivalent to saying that one argument of greater weight may well have a sounder basis or foundation for trusting it than another of less weight. The clue here is the concept of 'confidence' upon which the conclusion of an argument rests. This concept 'does not appear explicitly in the TP, it being only in and after the GT that [its] connection [with weight] emerges clearly' (O'Donnell, 1982: 61). In the case of two arguments respectively of a/h and a/hh_1,[11] for example, the latter, as compared with the former, is associated with a higher degree of confidence, regardless of the comparability between them in respect of 'more' or 'less', for it is based upon more information, that is to say, $V(a/hh_1) > V(a/h)$. In this way, more information upon which probabilities are grounded would result in greater confidence in itself.

In view of the informational aspect of weight, it is worth paying attention to Keynes's metaphorical way of outlining the distinction between the weight and the probability of an argument: 'The weight . . . measures the *sum* of the favourable and unfavourable evidence, the probability measures the *difference*' (TP: 84; original emphasis). This distinction arises from 'the weighting of the *amount* of evidence [being] quite a separate process from the *balancing* of the evidence for and against' (ibid.: 80; original emphasis).

The more we acquire new pieces of evidence h relevant to an argument, the more solid is the foundation of the argument. This means that weight gives a representation of 'the degree of completeness of the information' (ibid.: 345) upon which to base the conclusion a of the argument. It follows that, given three new items of information h_1, h_2 and h_3 to which the probabilities a/hh_1, a/hh_1h_2 and $a/hh_1h_2h_3$, respectively, correspond, the best guide to deciding on the actual course of action would be to rely upon the probability $a/hh_1h_2h_3$ with the highest weight $V(a/hh_1h_2h_3)$.[12] However, there is a difficulty with using this type of guiding rule to make practical decisions. That is, when it is possible to get more information, 'there is no evident principle by which to determine *how far* we ought to carry out our maxim of strengthening the weight of our argument' (ibid.: 83; original emphasis). Thus this difficulty would lead to uncertainty related to one of three kinds of uncertainty which are derived and classified by O'Donnell from *A Treatise on Probability*[13] (see next section, below); it is uncertainty about weight, for 'we may be uncertain or ignorant concerning the data h, not because we are doubtful about its truth or falsity, but in the sense that we know we only have a limited portion of all the information relevant to the argument' (O'Donnell, 1982: 63; 1989: 77).

In the *General Theory*, Keynes substituted the concept of confidence for the weight of arguments. This concept takes on the meaning of 'how highly we rate the likelihood of our best forecast turning out quite wrong' (GT: 148). But it is not easy to understand what Keynes meant by this statement. It seems to have a flavour of probable error, but in Keynes's scheme probable error has no theoretical connection with weight, although it may have some limited connection in practice.[14] In situations of low weight, for example, large probable errors may arise, with both aspects adversely affecting confidence. Keynes also adds a clarifying sentence after the above quotation: 'If we expect large changes but are very uncertain as to what precise *form* these changes will take, then our confidence will be weak' (ibid.: 148; emphasis added). Keynes's reference here indicates that, to have a major effect on confidence, evidence should contain information regarding the form in which future changes are expected to occur.

IV INFORMATION AND A SOURCE OF UNCERTAINTY

Let us proceed to an examination of how far a shortfall in or lack of information can be considered as a source of uncertainty in Keynes's thought. As a starting point for such an examination, it would be greatly beneficial to utilize O'Donnell's *schema*[15] of grouping possible uncertainties which appear in *A Treatise on Probability*. In this *schema*, types of uncertainty (arising from ignorance) are classified into three categories, according to whether an object of ignorance is *a*, *h* or *q*, each of which is a basic component of the framework shown in section II for analysing information.

Among those objects of uncertainty, the data *h* and the probability-relation *q* should be deemed candidates for information, that is, as a guide to an uncertain actual life, whereas the truth or the falsity of the conclusion *a* could not be considered such a guide. Uncertainties about *h* and *q* are termed by O'Donnell (1991: 29, 30) 'low weight uncertainty' and 'irreducible uncertainty' respectively. The former weight concept means that 'we only have a limited portion of all the information relevant to the argument' (O'Donnell, 1982: 63; 1989: 77). This type of uncertainty appears in the famous footnote of the *General Theory* where Keynes distinguished 'very uncertain' from 'very probable' (GT: 148, n.1). In his note, the phrase 'very uncertain' bears the meaning of (in effect) very little information. Low weight uncertainty is thus defined not in terms of probability but in terms of weight.[16] On the other hand, the latter uncertainty, concerning the probability-relation, signifies that 'we may be ignorant or uncertain about the probability-relation *q* in that we simply do not know what it is' (O'Donnell, 1982: 63; 1989: 78). Irreducible uncertainty is introduced in the passage often cited in the literature, as follows:

> By 'uncertain' knowledge, let me explain, I do not mean merely to distinguish what is known for certain from what is only probable. The game of roulette is not subject, in this sense, to uncertainty; nor is the prospect of a Victory bond being drawn. Or, again, the expectation of life is only slightly uncertain. Even the weather is only moderately uncertain. The sense in which I am using the terms is that in which the prospect of a European war is uncertain, or the price of copper and the rate of interest twenty years hence, or the obsolescence of a new invention, or the position of private wealth owners in the social system in 1970. About these matters there is no scientific *basis* on which to form any calculable probability whatever. We simply do not know. (CW XIV: 113–14; emphasis added)

The term 'basis' in this quotation seems to give an important clue to understanding what type of uncertainty Keynes meant by some illustrations adduced by himself in the passage cited above. It is clear that this term corresponds to the evidence *h* upon which to rest the conclusion *a* of an argument. Then, how does such an interpretation of the term 'basis' connect with a suggestive expression in the last sentence of the same passage 'We simply do not know'? They could be connected by Keynes's unknown probability (see TP: 406). We do not know probabilities, for we may not have enough ordinary reasoning power to perceive the probability-relation owing to negligible evidence. Therefore, '[t]his kind of uncertainty is irreducible, not because the probabilities do not exist, but because they are unknown'

(O'Donnell, 1991: 31. Also cf. 1982: 63; 1989: 78). Given ordinary reasoning power capable of perceiving *a/h*, what produces irreducible uncertainty is a degree of scantiness of relevant data *h* available.[17] Such a careful consideration of both kinds of uncertainty makes it clear that scarcity of information is a source of uncertainty.

Lack of relevant information, which is a source of the uncertainties described above, makes it impossible for agents to have recourse to the probabilities themselves. Under these adverse circumstances, what do they have to rely upon in order to make decisions when they lack a sound basis for expectations? In the *General Theory*, expectations are divided into two categories: short-term and long-term. According to Keynes, short-term expectations are concerned with the price and the level of output planned by entrepreneurs, while long-term expectations are related to additions to their capital equipment. There is one fundamental difference between the two kinds of expectation. In the case of short-term expectations, as they are 'expectations as to the cost of output on various possible scales and expectations as to the sale-proceeds of this output' (GT: 47) and thus are moulded for *shorter* time horizons, they are based on *more* information. By contrast, in the case of long-term expectations, this category of expectations cannot help being grounded on *less* information which inevitably comes from buying long-lived assets with *longer* time horizons. The availability of more information in the former type of expectations results in the detection of probabilities. On the other hand, in the latter type which underlies decisions on investment, the scarcity of information may prevent probabilities from being calculated and hence low weight uncertainty or irreducible uncertainty exists and pervades. In the case of decision-making about investment especially, even though agents can always form expectations, they cannot always form probabilities.

In order to 'defeat the dark forces of time and ignorance which envelop our future' (ibid.: 155) which exists in the real world, while 'behav[ing] in a manner which saves our faces as rational, economic men' (CW XIV: 114), what did Keynes actually suggest we need to have recourse to? In this connection, to quote Keynes:

> The future never resembles the past – as we well know. But, generally speaking, our imagination and our knowledge are too weak to tell us what particular changes to expect. We do not know what the future holds. Nevertheless, as living and moving beings, we are forced to act. Peace and comfort of mind require that we should hide from ourselves how little we foresee. Yet we must be guided by some hypothesis. We tend, therefore, to substitute for the knowledge which is unattainable *certain conventions, the chief of which is to assume, contrary to all likelihood, that the future will resemble the past*. This is how we act in practice. (CW XIV: 124; emphasis added)

What Keynes suggested in this passage is that the last recourse should be convention as a guide to acting under great uncertainty, and that convention here is to 'assume the future to be much more like the past than is reasonable' (CW XIV: 125); in other words, as Keynes put it, '[t]he essence of this convention . . . lies in assuming that the existing state of affairs will continue indefinitely, except in so far as we have specific reasons to expect a change' (GT: 152). The essentials of such a convention as this consist of three assumptions: (a) taking the existing situation reflecting the past as continuing indefinitely, (b) modifying this practice according to the expectations of a definite change and (c) attaching more importance to the existing situation rather than expectations of definite changes in forming (long-term) expectations. In relation to the last assumption, Keynes claimed 'the facts of the existing situation enter, in a sense disproportionately, into the formation of our long-term expectations' (ibid.: 148); that is to say, it is foolish to fall back on vague and scanty knowledge about the future. This way of forming expectations by means of projecting the existing knowledge into the future is a type of inductive method, that is, extrapolation.

All the assumptions mentioned above on which convention is moulded together produce a combination of two of Keynes's three techniques by which agents pretend to behave rationally: '(1) We assume that the present is a much more serviceable guide to the future than a candid examination of past experience would show it to have been hitherto . . . [and] (2) [w]e assume that the *existing* state of opinion as expressed in prices and the character of existing output is based on a *correct* summing up of future prospects, so that we can accept it as such unless and until something new and relevant comes into the picture' (CW XIV: 114; original emphasis). His remaining technique, however, describes another way to form expectations, or rather a way to make decisions, especially in the share market: '(3) Knowing that our own individual judgement is worthless, we endeavour to fall back on the judgement of the rest of the world which is perhaps better informed. That is, we endeavour to conform with the behaviour of the majority or the average. The psychology of a society of individuals each of whom is endeavouring to copy the others leads to what we may strictly term a *conventional* judgement' (ibid.: 114; original emphasis). This passage suggests that one source of convention springs from an agent's psychological propensity to study and conform voluntarily to what others are doing. Imitating behaviour under uncertainty such as this pays off in itself. As Littleboy (1990: 271) notes, convention thus comes from 'rational or purpose-oriented behaviour'.[18] Agents' conformity to the actions or views of others turns out to their advantage. As a result, convention may reduce the possibility of unexpected changes and thereby enhance the stability of the system. Furthermore, Littleboy stresses the importance of convention in that it is capable of promoting stability; and convention in turn brings out inflexibilities in the markets and therefore results in the persistent existence of involuntary unemployment.[19]

Summing up, convention is a kind of device created by human beings in history to cope with the precariousness of knowledge arising from uncertainty regarding the future. Keynes himself never regarded conventional behaviour in an uncertain environment as inconsistent with rationality. It follows that his rational behaviour should be explained in terms of the concept of rationality different from 'an extraordinary contraption of the Benthamite School' (CW XIV: 124) which is equivalent to an imaginary probability by which the future could be reduced to the same calculable status as the present. His rationality thus requires that, given all the relevant information available to them, agents select from alternative courses of action on a *reasonable* ground. The more stable is convention, the smaller is disquiet about the future and hence the stronger is conformity to the rest of the world. For Keynes, the reason why agents rely on convention in making decisions under pervasive uncertainty is that there is no choice left to them other than reliance on such conventional judgments whenever relevant information is sparse. This reliance results in a considerable degree of *continuity and stability* as long as convention turns out to be firmly maintained. In this sense, even conventional behaviour is not irrational under uncertainty.

V   CONCLUSIONS

In this chapter we have examined Keynes's treatment of information mainly in *A Treatise on Probability* and the *General Theory*. We arrive at three conclusions:

1. Premises represent information as the foundation for rational arguments in *A Treatise on Probability*, and the premises of those arguments by themselves make it possible to intuit a probability-relation, given ordinary reasoning power. In this sense, they are a basic and pivotal concept in Keynes's general approach to information.
2. Keynes approached information in terms of the weight of argument rather than evidence in *A Treatise on Probability*. Weight has normally (but not always) a positive correlation with evidence, but it is independent of probability. However, in the *General Theory* he relied more on the concept of confidence, a concept which appears to be underpinned by the weight of argument.

3.   When information is sparse or negligible, so that no probability can be discerned, Keynes adopted the concepts of irreducible or radical uncertainty and convention instead of probability. Keynes's irreducible uncertainty results from probability being unknowable owing to absence of information.

As the degree of availability of information changes, Keynes altered his method of approaching the question of information. In the case of great difficulty in getting information, he attempted to deal with information more in terms of the concepts of uncertainty and convention than in terms of the premise or the weight of argument. Because the main purpose of the *General Theory* was to analyse the behaviour of investment, which is a major component of the theory of output as a whole and is governed by a deficiency of information, it would seem that he was inclined to utilize uncertainty and convention rather than the weight of argument as in *A Treatise on Probability*. His intention to build a general and 'practical theory of the future' (ibid.: 114) caused him to prefer the concepts of expectation and convention to that of probability. And this preference results from the lack of information.

NOTES

1.   I am extremely grateful to Rod O'Donnell and Jochen Runde for helpful comments on an earlier version of this chapter and to the editors for useful comments and suggestions in the preparation of the manuscript. The responsibility for any remaining errors is mine alone. I also wish to thank Howard Vane and Warren Young, who helped me improve the English.
2.   It should be noted that there is an important difference between Keynes's two explanations of how agents behave under uncertainty in *A Treatise on Probability* and in the *General Theory*: an account of how to behave under uncertainty in the former is normative, while that of the latter is predominantly descriptive. This point was suggested to me by Jochen Runde in correspondence.
3.   Although Keynes used the term 'information' in *A Treatise on Probability*, he adopted the term 'news' instead of 'information' in the *General Theory*. Why did the word 'information' fall out of use in the book? The reason is that it was not much used in Keynes's time, as pointed out by O'Donnell in correspondence. Furthermore, O'Donnell suggested that 'knowledge' is the key term used commonly in both *A Treatise on Probability* and the *General Theory*, and usually has the same meaning as 'information' or 'news' in both books. Incidentally, the term 'news' appears eight times in the *General Theory* (cf. Glahe, 1991: 106).
4.   Keynes differentiated certainty from truth: the former is a logical relation between propositions, while the latter is a property of a proposition. In this connection, O'Donnell asserts that 'a certain conclusion (that is, one based on the logical relation of certainty) becomes a *true* conclusion when the premises are true' (O'Donnell, 1989: 36; emphasis added).
5.   Cf. TP: 77.
6.   After *A Treatise on Probability*, the concept of weight is discussed in GT: 148, n.1 and CW XIV: 293–4).

7. For a fuller discussion of the properties of weight, see also O'Donnell (1982: 58–62; 1989: 67–74) and Runde (1990: 279–83).
8. Runde (1990) points out the possibility that changes in the weight of argument are not directly related to changes in information. He argues that there are two notions of weight in *A Treatise on Probability*. The notion of what he calls 'weight 2', which is defined not only in terms of relevant knowledge but also in terms of 'relevant ignorance', may make it possible for additional information to decrease the weight of argument. He says that 'The possibility that weight may decrease with the acquisition of more evidence does not appear in the *Treatise*' (Runde, 1990: 283) and that weight 2 may be relevant to investor confidence in the *General Theory*. Although Runde lays stress on the difference between this kind of weight and the one discussed in the text, I shall proceed in the text of this chapter exclusively on the assumption of the monotonic relation between the relevant evidence of argument and its weight.
9. See TP: 130; cf. also CW XXIX: 289. For a more detailed explanation of Keynes's earlier uses of the term 'value', see O'Donnell (1982: 58; 1989: 69).
10. Keynes restricted the cardinal measurement of weight to very few cases, while he regarded the impossibility of numerical measurement as a matter of course. On the issue of the measurement of weight, see TP (77–80).
11. This is one of the two cases where it is possible to compare two arguments with respect to their weight (Cf. TP: 77–8).
12. Keynes seemed to be doubtful about the relevance of such a guiding rule in making practical decisions. In particular, where it is possible to obtain more information, he confessed to being unable to give a definite answer regarding 'to what point the strengthening of an argument's weight by increasing the evidence ought to be pushed' (TP: 83). Therefore, Keynes was forced to say that 'when our knowledge is *slight but capable of increase*, the course of action, which will, relative to such knowledge, probably produce the greatest amount of good, will often consist in the acquisition of more knowledge' (ibid.: 83; emphasis added) and that 'if, *for one alternative*, the available information is necessarily *small*, that does not seem to be a consideration which ought to be left out of account altogether' (ibid.: 346; emphasis added). Cf. also ibid.: 83–4, 345–6.
13. Other kinds of uncertainty are those concerning *a* and the probability-relation *q*. For the details of all kinds of uncertainty including that about the data *h*, see O'Donnell (1982: 62–6;1989: 77–9).
14. See TP (80–82) and O' Donnell (1989: 73; 1991: 38).
15. For his explanation of this schema, see O'Donnell (1982: 62–3; 1989: 77–9).
16. Brady (1987) and Stohs (1980) are listed by O'Donnell (1991: 26–33; cf. also pp. 46–7 and 54–5, n.14) among the adherents of low weight uncertainty; we can add Hoogduin (1987) to them. O'Donnell also makes mention of one more kind of uncertainty, namely 'unrankable uncertainty' (O'Donnell, 1991: 31–2).
17. Conversely, even though the relevant information is very scanty, given sufficient mental ability to detect the probability-relation, the probability can become known. Cf. O'Donnell (1991: 32).
18. Littleboy distinguishes convention from mere custom or habit: 'Herding is not always instinctive . . . It is not simply a matter of unthinking habit or custom'(1990: 272). His statement, 'Agents learn that conformity avoids losses' (ibid.: 272) is also very helpful for understanding the rational or purpose-oriented nature of convention.
19. On the stabilizing roles played by convention, see Littleboy (1990: 30–32). In this respect, Littleboy says that '[i]t is the existence of the conventions that lie behind the propensity to consume, the willingness to invest, the desire to hold money and the behaviour of the money wage [all of which are independent variables of Keynes's system] which together can explain stability in a system' (ibid.: 32).

8. The role of econometrics in a radical methodology

Bill Gerrard[1]

I INTRODUCTION: WHAT ARE THE ISSUES?

There has always been a methodological debate in economics. But only periodically has the debate been deemed significant enough to be taken seriously by economists themselves. Most of the debate has been *about* economists but not *by* economists. However, there have been at least two major exceptions, the *Methodenstreit* between the early neoclassical economists and the historical school in the 1880s and the marginalist controversy in the late 1940s and early 1950s. The current phase of the methodological debate in economics, from 1970 onwards, also has claim to major significance.

The origins of the current phase of the methodological debate lie in the crisis following the breakdown of the Keynesian–neoclassical consensus in the 1960s and an increasing concern about the 'technological' failure of economics to produce practical tools for policy makers. The crisis led some distinguished economists such as Leontief (1971), Phelps Brown (1972) and Worswick (1972) to question the credentials of economics as a science on two main grounds: (a) large parts of abstract economic theory had little or no empirical relevance, and (b) economics showed a lack of cumulative progress compared to other (natural) sciences. Thus the current phase of the methodology debate in economics initially sought to answer the question: is economics a science?

As I have argued elsewhere (Gerrard, 1995), it is useful to characterize the current methodological debate in economics as dealing with both 'traditional' and 'new-view' issues. The traditional methodological issues concern the objectives of economic theory and the methods of theory appraisal. With respect to the objectives of economic theory, a key issue is whether or not economic theory should attempt to describe and explain the underlying mechanisms generating observed phenomena or, alternatively, limit itself to simulating and predicting observed phenomena with no necessary requirement that economic theory should correspond to causal reality. Much of this debate over objectives has been associated with the 'as if' or 'black box' methodological defence of the assumption of profit max-imization by Friedman (1953b), who argued that ultimately an economic theory should be judged by its predictive power, not by the realism of its assumptions.

As evidenced by Friedman's argument, the issue of the appropriate objectives for economic theory cannot be separated from the issue of the appropriate methods of theory appraisal. It is conventional to characterize this part of the debate as deductivism versus empiricism. Deductivist argu-ments stress the importance of 'internal' criteria in theory appraisal such as the axiomatic basis, logical consistency, mathematical technique, sim-plicity and generality. Empiricist arguments, on the other hand, stress an 'external' criterion: the consistency of theory with observed data.

New-view issues arise from a more general view of science as consisting of conglomerate theoretical structures reproduced and transformed in a social context. The emergence of the new view of science originates in the Popper–Kuhn controversy in the philosophy of science in the 1960s and 1970s. Popper (1959, 1963) proposed the falsificationist view of science. Popper argued that there is a demarcation criterion by which science can be distinguished from non-scientific belief systems such as religion and ideol-ogy. The form of justification (that is, the method of theory appraisal) pro-vides the demarcation criterion. For Popper, the defining characteristic of science is the use of empirical testing for theory appraisal. Science is a process of conjecture and refutation. Scientific theories must provide test-able conjectures which can be subjected to attempted falsification by empir-ical evidence. Science progresses by rejecting falsified theories and retaining (and continuing to test) those theories which have not yet been falsified.

Kuhn provided an alternative view of science in his book, *The Structure of Scientific Revolutions* (1962). Kuhn argued that the essence of science cannot be captured by a purely rational calculus (that is, the scientific method) such as Popper's falsificationism. Science has a conglomerate structure, what Kuhn called a paradigm, and is developed in a social process in scientific communities. In normal science, a scientific community has a single dominant paradigm which defines the research agenda and the analytical methods. Very occasionally, scientific communities experience revolutionary paradigmatic changes as a response to a deep scientific crisis engendered by the accumulation of anomalous empirical evidence. Kuhn's description of the scientific progress stimulated an increasing concern with the history and sociology of science, as well as provoking renewed debates in the philosophy of science on the objectives of science and methods of theory appraisal.

The Popper–Kuhn controversy has had a considerable impact on the methodological debate in economics. As Backhouse (1994) persuasively argues, much of the agenda for the current debate was set by Blaug's *The Methodology of Economics* (1980). As well as providing a systematic treatment of the methodological debate in economics, Blaug makes two related methodological prescriptions, one aimed at economists and one aimed at historians of economic thought. Blaug's prescription for economists is to be more thoroughly falsificationist in practice. Blaug's prescription to historians of economic thought is to use Lakatos's methodology of scientific research programmes (Lakatos, 1974) as the appropriate framework for rational reconstructions of the history of economic thought. Lakatos's framework of hard-core assumptions, auxiliary hypotheses and progressive/degenerating research programmes can be seen as a development of the Popperian perspective to take account of the conglomerate nature of science. Blaug's arguments for the applicability of Popper and Lakatos to economics can be seen as a traditional–conservative response to the Popper–Kuhn controversy. The alternative radical response has involved the articulation of a variety of new views of economics such as the rhetorical approach (McCloskey, 1983, 1986), science as a socialization process (Colander and Klamer, 1987) and science as a reputational system (Whitley, 1984).

Despite the intensity and wide-ranging nature of the current methodological debate, it has remained a minority interest in mainstream economics. The coverage of the debate in the 'core' economics journals has tended to be limited to a continuing concern with Friedman's methodological arguments (Boland, 1979, 1981; Frazer and Boland, 1983; Hirsch and De Marchi, 1984; Hoover, 1984) and the rhetoric of economics (McCloskey, 1983, 1995; Caldwell and Coats, 1984; Mäki, 1995). However, the methodological debate has been much more central to radical schools of thought such as Post Keynesian economics. This is not surprising. Radical schools, by their very nature, need to justify their existence as an alternative to the mainstream. This inevitably involves a methodological dimension as radical schools argue against the limitations of the orthodox research agenda and analytical methods and argue for a different research agenda and different analytical techniques. In particular, Post Keynesian economists have argued for greater pluralism. Dow (1985), for example, has argued for the adoption of the pluralist Babylonian mode of thought as an alternative to the objectivist and reductionist Cartesian/Euclidean mode of thought adopted by orthodox economists. More recently, Lawson (1994a) has argued that critical realism is the appropriate philosophical framework for Post Keynesian economics, providing coherence at a methodological level to the wide diversity of substantive theoretical work.

Running in parallel to the current methodological debate in economics, there has been an equally intense methodological debate in econometrics. This debate has focused on the appropriate relationship between economic theory and econometrics. It has its origins in the perceived failure of econometric methods to produce stable estimated empirical relationships. Another impetus has been the development of econometric techniques, especially in the field of time-series analysis. Econometric techniques such as Box–Jenkins methods and vector autoregression (VAR) analysis are largely data-driven statistical modelling techniques with little or no input from economic theory. The emergence of atheoretical time-series analysis has revived the 'measurement-without-theory' controversy between Koopmans and Vining which took place in the late 1940s. Various econometric methodologies have been proposed. Pagan (1987) provides a critical survey of three econometric methodologies associated with Hendry, Leamer and Sims, respectively. However, the links between the methodological debates in economics and econometrics have tended to be rather one way. The methodological debate in econometrics has been informed by the philosophy of science and the general methodological debate in economics (see, for example, Hendry, 1995: ch.1) but there has been little flow in the opposite direction. Partly this has been a result of the substantial intellectual 'barriers to entry' created by the technical knowledge required to gain access to the modern econometrics literature. Methodological arguments in economics relating to empirical work have thus tended to be rather abstract and superficial, lacking any detailed knowledge of the actual empirical methods employed by econometricians. (See Darnell and Evans, 1990; Gerrard, 1995, for two recent attempts to bring the methodological debate in econometrics into the more general methodological debate in economics.)

Post Keynesian economists seem to have become increasingly hostile to econometrics. This hostility can be traced back to Keynes's criticisms of Tinbergen's use of econometric methods. There has been renewed interest in Keynes's criticisms of econometrics in recent years within the 'new' Keynesian fundamentalist research programme which seeks to ground Keynes's later economic writings in his earlier philosophical writings, especially *A Treatise on Probability*. From this perspective, Keynes's criticisms of econometrics are a corollary of his earlier related arguments against the general applicability (particularly within the social realm) of both the concept of a well-defined probability distribution and an atomistic presupposition about the nature of the world. Modern extensions of these arguments include Davidson (1991) on the non-ergodic nature of economic processes and Lawson (1989a) on the inherently instrumentalist nature of econometrics. But not all Post Keynesians have repudiated the use of econometric methods. Downward (1995), for example, argues that econometric methods are compatible with a critical realist perspective and applies VAR analysis to the investigation of Post Keynesian theories of pricing using data for the UK manufacturing sector.

The objective of this chapter is to argue for a more constructive approach to econometrics by Post Keynesians. Econometrics can, and should, be part of a radical methodology. The structure of the chapter is as follows. Section II sets out two alternative clusters of methodological beliefs in economics: a 'conservative' cluster, generally protective of mainstream economic theory, and a 'radical' cluster with a more fallibilist approach to economic theory. Section III shows how the conservative cluster of methodological beliefs is embodied within two econometric methodologies: the AER/textbook approach and VAR analysis. Section IV argues that the LSE approach to econometrics, particularly the 'general-to-specific' methodology associated with Hendry, incorporates a radical, fallibilist perspective on economic theory, allowing for a more meaningful, critical interaction between theory and empirical evidence. Section V provides a summary and conclusions.

II   TWO ALTERNATIVE CLUSTERS OF METHODOLOGICAL BELIEFS IN ECONOMICS

Knowledge consists of sets of justified beliefs about the nature of the world. Methodology is the study of the methods by which knowledge is attained. Methodology may be merely descriptive of the methods actually employed or may also involve a prescriptive aspect. Prescriptive methodology seeks to prescribe the methods that should be adopted in order to determine whether or not a theory is sufficiently justified to be considered as knowledge. In a sense, prescriptive methodology is meta-knowledge, in that it seeks to justify or repudiate the methods of justification employed by scientists. Traditional methodological perspectives such as falsificationism are both descriptive and prescriptive. New-view perspectives, deriving from a post-positivist/post-modernist critique of the notion of the Scientific Method as the only means of acquiring knowledge, are primarily descriptive of the processes by which scientists justify their knowledge claims. McCloskey (1983, 1986), for example, views the justification of economic knowledge as a social process of rhetoric rather than merely a matter of logic. One of the key methodological issues in the process of justification is the relationship between theory and empirical evidence.

Despite recent claims in economics to the contrary, methodology is not, never can be, and never should attempt to be non-prescriptive. In studying the methods of analysis, methodologists, at the very least, provide descriptions of the means by which scientists seek to justify their knowledge claims. Often this may involve making explicit implicitly held methodological beliefs and presuppositions. These descriptions provide the basis for critical evaluation, for questioning the justification of the justifications. This is an important, indeed essential, role of methodology as a source of critical awareness of the foundations of knowledge claims. A non-prescriptive methodology, if such a thing could exist, would be mere scholasticism at best and at worst a legitimization through neglect of dogmatic (non-scientific) belief.

In considering the methodology of economics, it is important to distinguish between 'abstract' methodology and 'practical' methodology, akin to McCloskey's distinction between official and unofficial rhetoric (McCloskey, 1983). Abstract methodology is an outsider's view of the methods employed by economists. It is produced by philosophers and consists of a set of explicit, philosophically coherent and internally consistent methodological beliefs. Practical methodology, on the other hand, is an insider's view. It is the cluster of methodological beliefs held by economists and econometricians with which to justify their research methods, if required. Practical methodology is often largely implicit, a tacit dimension of knowledge (Polanyi, 1973) and, as a result, a cluster of methodological beliefs may include elements seemingly drawn from philosophically incompatible belief systems. The tacit nature of methodological beliefs arises from the educational process. Research methods are acquired through a learning-by-doing process (Kuhn, 1962) and embody presuppositions about the nature of the world and how to acquire knowledge.

These presuppositions are seldom discussed unless economists and econometricians are challenged to justify their research methods. In trying to understand the research methods of economists and econometricians, it is important as a first step to identify the clusters of methodological beliefs before subjecting these clusters to critical evaluation. Abstract methodology provides an essential guide to the identification and evaluation of methodological beliefs. But, unless the methodological analysis starts with the identification of clusters, there is the danger that economists and econometricians will be 'pigeon-holed', quite misleadingly, within a fully consistent philosophical belief system. Thus, for example, the debates over whether or not Friedman is an instrumentalist are wrong-headed if the intention is to classify Friedman as belonging to a well-defined philosophical approach called instrumentalism. Friedman's methodological beliefs may involve aspects of instrumentalist thought, but that is quite a different claim with no necessary requirement of exclusivity and, hence, no implied criticism of inconsistency if this exclusivity is violated.

From the perspective of methodological clusters, two broadly defined clusters can be usefully distinguished within economics: a 'conservative' cluster and a 'radical' cluster.

The Conservative Cluster of Methodological Beliefs

The conservative cluster of methodological beliefs is the dominant cluster in economics and is characterized by a general defensive orientation towards mainstream economic theory. There is a strong *a priori* belief in the essential correctness and adequacy of the theoretical foundations of economics. Conservative methodological beliefs act as in-built immunizing stratagems against criticisms of mainstream economic theory.

There are four principal elements of the conservative methodological cluster: the axiomatic approach, 'as-if' modelling, objectivity, and empirical evidence as confirmatory. The axiomatic approach is justified by an amalgam of deductivist and Platonist arguments. Deductivism is the view that knowledge can be attained by the application of logical methods to axioms that are true *a priori*. It is a methodological view originally advocated in economics by J.S. Mill (1836). The truth status (that is, objectivity) of economic theory is ensured by its logical consistency and the self-evident truth of its axioms. From this perspective, empirical evidence plays a secondary role of confirming or otherwise the applicability of economic theory in specific situations. Applicability depends on the absence of disturbing causes, that is, transitory influences that are excluded from the theory. Lack of confirmation does not falsify an economic theory, but signifies the presence of significant disturbing causes.

There are also elements of Platonism within the conservative cluster (see Roy, 1989). Mathematical models are often justified as ideal abstractions that transcend the imperfect forms of empirical reality. This can be seen as another variant of the 'disturbing causes' defence against anomalous empirical evidence. It is also a defence against criticisms of the axiomatic basis of economic theory as unrealistic. An alternative defence is the instrumentalist argument that economic theory is not intended to be a realistic description of the economic mechanism but merely a predictive tool. Models are 'as-if' constructs to be judged empirically. It is a line of argument most famously associated with Friedman (1953b), but one at odds with the implied realism of the axiomatic approach.

A recent representative statement of the methodological defence of mainstream economics is provided by Hausman (1992) who considers that the justification of economic theory derives from its axiomatic foundations, not from empirical testing. Hausman defends the deductivist outlook as the only feasible scientific approach, given that economics is largely a field study rather than an experimental science. Hausman (1992: 226) concludes that its 'apparent dogmatism can arise from the circumstances in which economists find themselves blessed with behavioural postulates that are plausible, powerful, and convenient, and cursed with the inability to learn much from experience'.

Lawson (1989b, 1994a, 1994b, 1994c) argues that the methodological beliefs of mainstream economists are informed by Humean positivism. In particular, Lawson considers mainstream economists as empirical realists, concerned with event regularities. This implies a closed-system view in which empirical work in economics attempts to emulate the method of experimental control used in the natural sciences. Undoubtedly there are elements of empirical realism in the conservative cluster, particularly the advocacy of 'as-if' modelling and the importance attached to predictive power as a criterion of theory appraisal. But mainstream economists also exhibit deductivist and Platonist beliefs that the axiomatic foundations of economic theory embody the essential aspects of the economic mechanism. Friedman, for example, justifies the predictive power of models based on the axiom of profit maximization in terms of the economic mechanism of the competitive process acting as an evolutionary selection device. Empirical realism does not allow for this concern with causal reality and, therefore, is too restrictive as a description of mainstream methodology in economics.

The Radical Cluster of Methodological Beliefs

An alternative cluster of methodological beliefs is the radical cluster. The defining characteristic of the radical cluster is its fallibilist attitude to economic theory. It is particularly associated with non-mainstream schools of thought such as Post Keynesian economics, but not exclusively so. The radical cluster represents the recognition that the theoretical foundations of economic theory may be inadequate and, therefore, must be subject to empirical testing. There is a belief in the possibility that the 'world may bite back' in the sense that empirical evidence may cast doubt on the validity of economic theory. Economic theory can only be justified if it is shown to be consistent with observed phenomena. This requires that empirical evidence must not be relegated to a secondary role of identifying actual examples of the empirical regularities predicted by economic theory. Rather, there must be a meaningful interaction between economic theory and empirical evidence which involves the possibility that economic theory may need to be reconstructed to a greater or lesser extent in the light of empirical anomalies that are judged to be significant.

The radical cluster of methodological beliefs has four main elements: empirical testing, mathematical models as non-empirical, the importance of causal explanation, and pluralism. The stress on empirical testing as a means of theory appraisal within the radical cluster could be seen as a sophisticated form of falsificationism which recognizes the inconclusiveness of empirical testing: the Duhem–Quine thesis (Cross, 1982). Theories can never be conclusively falsified owing to their conglomerate structure. Target hypotheses are always tested in conjunction with a range of auxiliary hypotheses including the definition and measurement of variables, functional form and the stochastic properties of the estimated model. A falsification is a falsification of the whole conjunction, not the target hypothesis. Hence empirical testing always involves interpretation. This, in turn, can lead to an acknowldgment of the possibility of alternative interpretations. Furthermore, if the world is assumed to be inherently complex, alternative interpretations may be seen as complementary parts of an organic whole, implying the need for a pluralist (or Babylonian), rather than a reductionist (or Cartesian/Euclidean), approach.

The recognition of the difficulties of empirical testing is linked with a formalist view of mathematical models. Models are formal in the sense of being extended definitions which make no empirical claims about observed economic phenomena. Models allow conceptual exploration of the logical implications of a particular set of assumptions. Models only become theories with testable implications about economic phenomena when 'bridging' hypotheses are postulated asserting a correspondence between the formal model and empirical reality.

Lawson (1989b, 1994a, 1994b, 1994c) argues that transcendental realism provides the appropriate methodological alternative to mainstream economics. Transcendental realism (known as critical realism when applied to the social realm) treats reality as consisting of three domains: the empirical domain of experience, the actual domain of events and the 'deep' domain of structures and generative mechanisms. These domains are distinct and out of phase with each other. Structures and generative mechanisms are the intransitive features of reality which science aims to identify and explain. But structures and mechanisms are non-empirical entities which at best manifest themselves empirically as partial event regularities. The appropriate mode of inference is retroduction or abduction. Analysis begins with the identification of stylized facts – partial empirical regularities deemed to be sufficiently significant to warrant explanation – and proceeds from the manifest phenomena to deep structures. The research objective is to relate the stylized facts to the underlying structural tendencies.

Critical realism as a critique of 'as-if' modelling can be interpreted as part of a radical cluster of methodological beliefs, but not necessarily so. The concern for causal reality is not unique to radical schools of thought in economics. The axiomatic approach in mainstream economics can be viewed as dealing with deep structures and mechanisms. Indeed, one of the major criticisms of conventional econometric methods by real business cycle theorists and the move to greater use of calibration methods has been the failure of econometric models to identify deep structural parameters (see, for example, Wickens, 1995). Critical realism can also be interpreted as a defensive methodological belief to the extent that its concerns with non-empirical structures can be used to justify immunity from empirical testing.

III CONSERVATIVE APPROACHES TO ECONOMETRICS

A conservative approach to econometrics is based on the presupposition that the role of empirical investigation is the description of observed phenomena and/or the estimation of theoretically derived models. From this perspective, empirical investigation does not provide a means of testing the empirical validity of theories. Hence a conservative approach to econometrics is associated with the view that econometric modelling is a theory-driven estimation process or a data-driven description process. There is little or no allowance for an interactive confrontation of economic theory and empirical evidence. The theory-driven estimation process is exemplified by the AER/textbook approach to econometrics. The data-driven description process is exemplified by atheoretical time-series analysis.

The AER/Textbook Approach to Econometrics

The dominant approach to econometric modelling, particularly in North America, has been described by Gilbert (1986) as the AER (average economic regression) or textbook approach. It is an approach characterized by a strong *a priori* belief in the adequacy of the theoretical foundations of the model to be estimated. Economic theory is seen as providing an insight into the nature of the economic mechanisms. The role of econometric modelling is to estimate the theoretical model. The major concern is to discover whether the estimated coefficients are statistically significant. If the estimated coefficients are statistically significant, this is interpreted as confirmation of the importance of the economic mechanisms posited by the theory. Lack of confirmation is usually explained as arising from the effects of disturbing causes, that is, sample-specific transitory influences that mask the effects of the permanent economic mechanisms.

The AER/textbook approach begins with economic theory providing the specification of the deterministic component of the econometric model to be estimated. This includes specifying the dependent variable and the set of potentially relevant explanatory (or independent) variables representing the permanent effects of the economic mechanisms. A stochastic error term is added to capture the sample-specific transitory influences. It is seen as the field study equivalent to experimental control. It is assumed to possess a number of properties to justify the chosen estimation procedure as yielding the optimal estimators. The usual set of assumed properties is that the stochastic error term is a random variable with a normal distribution, zero mean, constant variance (that is, homoskedasticity) and serial independence. It is also assumed that the deterministic component of the model is correctly specified and that the variables are free from measurement error. Under these assumptions the ordinary least squares (OLS) regression technique is optimal. Formally, it can be shown that the OLS estimator is the best linear unbiased estimator (BLUE). The proof of this proposition is provided by the Gauss–Markov theorem.

After the econometric model is estimated, it is subjected to several criteria of evaluation: economic, statistical and econometric. The principal economic criterion is whether the estimated coefficients have the predicted sign. For example, is there a negative coefficient on the relative price variable in an estimated demand model? In addition there may be *a priori* beliefs about the size of the estimated coefficients suggested either by economic theory or by other empirical studies. The statistical criterion of evaluation is whether the estimated coefficients are individually and jointly significantly different from zero. Individual significance is tested by t-ratios. Joint significance is indicated by goodness-of-fit measures such as R^2 and formally tested by F-tests. The econometric criterion of evaluation is whether or not the residuals (that is, the unexplained variation in the dependent variable) conform to the assumed properties of the unobserved stochastic error term. This is the process of diagnostic testing. Standard tests include the Durbin–Watson (DW) test for serial dependence, White and Goldfeld–Quandt tests for heteroskedasticity (that is, non-constant variance), the Bera–Jarque test for non-normality and the Ramsey RESET test for model misspecification.

If the model is deemed to be inadequate because of 'wrong' signs, statistically insignificant estimates, or poor diagnostics, then the model is re-specified and re-estimated. Poor diagnostics tend to be interpreted as indicative of the stochastic error term not possessing all of the properties required for the estimation procedure to yield the optimal estimators. Thus poor diagnostics are seen primarily as an estimation problem requiring that the model be estimated by another, more optimal, estimation method. For example, if the DW test statistic is low, this is interpreted as evidence that the stochastic error is an autoregressive (AR) process (that is, serially dependent) and, hence, necessitating the use of the Cochrane–Orcutt estimation procedure. Similarly, if there is multicollinearity within the set of explanatory variables, this is interpreted as primarily a data problem. The sample data are seen as inadequate to allow precise and stable estimates to be obtained. Omitted-variable and bounded-influence estimation techniques may be considered more appropriate.

The major deficiency with the AER/textbook approach is that it is ultimately based on a very strong *a priori* belief about the ability of economic theory to deduce the essential nature of the economic mechanisms underlying the observed phenomena. It is this *a priori* belief that Leamer (1983) has called 'the axiom of correct specification'. The interpretation of diagnostic tests as indicating specific forms of estimation problem necessitates the assumption that the estimated model is well specified in all other ways. Correct specification requires the correct set of relevant explanatory variables as well as the correct functional form. This is a very strong requirement. But if the axiom of correct specification does not hold, then the results of the diagnostic tests cannot be interpreted in any definitive way. A low Durbin–Watson test statistic may be due to an AR error process, but it can also be caused by a number of other specification problems in either the deterministic component of the model or the stochastic component. Serial dependence in the residuals can be caused by incorrectly specifying the dynamic structure of the model or by using the incorrect functional form. Both of these are specification problems concerning the deterministic component of the model and necessitating respecification of the model rather than an alternative estimation procedure.

To the extent that the AER/textbook approach considers the possibility of specification problems rather than pure estimation problems, it does so in a rather *ad hoc* manner. Additional explanatory variables and alternative functional forms may be introduced in a very mechanical process, a case of 'if at first you don't succeed, try, try and try again'. Various algorithms, such as stepwise regression, provide search routines to identify models with high goodness-of-fit performance. There is little or no theoretical justification for the adjustments to the initial model specification. The specification search is driven entirely by statistical considerations. It is a specific-to-general modelling strategy in which the initial model is extended until the economic, statistical and econometric criteria for an adequate model are satisfied. The *ad hoc* nature of the modelling strategy implies that the specification of the final model may be path-dependent. There is no necessity that alternative specification searches converge on the same 'best' model.

The specific-to-general modelling strategy has the inherent danger of becoming an exercise in data mining. The specification search seeks to identify the 'best' model for the particular data set under investigation. But this can lead to a problem of overfitting, in the sense that, although a good sample-specific fit is achieved, there is little or no attempt to assess whether or not the estimated model has general applicability.

The AER/textbook approach is thus consistent with the conservative cluster of methodological beliefs in economics. In particular, it is closely associated with the axiomatic approach to economic theory. Economic theory is seen as solving the basic specification problem by providing an insight into the economic mechanisms and, thereby, identifying the dependent variable and the relevant set of explanatory variables. Econometrics is restricted to providing good estimates of the theoretically identified model. Gilbert (1986: 284) has recognized the problem:

> The problem with the AER approach is that we are using econometrics to illustrate the theories which we believe independently. The alternative might be to use econometrics to discover which views of the economy (or market) are tenable and to test, scientifically, the rival views.

The AER/textbook approach illustrates rather than tests theories. Consequently, it provides economic theory with a defence against anomalous empirical evidence. If an empirical model is deemed inadequate, this is attributed to estimation problems and/or transitory influences; it is not interpreted as a potential falsification of the underlying economic theory. Ultimately the AER/textbook approach to econometrics views the validity of economic theories as being grounded in their logical properties, not their empirical properties.

Atheoretical Time-series Analysis

Atheoretical time-series analysis is a data-driven approach with little role for economic theory other than identifying individual or groups of time-series variables of analytical interest. Econometrics is rejected as a means of either estimating or testing economic theories because of the inevitable problems of identification. In particular, Sims (1980) has been a strong opponent of the notion that econometrics can provide estimates of the structural parameters of economic mechanisms. He dismisses the heroic assumption that estimated coefficients can be interpreted as estimates of structural parameters as 'incredible identification' (Sims, 1980: 2). Such identification requires the imposition of a set of restrictions that are not supported empirically. Sims also believes that the advent of rational expectations has further highlighted the almost insurmountable difficulties posed by the identification problem. To the extent that agents' behaviour depends on their expectations about future outcomes, it follows that their behaviour may depend on all variables within their information sets. This being the case, it is no longer feasible to model economic behaviour as dependent on a relatively small set of determining variables. Sims illustrates his argument with the example of US consumers stockpiling coffee in anticipation of the effects of a frost in Brazil. In this case rational expectations render the distinction between the demand and supply effects on prices and quantities almost empirically meaningless, since these effects cannot be identified separately.

One reaction to the identification problem has been to reject econometrics as a useful means of empirical investigation. This view is principally associated with real-business-cycle theory and started with the work of Kydland and Prescott (1982). Real-business-cycle theorists tend to advocate calibration methods (often called 'quantitative theory') as an alternative to econometric modelling. Quantitative theory involves building a general equilibrium model with specific functional forms and, through the appropriate selection of parameter values (that is, calibration), attempts to mimic the behaviour of the actual economy by running computer simulations of the model subjected to a series of random, usually technological, shocks. Calibration is seen as a more effective means of quantifying the deep structural parameters. But, despite the claims made on its behalf, calibration is a complement to, rather than a substitute for, econometric modelling. Econometric studies provide the main source of empirical estimates of the parameter values used to calibrate the models. Furthermore, to be a practical tool, calibration must undertake sensitivity analysis to assess the robustness of its results. This requires knowledge of the statistical properties of the parameter values and again necessitates an input from econometrics.

Sims's own response to the identification problem has been to develop the vector autoregression (VAR) approach to the econometric modelling of time-series data. The VAR approach provides an alternative methodology to that of structural estimation. The objective is not to identify the structural equations derived from economic theory; rather, the VAR approach is essentially a descriptive approach in which the aim is to produce an adequate statistical summary of the data. The VAR approach involves the estimation of a system of equations, with each variable being modelled as a function of its own lagged values and the lagged values of all of the other variables in the system. Consequently, it represents an extension of the single-equation Box–Jenkins methodology to the estimation of systems of equations. The VAR is a system of unrestricted reduced-form equations. Economic theory plays a purely minimal role of suggesting the variables to be included in any particular VAR. Economic theory is not used as a source of restrictions to be imposed on the VAR. After the initial estimation of the VAR, the next step is to simplify the VAR by imposing data-driven restrictions such as eliminating statistically insignificant lagged values. The estimated VAR is evaluated with respect to two principal criteria: goodness-of-fit and the randomness of the residuals. If the estimated VAR is deemed satisfactory, it may be used subsequently to investigate the reduced-form implications of economic theories. This investigation does not constitute empirical testing of economic theory, since the lack of structural restrictions precludes adequate differentiation between competing theories. Rather, it is an exercise in empirical illustration of economic theories through the quantification of the reduced-form implications.

There have been attempts to move beyond the 'pure' VAR approach through the development of the structural VAR approach. Here additional theory-driven restrictions are imposed to identify structural parameters. One notable example of the structural VAR approach is the Blanchard–Quah decomposition (Blanchard and Quah, 1989). Blanchard and Quah show how it is possible to decompose a bivariate VAR to obtain estimates of permanent and temporary shocks by imposing the long-run restriction that only real shocks have permanent real effects. This restriction is derived from the natural-rate hypothesis. Blanchard and Quah apply their procedure to US post-war quarterly data on output growth and unemployment to estimate the time paths of the impact of aggregate demand and supply shocks.

The development of the structural VAR approach represents a move towards a greater role for economic theory in the specification of the system of equations to be estimated. But the VAR approach remains primarily a process of data description in which the aim is to estimate reduced-form equations with little testing of (structural) economic theories. The structural VAR approach extends the process of empirical illustration of economic theories towards the quantification of structural parameters. But this is not empirical testing. For example, the Blanchard–Quah decomposition presupposes the validity of the natural-rate hypothesis; it does not subject this hypothesis to critical empirical evaluation.

IV   THE LSE APPROACH: A RADICAL METHODOLOGY

The LSE approach originated at the London School of Economics primarily in the work of Denis Sargan. (See Gilbert, 1989, for an account of the historical development of the LSE approach.) The approach to econometric modelling that began to emerge from Sargan's work was further developed by David Hendry (1993, 1995), a student of Sargan, along with various collaborators including Ericsson, Mizon and Richards. As a result, the LSE approach has become synonymous with Hendry's 'general-to-specific' methodology of econometric modelling. Gilbert (1989: 108) summarizes the principal characteristics of the LSE approach as follows:

> There is an emphasis on relatively free ('databased') dynamic specification in conjunction with a commitment to extensive specification tests. The error correction dynamic adjustment specification is frequently adopted, and found acceptable. And there is a tendency to identify residual autocorrelation with equation misspecification.

The general-to-specific approach to econometric modelling involves the formulation of a very general model, followed by its simplification through the imposition of both theory-driven and data-driven restrictions. At the basis of the general-to-specific approach are the twin concepts of the data generating process (DGP) and the statistical generating mechanism (SGM). The DGP consists of two components: the economic mechanism and the measurement process. The economic mechanism is the decisions and actions of economic agents. The measurement process is the means by which the realized outcomes of these decisions and actions are transformed into observed and measured values (that is, data). Thus the DGP is the economic reality, the structure that generates the data to be modelled. The SGM, on the other hand, is a convenient fiction in the sense of being a conjecture about the joint probability distribution of a stochastic process that could have generated the data. It is not implied that the DGP is inherently stochastic. Rather, it is a recognition that the modelling process necessarily involves a limited representation of reality combined with the contention that the appropriate way to capture this limitation is to assume that reality behaves in the manner of a stochastic process. Hence the SGM is the justification for the introduction of a stochastic error term in the empirical model to be estimated. The SGM provides the basis for statistical estimation and inference. As Lawson (1989a) has noted, the stochastic error term is instrumentalist in nature, a necessary fiction to justify the modelling of one part of reality in isolation (what Lawson calls 'the extrinsic closure condition').

Given the assumed properties of the SGM, the next step is to specify the empirical model to be estimated. The empirical model is formulated as a theoretically meaningful and statistically adequate representation of the DGP. The general-to-specific approach adopts the modelling strategy of specifying a very general empirical model and using extensive diagnostic testing to ensure that the estimated model is statistically adequate. If the estimated model is statistically adequate, it is said to be congruent with the DGP. Congruence is a necessary condition for the estimated model to be a 'true' representation of the DGP, but it is not a sufficient condition. The concept of congruence is a recognition of the fallibility of human knowledge. We can never know if we have discovered a true model of the DGP.

Rather, all we can continually strive for are adequate representations. Having estimated a congruent model, the modelling objective becomes that of parsimony. Theoretically meaningful reparameterizations and linear restrictions are introduced to produce a simplified model. Data-driven restrictions are also imposed, such as the marginalization of irrelevant (that is, statistically insignificant) variables. Provided that the imposed restrictions are statistically valid, the simplified model will retain the congruence property. Thus the ultimate objective of the general-to-specific modelling strategy is to produce parsimonious empirical models with theoretical meaning. These models can then be used for the empirical testing of economic theories.

Economic theory plays two key roles in the modelling process. It provides the focus of interest, identifying the DGP to be investigated and designating a set of potentially relevant variables. Economic theory is also a source of long-run (equilibrium) restrictions. In contrast, short-run dynamics are data-determined. Economic theory tends to have little to say on the precise nature of adjustment processes. The general-to-specific approach is particularly associated with the use of the error correction mechanism (ECM) as a formulation of the short-run dynamics of economic processes. The ECM is linked with the concept of cointegration. Two variables are said to be cointegrated if they move together over time. Technically, cointegration requires that there exist a linear combination of the set of variables under investigation that is stationary. Cointegration is consistent with the notion of long-run equilibrium relationships. Hence a key step in the modelling process is to establish whether or not a set of variables is cointegrated. The Engle–Granger representation theorem proves that the short-run dynamics of a cointegrating relationship can be modelled by an ECM.

The epistemological basis of the LSE approach is set out by Hendry (1995: ch.1) in terms of four levels of knowledge. Level A is the situation in which the structure and parameters of the DGP are known. This is the realm of probability theory. Level B is the situation in which the structure of the DGP is known but the parameter values are unknown. In this case the problem is one for estimation theory: how to acquire the best statistical estimates of the unknown parameter values. Level C involves a further degree of uncertainty: both the structure and the parameter values of the DGP are unknown. This is the level of modelling theory in which both an adequate specification of the structure of the DGP has to be discovered and the parameter values have to be estimated. Level D represents the highest degree of uncertainty in which the data outcomes are unknown. In this case there is a forecasting problem; the theory of forecasting becomes relevant. Levels C and D are the empirically relevant situations. The econometrician is trying to estimate an empirical model of a DGP with unknown structure and unknown parameter values and may be concerned with predicting future data outcomes. Levels A and B are theoretical abstractions which underpin levels C and D, but are not empirically relevant in themselves.

From the perspective of these four levels of knowledge, the general-to-specific approach to econometric modelling involves an iterative cycle between levels A, B and C. Initial specification assumptions are made about the structure of the DGP and the nature of the stochastic process. The empirical model is estimated and diagnostic testing is used to evaluate the validity or otherwise of the specification assumptions. If the diagnostic properties of the estimated model are poor, the model is respecified and re-estimated. Thus the LSE approach views the modelling process as a spec-ification problem. The AER/textbook approach, on the other hand, views the modelling process as predominantly a level-B problem, that is, an esti-mation problem. Economic theory is seen as providing well-specified models to be estimated. This fundamental difference between the two approaches to econometric modelling is most apparent in the interpreta-tion of diagnostic tests. The LSE approach treats poor diagnostic proper-ties as a possible indication of a misspecified model, whereas the AER/textbook approach treats poor diagnostic properties as most likely being caused by the use of an inappropriate estimation procedure.

The difference is one of degree – differences in the relative prior probabil-ities attached to whether poor diagnostic properties are a specification or estimation problem – but reflects a fundamental methodological difference between empiricist and deductivist outlooks. The interpretation of a low Durbin–Watson test statistic provides a good illustration of this fundamen-tal difference. The LSE approach interprets a low Durbin–Watson test sta-tistic as indicative of a specification problem, particularly an inadequate characterization of the dynamics of the DGP, requiring that the model be respecified. As discussed previously, the AER/textbook interpretation is that the stochastic error process is serially correlated, implying that the optimal estimation procedure is no longer OLS but rather the Cochrane–Orcutt (or autoregressive least squares) estimation procedure. Similarly, the LSE approach does not interpret multicollinearity as a data-based problem but as an indication of a model specification that does not exploit efficiently the available sample information.

An alternative way of characterizing the difference between the two approaches is with respect to whether or not econometric modelling is seen as analogous to experimental control. The AER/textbook approach views econometric modelling as seeking to emulate the experimental method. Consider the empirical model

$$y_t = bx_t + u_t \qquad (8.1)$$

where $y_t \equiv$ dependent variable at time t; $x_t \equiv$ independent variable; $b \equiv$ parameter; and $u_t \equiv$ stochastic error term.

The AER/textbook interpretation of equation (8.1) is to view the left-hand side (LHS) of the equation as the outcome of the right-hand side (RHS). The estimation problem is to derive an estimate of the parameter, b, given a set of observations of (y_t, x_t). The alternative LSE interpretation is that equation (8.1) is a misleading analogy and is more appropriately written in the following form:

$$y_t - bx_t = u_t, \tag{8.2}$$

where the stochastic error process, u_t, is the outcome of the observed values of the variables and the assumed specification of the DGP. The stochastic error process depends on the model specification imposed by the econometric modeller. In a sense, the causation runs from the LHS to the RHS, and not vice versa.

Within the general-to-specific modelling framework, there are two main criteria of evaluation of estimated models: congruence and encompassing. Congruence implies that the estimated model is an acceptable representation of the DGP, both economically and statistically. This requires that the sign and magnitude of the estimated parameters are consistent with economic theory, the estimated parameters are individually and jointly statistically significant and the diagnostic properties are good. Encompassing is the requirement that the estimated model be able to account for the explanatory power of rival models. Encompassing ensures that there is cumulative progress in the econometric modelling process. In addition, considerable emphasis is placed on the need to identify structurally stable empirical models, that is, empirical models in which the values of the estimated parameters are not dependent on the length of the sample period. Recursive estimation techniques are used to evaluate how the parameter estimates change as the sample period proceeds. Chow tests, one-step residuals, innovations and cumulative measures of goodness-of-fit provide a variety of means for describing and testing for structural change. Another important aspect of the model evaluation process is to determine whether the estimated model has good out-of-sample forecasting ability. This acts as a safeguard against data mining and overfitting. Taken together, encompassing, structural stability and out-of-sample forecasting provide a set of criteria consistent with the ultimate objective of econometric modelling in the LSE approach, namely, the discovery of empirical models that are generally valid across both time and space.

The LSE approach, as developed in the general-to-specific modelling strategy, offers a radical methodology in the sense of allowing for an inter-active approach between economic theory and empirical evidence. Unlike the more conservative approaches, the LSE approach assumes neither that the economic structure is known *a priori* nor that the economic structure is unidentifiable. Economic theory is used to provide initial hypotheses about the general form of the DGP and its long-run properties. A specifi-cation search is undertaken guided by both economic theory and sample information. The aim is to produce congruent simplifications that are eco-nomically meaningful and progressive. The emphasis on the fallibility of knowledge, particularly evidenced by the recognition of congruence rather than 'truth' as the research objective, places the LSE approach within the post-positivist/post-modernist philosophical outlook. Hence the LSE approach is consistent with the methodological principles of Post Keynesian economics and, as a consequence, should be used much more widely for empirical research by Post Keynesian economists.

However, there is a long history of Post Keynesian antagonism towards econometrics. The origins of this antagonism lie in Keynes's critique of Tinbergen's early applications of econometric techniques (Keynes, 1939, 1940). Keynes set out a long list of potential problems which may bedevil any estimated economic model. As a consequence, an estimated model must be interpreted with considerable care and sufficient emphasis must be placed on its fallibility. Indeed, Keynes considered the problems so great as to call into question whether it is worthwhile to employ econometric methods. The problems that Keynes identified included omitted variables, unobservable variables, simultaneity, non-linearity, dynamic specification, the lack of uniformity over the sample period and the inadequacy of the data. As Hendry (1993: 20) recognizes, Keynes's criticisms of Tinbergen's econometric methods provide an 'excellent list' of the 'problems of the linear regression model'. Many of the developments in econometrics over the last fifty or so years can be seen as a continuing attempt to study the consequences of the problems identified by Keynes, to design diagnostic tests to detect the occurrence of these problems and to develop the appro-priate methods of dealing with these problems. The LSE approach, in par-ticular, is founded on the presupposition that the nature of the DGP is not known *a priori* but has to be discovered during the modelling process.

Keynes's critique of Tinbergen's method has been interpreted by many Post Keynesian economists as a complete rejection of econometric methods. This attitude continues to prevail and has been given substance in many different forms. For example, Lawson (1981) criticizes Hendry's approach to econometric modelling as being characterized by the assump-tion of true, correctly specified equations. Later, from a more explicitly realist perspective, Lawson has criticized econometrics as instrumentalist

(Lawson, 1989a) and underpinned by Humean positivism (Lawson, 1994b). Davidson (1991) has focused on the non-ergodicity of economic processes which precludes the usefulness of econometric methods. Foster and Wild (1995) are critical of the use of cointegration, which they consider to be inextricably linked to an equilibrium interpretation of economic outcomes and hence incompatible with the evolutionary approach widely advocated by Post Keynesian economists. There is some substance to these Post Keynesian criticisms when directed at the AER/textbook approach to econometric modelling, but the inappropriateness of many of these criticisms with respect to the LSE approach has usually not been recognized, leading to a complete rejection of econometric methods by many Post Keynesian economists which is both unwarranted and, more importantly, hinders the development of Post Keynesian economics as a significant contribution to the understanding of economic processes.

As has been argued above, the LSE approach is consistent with the methodological perspective of Post Keynesian economics. The LSE approach recognizes the fallibility of human knowledge, both in the concept of congruence and in the primacy attached to the specification (that is, level-C) aspect of the modelling problems. The LSE approach does not assume that true, well-specified models exist and are known to the econometrician. This would limit the modelling problem to a purely level-B estimation problem. Furthermore, the LSE approach adopts a realist epistemology. The realism of the LSE approach is embodied in the notion of the DGP which represents the unknown fundamental economic structure to be investigated. This fundamental economic structure is assumed to be invariant. Hence considerable importance is attached to testing whether or not estimated models are structurally stable, using, for example, recursive least squares. Structural instability is evidence that the estimated model has not adequately captured the fundamental invariant structure of the DGP. This emphasis on structural instability can be interpreted as the principal prescription for econometricians to be derived from critical realism (Smith, 1994). To say that the LSE approach is realist is not to imply that it is devoid of instrumentalist assumptions. Instrumentalist assumptions (that is, convenient fictions) in one form or another play a necessary justifying role in all methods of analysis. Temporary independence assumptions are required as the extrinsic closure condition in order to justify the focus of analysis on one part of reality. In the LSE approach, the concept of the SGM fulfils this role. These temporary independence assumptions need to be recognized and their appropriateness evaluated. The extensive use of diagnostic tests in the LSE approach represents an attempt to evaluate the empirical validity of the assumptions of the SGM.

The Post Keynesian criticisms about the non-ergodicity of economic processes and the equilibrium-theoretic nature of cointegration are also exaggerated. A major focus in recent econometric theory has been the analysis of non-stationary time series, an important subclass of non-ergodic processes (see Banerjee *et al.*, 1993). Considerable advances have been made in developing unit-root tests to detect non-stationarity under various conditions. Cointegration and error correction mechanisms are important developments for modelling non-stationary time series. Cointegration need not necessarily be treated as an equilibrium-theoretic concept. Cointegration tests are a *statistical* technique for detecting long-run co-movements between time series. This is an important element of exploratory data analysis prior to the econometric modelling process. Alternative *theoretical* interpretations of long-run co-movements are possible. Admittedly, the predominant interpretation of cointegrating relationships is an equilibrium interpretation, but this need not be the case. To the extent that evolutionary processes may produce long-run co-movements between economic time series, this can be investigated by the use of cointegration tests.

V   SUMMARY AND CONCLUSIONS

All research methods involve implicit presuppositions about the nature of the objects of study, the nature of knowledge and the means by which knowledge can be attained. It is the role of methodology to evaluate these presuppositions critically. In this chapter two alternative clusters of methodological beliefs in economics have been identified: a conservative cluster that is generally protective of mainstream economic theory and a radical cluster with a much more fallibilist (and, hence, 'scientific') approach to economic theory. It has been shown that these clusters of methodological beliefs are embodied in alternative econometric methodologies. The conservative cluster of methodological beliefs is embodied in the theory-driven AER/textbook approach and the data-driven atheoretical time-series approach. Both of these econometric methodologies inhibit the critical empirical evaluation of economic theory and, as a consequence, encourage a dogmatic belief in the adequacy of economic theory. In contrast, the LSE approach incorporates a more radical, fallibilist perspective on economic theory, allowing for a more meaningful, critical interaction between economic theory and empirical evidence. It has been argued that econometrics and Post Keynesian economics are not inherently antagonistic. The LSE approach to econometrics is compatible with the radical outlook of Post Keynesian economics. In particular, the LSE approach is post-positivist/post-modernist in its fallibilist concern for congruence rather than truth. The LSE approach is also inherently realist, seeking to discover adequate statistical representations of the fundamental economic structure (that is, the DGP). Economic theory is seen as a source of hypotheses about the nature of economic structure. These structural hypotheses need to be subjected to critical empirical evaluation rather than accepted as true *a priori*. It is, therefore, concluded that econometrics is not a school-specific, 'orthodoxy-only' methodology. Econometric methods can, and should, be used more extensively within Post Keynesian economics as an essential part of a radical methodology.

NOTE

1. Subject to the usual disclaimer, I wish to acknowledge the comments of John Hillard as well as the useful discussions related to the original paper at the second Keynes, Knowledge and Uncertainty Conference held at the Hilton Hotel, Leeds in March 1996. Thanks are also due to the participants in the Applied Economics Workshop at the University of Leeds and a staff seminar at Staffordshire University to whom an early draft was presented. I am also grateful to Philip Arestis for detailed and helpful comments on a draft of this chapter.

9. Post-orthodox econometrics

Paul Ormerod

I INTRODUCTION

Presenting a paper to any conference with the name 'Keynes' in the title, particularly to one sponsored by the Post Keynesian Study Group, is fraught with danger. For the exegitical debate about 'what Keynes really meant' is often carried out with as much fervour as the arguments between the Fathers of the early Church. Indeed, some of the latter material has a familiar sound. Origen, for example, proposed a theory of Redemption in which the soul fluctuated between Heaven and Hell, a suggestion sternly denounced as heresy by Augustine, who specifically denied the existence of endogenous cycles.

It is as well to make my own position clear from the outset. Keynes is obviously a very important figure in economics. But it is now sixty years since the *General Theory* was written, and the world has moved on. Particularly outside the discipline of economics, scientific methodology has changed. We should be concerned to use advances in knowledge to increase our understanding of the dynamics of capitalism, regardless of whether Keynes – or Smith or Ricardo or Marx, for that matter – really meant the same thing. So I do not intend to enter into definitional arguments about Keynesianism. The aim instead is to review how we should approach applied macroeconomic analysis.

Section II of the chapter considers briefly the post-war research programme in conventional macroeconomic modelling. Both in terms of forecasting accuracy and of structural understanding of the economy, very little progress has been made. Section III points out that the failures of forecasting are inherent in the nature of macroeconomic time series. It is simply not possible with most macro data series to generate forecasts over time which have an error variance significantly less than the variance of the data themselves. An important implication of this result is that conventional short-run stabilization policies cannot work in any meaningful sense, even if the structure of the economy were well understood. In Section IV, I argue that most existing applied macroeconomic relationships are overfitted. In local time neighbourhoods very simple linear models offer a good explanation of key macroeconomic relationships in the OECD economics. However, a small number of shocks have caused permanent shifts in key relationships, such as those between inflation and unemployment and between unemployment and growth. It is the task of political economy and not econometrics alone to understand the reasons for such shifts.

II   THE CONVENTIONAL RESEARCH PROGRAMME IN MACROECONOMICS

Most existing macromodels are based upon the synthesis which became 'Keynesian' economics. Depending upon the various strengths of key link-ages, these models are capable of generating a wide range of different policy simulation results, from ones close to the position of pure monetarism to ones in which fiscal policy can have a permanent effect on the economy. The criticisms which follow apply equally well, however, to the minority of models which describe themselves in alternative terms, such as 'monetarist' or 'supply-side'.

Such conventional macroeconometric models, whatever their theoretical and empirical leanings, are of little or no value. There are two aspects to discuss here: first, their forecasting record, and, second, their structural understanding of the economy. It is important to note that a great deal of public research money and effort has gone into these models in the post-war period, especially in the past twenty years. Despite this, no real progress has been made using this methodology.

The forecasting record is poor and shows no signs of improving. The OECD (1993), for example, note that over the 1987–92 period one-year ahead forecasts of GDP growth and inflation could not beat the naive rule that next year's growth/inflation will be the same as this year's. These fore-casts were carried out by the governments of the G7 countries, the IMF and the OECD itself. As examples of the one-year ahead forecasting record for GDP growth, for the US economy recessions have generally not been fore-cast prior to their occurrence, and the recessions following the 1974 and 1981 peaks in the level of output were not recognized even as they took place (Stekler and Fildes, 1999). Further, growth has generally been over-estimated during slowdowns and recessions whilst underestimates occurred during recoveries and booms (Zarnowitz and Braun, 1992). For the UK, the predictions of the Treasury over the 1971–96 period have been at least as good as those of other forecasters, but the mean absolute annual fore-cast error for these one-year ahead predictions was 1.45 per cent of GDP, compared to an actual mean absolute change of 2.10 per cent (Mellis and Whittaker, 1998). In 13 European countries over the 1971–1995 period, the average absolute error was 1.43 per cent of GDP, compared to the average annual change of 2.91 per cent (Oller and Barot, 1999).

Of course, the raw output of the models is adjusted by the forecasters, but such literature as exists on this topic suggests that the unadjusted forecasts of the models tend to be even worse (see, for example, Clements, 1995, for a list of such references).

Macro models in the UK, thanks to their reliance upon public funding, are the most sophisticated in the world, in the sense of being closest to academic work on economic theory and on econometrics. Yet their policy properties are still far from converging, despite the research effort devoted to them. Church *et al.* (1993) give simple properties of the six leading UK models of 1992 vintage, looking at straightforward questions such as the public spending multiplier. In some ways, the results are even more disparate than those reported for the models of 1977 vintage by Laury *et al.* (1978). On the issue, for example, of the impact on the price level of a change in the VAT rate, the models even give different signs. In some, prices rise, in others, they fall.

A technically more sophisticated exercise which demonstrates the point on policy properties was published recently by Bray *et al.* (1995). The research team used the London Business School, National Institute, Oxford Economic Forecasting and Treasury models of the UK economy to carry out a policy optimization exercise through to the year 2002. The broad objectives were to achieve low inflation, to reduce unemployment, to maximize growth, to keep government borrowing within certain constraints, to stabilize the exchange rate and to meet targets on the balance of payments. The available instruments spanned the range of conventional fiscal and monetary tools, being the standard rate of income tax, government expenditure and the short-term interest rate. The differences in the model results are, as with the simple exercise on a VAT change, not merely quantitative but are different in direction. Compared to the base forecast, for example, the Treasury, LBS and NI models require interest rates to be lower almost throughout the whole period, albeit by widely different amounts, whereas the OEF model requires them to be higher. As a percentage of GDP, government expenditure is higher in the NI model compared to the base forecast, much lower in the LBS model, virtually unchanged in the OEF, and both higher and lower over time in the Treasury model.

In summary, despite an intensive research effort over several decades, conventional macro models are capable neither of producing forecasts whose error variances are significantly less than the variances of the data series being forecast nor of making progress in understanding the impact on the economy of the orthodox instruments of fiscal and monetary policy.

III   FORECASTING IN ECONOMICS

Despite the accumulation of evidence, conventional macroeconomic modellers continue to work under the illusion that the application of yet more
sophisticated orthodox economic theory and yet more sophisticated econometrics of this kind will enable them both to make better forecasts and to
understand the structure of the economy better (see Hall, 1995, for a recent
example). In this section I address the question of the inherent forecastabil-
ity of macroeconomic time-series data and suggest that, in the current state
of scientific knowledge, it does not appear possible to generate macro forecasts in which the variance of the forecast error is significantly less than the
variance of the data themselves.

The idea that the business cycle is intrinsically unpredictable is not new.
Fisher (1925) suggested more than seventy years ago that the business cycle
was inherently unpredictable because, in modern terminology, the dimension of the problem is too high relative to the available number of observations. He argued that movements over time in the volume of output were 'a
composite of numerous elementary fluctuations, both cyclical and non-
cyclical', and quoted approvingly from his contemporary Moore, who
wrote that '[business] cycles differ widely in duration, in intensity, in the
sequence of their phases and in the relative prominence of their various
phenomena'. In such circumstances, even though deterministic structure
exists, given the limited amount of data available, it would be virtually
impossible to distinguish data generated by such a system from data which
were genuinely random in terms of their predictability.

Interestingly, David Hendry, the major econometric theoretician of the
conventional macroeconomic modelling research programme over the past
twenty years, appears to be moving to a view which is close to this.
Clements and Hendry (1995) suggest that there is 'a limit on our ability to
forecast even with parameter constancy'. They give as their major reason
the inherent uncertainty of the model structure. This is a point which
Chatfield (1995), a mathematical statistician rather than econometrician,
has emphasized for some time. The estimation of model parameters traditionally assumes that the model has a prespecified known form, and takes
no account of possible uncertainty regarding the model structure. In particular, this approach postulates implicitly the existence of a single, 'true'
model, an assumption which both Clements and Hendry and Chatfield
question, the latter writing: 'in practice model uncertainty is a fact of life
and is likely to be more serious than other sources of uncertainty which
have received far more attention from statisticians'.

Clements and Hendry speculate that 'it may be that only a few periods
ahead are necessary for economic stabilisation policy (e.g. 4–8 quarters)

and that forecasts are informative over this horizon'. Unfortunately, the evidence suggests that this is probably not the case. In the last few years, for example, statisticians have begun to apply non-linear estimation techniques to macroeconomic data series. Potter (1995) and Tsay and Tiao (1994) investigated quarterly changes in real US GNP from 1947 to 1990, using the first difference of the natural log of GNP. Tiao and Tsay used a threshold autoregressive model in which the data series was partitioned into four regimes determined by the patterns of growth in the previous two quarters. Potter also takes the threshold autoregressive approach, partitioning the data into just two regimes on slightly different criteria with respect to past growth than Tiao and Tsay.

Both the above papers showed that non-linear techniques were decisively superior to linear autoregressive representations of the data in terms of in-sample fit to post-war quarterly data on US GNP growth. However, the variance of the model error is barely less than the variance of the data, the former being 90 per cent of the latter in the Tiao and Tsay model and 88 per cent in Potter's best model. And this is the weakest possible test of forecasts, given that the fitted values of the model represent one-step ahead in-sample predictions.

With Michael Campbell (1997), I applied a non-parametric non-linear technique, namely a form of kernel smoothing, to the same data series. The ratio of the mean squared error to the variance of the data was 90 per cent for quarterly changes in US GNP, effectively identical to the two papers quoted above. We also built models for two, four and eight quarter differences in the log of the data, and carried out direct 2-, 4- and 8-step predictions, respectively. In other words, in predicting the 4-quarter growth rate from time t to time $t+4$, for example, only information up to time t was used, as it would be in a genuine forecasting situation. The results for the 2-step ahead direct predictions were very similar to those of the one-step, but the 4- and 8-step ones were even worse.

Both the actual forecasting record of macro models over a twenty-year period and the recent results from non-linear representations of the data suggest that most macroeconomic data series are inherently unpredictable. Ormerod and Campbell (1997) argue that this is an intrinsic property of the data, and one which is consistent with the Fisher hypothesis described above. In the past decade or so, important advances have been developed in non-linear signal processing, which it is perhaps helpful to think of as trying to identify the ratio of signal to noise in a data series. The approach is not concerned with the estimation of any particular model, but with the more general question of the signal-to-noise ratio. A very high level of noise relative to signal, for example, would suggest that in practice the data series would be indistinguishable from a random data series and no meaningful forecasts could be carried out. If a signal of sufficient strength exists, the practical problems of finding an appropriate representation of the data in a model may still be formidable, but at least in principle the effort can succeed.

A clear summary of the technique, known variously as singular value decomposition or singular spectrum analysis, is given in Mullin (1993) and a much more formal mathematical exposition is provided by Broomhead and King (1986). Other techniques in the physical sciences which are concerned with the existence of deterministic structure, such as the calculation of correlation dimension or of Lyapunov exponents, require far more data points than are available in macroeconomic data series. But singular value decomposition can be applied to noisy data series with lengths typically encountered in macroeconomics.

A brief overview of the technique is as follows. The essential concept is to form a delay matrix from a single time series in the following way. Given a series x_t, where t runs from 1 to n, choose a maximum delay d, and the first row of the matrix is $x_1, x_2,..., x_d$. The second row consists of $x_2, x_3,...,$ x_{d+1}, and so on. Restricting ourselves for the purposes of illustration to three dimensions and avoiding formal mathematics, we can see that such a matrix contains rows (x_t, x_{t-1} and x_{t-2}). If we connect these points in sequence on a graph, the underlying structure of the data series may be revealed. For example, the attractors arising from the Lorenz equations can be reconstructed in this way.

The covariance matrix of the delay matrix is formed, and the eigenvalues of this matrix are calculated. The eigenvalues can be thought of heuristically as measuring the strength of movement of the series in the direction of the corresponding eigenvector. For example, if there were two eigenvalues which were large relative to the rest, this would indicate that a two-dimensional model might well give a good account of the series, since the series largely occupies, or fills out in, two directions only. The square roots of the eigenvalues are described as the singular spectrum. Noise which is present in the data series appears in the singular spectrum as a floor at the upper end. The significant values appear above the noise floor, and their number gives an upper limit on the embedding dimension of any attractor which might exist in the data.[1]

Applying this technique to the quarterly growth in real US GNP, for example, reveals a singular spectrum of the data which is similar, though not completely identical, to that of a random data series. There are no values which stand out clearly above the rest, nor do the values decline to a clear floor.[2] Similar results, which are even closer to those of random data series, are obtained by Campbell and Ormerod for annual growth in real GDP/GNP data for a range of OECD economies over a variety of sample periods.[3]

The interpretation of these findings is entirely consistent with the Fisher hypothesis. In practice, GNP data is indistinguishable in terms of the ratio of its signal to noise content from that of a random data series. There are simply too many factors which determine business cycles to enable forecasts to be made in which the variance of the error is significantly lower than that of the data.

It is very important to note that this does not necessarily mean that structural models of individual series cannot be built, using the word 'structural' in the following sense. To take a hypothetical example, suppose that fluctuations in GNP were determined solely by changes in the stock market index, with an error term whose variance was very small relative to that of the data. By construction a very good structural model of GNP could be built. But, as a vast literature shows, the stock market itself is unpredictable. So even though changes in GNP could be accounted for *ex post* by movements in the stock market, meaningful *ex ante* forecasts of GNP could not be carried out.[4]

The inherent unpredictability of movements in GNP undermines the concept of short-term, countercyclical policy. Criticisms of such policy are by no means new. The Lucas critique is well known, and many academics saw it at the time as dealing a fundamental blow to the use of conventional macro models in policy analysis. However, econometricians have rallied and have proposed ingenious ways of dealing with the criticism (see Clements and Hendry, 1995, for a summary of the key points).

Friedman argued against countercyclical policy many years ago on less esoteric grounds, invoking the simple formula for the variance of the sum of two series. If one series is GNP in the absence of countercyclical policy and the other is the effects of such policy, the variance of the two combined will only be less than that of GNP in the absence of policy if the covariance between the two is negative. Friedman was sceptical of policy makers having sufficient understanding of the economy to achieve such a result. Results obtained using modern non-linear signal processing techniques suggest that his intuition was correct, for if changes in GNP cannot be predicted successfully, it is only by chance that interventions designed to smooth out such fluctuations will succeed.

This latter point holds true even if good structural models of the economy can be built. Suppose, for example, that the conventional macro models were eventually able to agree on the impact on GNP of, say, a given change in government spending. This is far from being the case in reality, and even if it were, the results would not necessarily be true purely as a result of this hypothetical agreement. But suppose as well that the evidence amassed in favour of the result were impressive. Even in these circumstances it would not be possible to carry out short-term countercyclical policy which was consistently successful. For the unpredictable nature of the GNP data would mean that policy makers would often make the wrong kind of intervention, sometimes expanding or contracting when the economy would have moved the same way without intervention.

IV   STRUCTURAL RELATIONSHIPS IN ECONOMICS

The distinction is made frequently in applied macroeconomics between forecasting and policy analysis. Clements and Hendry (1995) go so far as to suggest that separate models should be used for the two tasks. This is an idea with which modellers in the physical sciences are familiar.

The Santa Fe Institute time series competition presented researchers with a number of unidentified, highly non-linear time series of data. From the outset, three distinct goals were specified, as Gershenfeld and Weigend (1993) point out in their introduction to a description of the competition: first, to forecast, or to 'accurately predict the short-term evolution of the system'; second, to model or to 'find a description that accurately captures features of the long-term behaviour of the system' (a clear distinction was made between these two aims, and indeed was demonstrated in the results of the competition); the third goal, described as 'system characterization', is much less familiar to economists but is the purpose, for example, of the signal processing technique described above. The aim is to determine fundamental properties of the system, such as the degree of randomness, which obviously overlaps with the aim of forecasting.

Conventional macroeconomic modellers increasingly make the distinction between forecasting and policy, but it is one which they have been compelled to make in the light of their actual forecasting performance. The econometric methodology of cointegration which underlies many of these models does, of course, place great emphasis on discovering long-run relationships. Each of the models used in the exercise of Bray *et al.* (1995), for example, is replete with such equations yet, as noted in section II above, despite over twenty years of intensive research effort, different models still give quite different results for the effects of various standard fiscal and monetary packages on the economy.

One possible explanation for the failure to agree on the effects of policies is that the models are overparameterized to a serious extent. Chatfield (1995) argues that this is a general fault of a great deal of statistical modelling. Advances in computer technology have far outstripped developments in statistical theory. As a result, not only are most models fitted to time-series data overparameterized, but the data-mining process by which they are selected means that there is no adequate statistical theory with which to judge the published models. Forty years ago, the physical process of computing even a simple regression was hard. Now, a graduate student, aided by menu-driven software, can generate a hundred versions of an equation in a single day.

This criticism applies with particular force to the data-driven approach which has dominated time-series econometric modelling in the UK for twenty years. The battery of tests which must be applied to equations before they are deemed fit to publish in respectable journals looks impressive, but the equations which are reported are invariably the result of intensive trawling of the data. The quoted test statistics can be thought of as design criteria. Models cannot be published unless they pass the currently fashionable list of tests. But the fact that the data are mined in order to produce a model which satisfies such tests undermines the whole value of the test procedure.

An important way in which this is reflected is in the parameter stability and forecasting performance of such equations once they confront genuine out-of-sample data – in other words, data which have not been used as part of the overall data sample with which apparent tests of stability have been constructed. Even inserting correct values of all the explanatory factors, the standard error of the model with genuine out-of-sample data exceeds that of the in-sample fit, both rapidly and substantially in many cases. This phenomenon is very well known amongst the practical model-building fraternity – purer academics are not often obliged to revisit the scene of their crimes once their article is published – but is rarely articulated in the public domain.

Overfitting can often be seen within the data sample used for estimation by applying simple techniques such as 'leave-one-out' regression. The 'leave-one-out' standard error of a regression is calculated as follows. If the equation is fitted on a sample of 1 to n data points, calculate the error for period 1 by fitting the equation on the sample 2 to n and backcast the first data point; for period 2, fit the model using period 1, and 3 to n, and so on. The resulting standard error is often distinctly larger than the one obtained fitting the model from 1 to n only. (The resulting residuals are often known as 'studentized' or 'deletion' residuals; see, for example, Atkinson, 1985.)

Another reflection of overfitting is the way in which published equations for, say, the consumption function change over time. A paper is published which heralds the 'truth' – the discovery of 'the' structural model which determines consumption. But a constant stream of such discoveries appears to be needed.

Despite these problems, conventional modelling proceeds on the basis of assumptions which implicitly rule out structural change, or regime shifts, in the economy. Mizon (1995), for example, describes the history of the

'LSE' econometric methodology, of which Hendry has been the foremost exponent, and the importance attached to parameter constancy over time. Interestingly, Hendry appears to have moved sharply away from this position very recently (see, for example, Clements and Hendry, 1995). He now argues that the assumption of parameter constancy is not appropriate, and that regime shifts are 'an important feature of the actual economy'.

A wider recognition of this fundamental feature of capitalist economies by what might be termed the conventional modelling community would represent a very important step forward in the research agenda. Ormerod (1994a), for example, examines Phillips curves in a wide range of OECD economies over the post-war period from the early 1950s to the early 1990s. For around 90 per cent of the time, very simple relationships between inflation and unemployment give a good account of behaviour. But the relationships are characterized by a small number of major shifts, which can be very abrupt in the sense that an economy can move from one apparently settled Phillips curve to another without a transition period. Mizon (1995), using quarterly data for the UK since 1966 to build a wage–price system, obtains a similar result in terms of the stability of his estimated relationships.

More generally, Ormerod (1994b, 1995) argues that, in local time neighbourhoods, straightforward linear models estimated with a very small number of parameters offer a good explanation of key macroeconomic relationships in the OECD economies. As well as the inflation/unemployment relationship, movements in unemployment itself, for example, can be accounted for by a simple relationship between unemployment and GDP growth (current and lagged) and lagged unemployment.

But such models almost invariably offer very poor explanations over longer time periods. Both these relationships have experienced a number of major shifts during the post-war period. There is a certain amount of common ground in the timing of these shifts, but the historical experience of each country is important in understanding both the timing and magnitude of the shifts. A small number of shocks in the post-war period, with the exact number varying from country to country, have caused permanent shifts in the inflation/unemployment and unemployment/growth relationships. But, by implication, the vast majority of the numerous shocks which affect on the economic system have had no such impact. The fashionable concept of hysteresis implies that every shock has a permanent effect, which is by no means the case.

A key task of any applied work should be to screen the data before any estimation is done at all, in order to identify periods when stable relationships might exist. Over such periods, very simple equations should be estimated which have a good theoretical basis, and with an absolute minimum of data mining. The role of statistical estimation is to parameterize such relationships, and to test the appropriateness of the shifts identified by prior screening of the data.

But the main task is to understand how and why shifts in such relationships take place, which requires careful analysis of the transition periods. It is here that a multidisciplinary approach becomes essential, and we move to questions which it is outside the power of time-series econometrics alone to resolve. And it is here that potentially the greatest policy gains can be made. An understanding, for example, of the circumstances in which the Phillips curve might shift would transform the potential power of governments.

NOTES

1. The eigenvectors associated with the dominant eigenvalues form the coordinate system onto which the data can be projected optimally.
2. This result is robust with respect to the choice of the delay factor, d. Even setting $d = 50$ fails to reveal any significant values. The potential criticism of the approach by Vautard and Ghil (1989), namely that as d increases the number of significant eigenvalues may increase, does not apply to its use on macroeconomic data series, for significant values do not appear to exist at all.
3. These results are confirmed by Ormerod and Mounfield (2000) who apply random matrix theory, developed for the study of complex nuclear spectra, to annual GDP data for 17 OECD countries over the 1871–1994 period.
4. More generally, the use of multivariate rather than univariate techniques for forecasting does not of itself overcome the problem of a high noise-to-signal ratio in a data series. Such a ratio could arise for a number of reasons. The data could be genuinely random (for example, rolls of true dice); they could be determined by factors whose numbers are large relative to the available observations; or they could be determined by a small number of factors which themselves have high noise-to-signal ratios.

10. Realism, econometrics and Post Keynesian economics

Paul Downward

I INTRODUCTION

This chapter explores the role of econometrics as a research tool for econ-omists. In a related manner the purpose of economic theory is also dis-cussed. In discussing such methodological issues the econometric literature on pricing is used as a reference point. In some respects this limits the gen-erality of the discussion. On the other hand, too often methodological dis-cussion is confined to highly abstract discourse. Those impatient to 'get on with things' often ignore the full (potentially weak) basis of their knowl-edge claims.[1] In this respect there is much to be gained by integrating methodological discussion with applied work. This is, of course, of para-mount importance to economic approaches outside the mainstream,[2] par-ticularly in attempting to develop convincing alternative analyses of economic phenomena based on realism, which is an aspiration of Post Keynesian economics.[3] Concern for the adequacy of knowledge claims as well as the provisions of concrete results go hand in hand in moving towards this objective.

The general problems associated with econometric evidence are of more concern for neoclassicals who have tended exclusively to cite or invoke this type of analysis. The main argument of this chapter is that econometric work cannot be decisive in distinguishing between Post Keynesian theories of pricing, though some distinction from neoclassical pricing theory is pos-sible. Nonetheless, as part of a broader, realist, empirical research agenda, econometric evidence may have a constructive role to play for Post Keynesians. The chapter proceeds as follows. Section II presents a set of (distinguishing) metatheoretical characteristics for neoclassical and Post Keynesian economics. It is argued that each approach reflects particular ontological bases, which have specific epistemological implications.[4] Section III illustrates these ideas in exploring neoclassical and Post Keynesian pricing theory. Section IV investigates the methodological role of evidence from Post Keynesian and neoclassical perspectives in some detail. In particular the concerns of Keynes for econometrics are raised and an evaluation of the econometric evidence on pricing is presented. Finally some conclusions are drawn in Section V.

II SOME METATHEORETICAL DISTINCTIONS: CLOSED SYSTEMS VERSUS OPEN SYSTEMS

It soon becomes clear to those interested in doing applied economics that, prior to engaging in data analysis, clear theoretical premises need establishing. It is important to be explicit about the nature of the proposed theoretical/data interaction. As argued below, discussion of precisely how this interaction occurs does not readily exist in Post Keynesian economics, unlike neoclassical economics (see, for example, Lawson, 1994b, Steedman, 1995). A precondition for undertaking applied work in Post Keynesian economics thus necessarily involves some prior theoretical discussion. To facilitate this discussion, this section presents some 'organizing' meta-theoretical concepts.

A central foundation of this chapter is that there is increasing recognition in Post Keynesian work that Critical Realism provides the philosophical framework for Post Keynesian methodology (Dow, 1985, 1990b, 1992; Arestis, 1992; Arestis and Sawyer, 1993; Lawson, 1994b; King, 1995; Dow and Hillard, 1995). In contrast, neoclassical theory embraces an instrumentalist methodology when theory is juxtaposed to data (Caldwell, 1989; Boland, 1979). The differences in approach this implies, as well as the definition of these terms, is best understood by contrasting them.

Lawson (1994a, 1994b, 1997), drawing heavily on Bhaskar (1978, 1989), argues that neoclassical economics has its roots in the philosophical system of positivism – and in particular a Humean version of ontology – whereby reality comprises the constant conjunction of atomistic events. It is a closed-system approach to theorizing. The essential epistemological feature of orthodox economics is to conceive of 'causal laws' or theoretical explanation in terms of a particular form of a generalized relationship between theoretical categories. This generalized relationship comprises statements of the form 'whenever event "X" then event "Y"'.[5]

In contrast, an adherence to realism and an open-system approach to theorizing is increasingly embraced by Post Keynesians.

Ontologically speaking, an open-system approach presents an 'organicist' view of the world (Dow, 1994a). This position holds that, to the extent that regularities in the social realm exist to be identified or theorized about, then, because of the continual interplay between (intrinsic) human agency and structure, these will be a plurality of partial regularities and processes and not predictable or universal event regularities. These processes are the 'generative structures, powers, mechanisms and necessary relations, and so on, that lie behind and govern the flux of events in an essentially open world' (Lawson, 1994a: 516).

Accepting this proposition has certain related (realist) epistemological implications. Dow (1994a) summarizes these. An open-system ontology carries with it the notion that uncertainty, based on the incomplete or partial understanding possible in an open system, is endemic both to the researcher and to the researched. This provides a rationale for, as well as reflects, the existence of multiple processes underlying events and thus justifies a pluralist approach to theorizing (which of necessity involves abstraction and partiality); the thrust of theory should be to discover these processes in reflecting this open-system thinking.

III   CORE PRICING THEORY: NEOCLASSICAL AND POST KEYNESIAN PERSPECTIVES

Hodgson (1988: xiv) notes that the key tenets, or meta-theoretical framework, of neoclassical economics are its sole reliance on a method of analysis that expresses theoretical explanation as the achievement of an agent's objective under effectively full information, elaborated upon by highlighting positions of attained equilibrium. It is clear, therefore, that the ontological presumptions of neoclassical theorizing are reflected in such core assumptions and can be summarized as comprising a 'closed' system. This is because in any given context one causal mechanism, that is, effectively full-information optimization, is isolated. There is a one-to-one correspondence between the way this mechanism acts and the events that ensue. In this case apparently diverse phenomena are *logically* reducible to the same form of decision making.

Here it is argued, along with Lavoie (1992a), that this produces a dualistic core/periphery distinction in neoclassical theory. As far as pricing is concerned, applied neoclassical economics, often referred to as the industrial organization literature, is in essence the periphery of neoclassical economics. It involves optimizing narratives and can be seen to be a logical extension of a purely axiomatic, general equilibrium, perfectly competitive core. Peripheral assumptions about market structure are relaxed but the applied work essentially shares the same fictitious and axiomatic view of decision taking, rather than offering a more literal view of decision taking. Dow (1990b) describes this juxtaposition of unrealistic core assumptions and associated truth claims essentially resting on prediction, or the constant conjunction of events, as an 'event-truth' realist perspective. Lawson (1997) describes this approach as empirical realism. In this sense neoclassical explanations are based on logical time.

This duality is not a comfortable state of affairs for neoclassicals. If one examines the literature on industrial organization, a whole plurality of models exist which differ at the concrete level, in terms of accounts of pricing, because of the realism of the approach's more peripheral assumptions. This pluralism entails a dilemma for neoclassical economists. Variety at the epistemological level is completely at odds with the methodological precepts of neoclassical economics detailed above. A lacuna now exists between much neoclassical theory and its truth claims or empirical agenda (Dow, 1994b). However, as argued below, using a variety of models to capture aspects of reality is perfectly explicable from a Post Keynesian perspective. Though the industrial organization literature is often presented as synonymous with neoclassical economics, particularly because at their core optimizing narratives are employed (Sawyer, 1990), one can, however, identify overlap in this literature with Post Keynesian economics. This is made evident below.

Standing in contrast to this core/periphery dual, one can argue from a critical–realist perspective that a core for Post Keynesian pricing theory exists, is different from neoclassical economics and does not presuppose any disarticulation from a periphery. The essence of this distinction lies in issues of ontology. A Post Keynesian core essentially represents what a variety of empirical insights can be reduced to, in reflecting, conceptually, some deeper causal processes *actually underlying* the events under study. The basic point, therefore, articulated by Mäki (1990), is that the ability to *infer* different phenomena from the same set of premises is not necessarily the same as arguing that different phenomena are literally *representatives* of a common set of behaviours. Dow (1990b) describes these latter epistemological aspirations as 'process-truth' realist, which this chapter treats as synonymous with critical realism, and this is what is emphasized by references to realism in this chapter. In this case, the realism of what Mäki (1990) calls the 'ontic furniture' of Post Keynesians is valued.[6]

As far as pricing is concerned, therefore, Downward (2000) argues that a behavioural 'core' of Post Keynesian pricing theory can be identified through the focus on the mark-up. In deference to research concerned with the literal process of agent decision making under conditions of uncertainty, Post Keynesians emphasize that prices are set by firms adding a mark-up to some measure of average costs.[7] The precise way in which the mark-up is determined depends upon circumstances, and may be represented differently by the theorist depending on the precise line of enquiry. Nonetheless, it is a defining feature of Post Keynesian pricing theory that the mark-up is determined *ex ante* in the uncertain pursuit of some (possibly multiple) objective(s).

Crucially, from such a methodological perspective, no distinction, or duality, between core theory and peripheral evidence remains. Such a distinction in essence mirrors Robinson's (1978) notion that neoclassical economics is based on 'logical time' and equilibrium rather than 'historical time' in which the theorist can only really suggest the possibilities in which economic variables may interact. As discussed below, this has interesting ramifications for issues of choice between Post Keynesian theories based on empirical evidence.

IV   THE METHODOLOGICAL ROLE OF EVIDENCE

General Issues

Stemming from the above discussion, for neoclassicals the isolation of empirical regularities in the social world defines applied work, whereas formal axiomatic reasoning defines theoretical work.[8] Notions applicable to the experimental realm are carried over to the social realm of economics. This is, of course, manifest in the dominant appeal to econometrics in applied work to test parametric representations of phenomena, and the use of mathematical techniques, particularly deducing the solution to optimization problems through calculus, in theoretical expression (see, for example, Blinder, 1991).

It is not surprising that econometrics is the dominant form of empirical work for neoclassical economists. It follows from the Humean/positivist ontology ascribed to neoclassical economics that theory is presented in a closed or determinate way entailing event regularities. The parametric form of neoclassical theory is a testimony to this. The development of econometrics has thus occurred, symbiotically, with the need to test these parametric forms statistically. While there is debate about whether or not the agenda of econometrics has been to attempt to confirm (conditionally) certain hypotheses rather than to falsify them (also conditionally), the essential thrust of econometrics has been to produce a model to account for a theoretically presupposed 'event-regularity' (see also Downward and Mearman (forthcoming) for a discussion of economic methods from a critical–realist perspective).

Haavelmo's (1944) extensive monograph, making the case for allying probability theory to economic modelling, is considered to be the earliest coherent statement of these aspirations. This essay strongly influenced the development of modern econometrics. For Haavelmo, the essence of econometrics is to build, identify, estimate and assess various models conforming to the optimizing behaviour given by neoclassical precepts. Of course these are reformulated stochastically. Importantly, he writes, 'The question is not whether probabilities exist or not, but whether – if we proceed as if they existed – we are able to make statements about real phenomena that are correct for "practical purposes"' (Haavelmo, 1944: 43).

Econometrics, so defined, can thus be described as a form of instrumentalist reasoning.[9] Coupled with neoclassical theory, the 'predictive' merit of models is most valued. Metaphorical, or *as if*, claims concern the outcomes of (implicit) processes. It is not typically argued that econometric models represent the real processes underlying these outcomes in any obvious way. On the contrary, the results are presented as if produced by the joint probability distributions governing particular economic variables, with little attention being paid to what actually may underlie their relationships. It is clear then that, inasmuch as neoclassical economics is couched in terms of event regularities, the truth claims of the approach reside purely in the ability of the econometric model, or version of that theory, to account for data regularities in a, classically defined, statistically significant way.

The issues raised here can be further elaborated upon using Lawson's (Lawson, 1997; Bhaskar, 1978: 76) distinction between 'intrinsic' and 'extrinsic' conditions for closure.[10] These conditions refer to the ways in which constancy of relations or regularities can be supposed to exist. Loosely speaking, the intrinsic condition for closure can be translated into the phrase 'every cause has the same effect'. As Lawson (1995a, 1997) argues, this can imply an assumption of atomic uniformity in explanation. This ensures the same outcome necessarily follows a cause, and that causal mechanism does not evolve or become transformed. The extrinsic condition suggests that 'every effect has the same cause'. This implies a closed system isolating causal mechanisms from external influence. Characterized in such a way the implicit, but inevitable, emphasis of econometrics motivated by neoclassical economics is that the salient outcomes of mechanisms producing economic events are captured in the data by the model. This 'identification' of the appropriate economic relationships is a result of, and reflects, the presupposition that economic relations can be presented in a parametric and probabilistic format. The magnitude of the key relationships between events is identified in estimated coefficients, linking variables additively, and peripheral influences, captured through a stochastic disturbance term, are presented as not, on average, affecting outcomes.

Notwithstanding these ideals, in practice econometrics has always failed to produce decisive demarcation between theories. Problems of identification exist and persist in econometrics. As far back as 1938, Frisch was concerned that multiple correlation was not capable of distinguishing 'unique' relationships between events. Frisch's (increasingly strong) criticism of econometrics parallels that of Keynes's (1939) almost contemporaneous criticism of econometric methods based on a review of Tinbergen's work for the League of Nations. He notes that 'the main *prima facie* objection to the application of the method of multiple correlation to complex economic problems lies in the apparent lack of any adequate degree of uniformity in the environment.' (Keynes, 1939: 567, original emphasis). For Keynes, the openness of economic systems places a fundamental obstacle in the way of regression techniques being applied to economic data. As Hendry and Morgan (1989) note, however, Keynes's and Frisch's concerns for econometrics were passed over by Haavelmo (1944) whose approach has been enshrined in the textbook approach to econometrics that persists today. Gilbert (1986) describes this approach to econometrics as the average economic regression (AER) approach. Theory provides the essential specification of the model and the main problem for the econometrician is to ensure that desirable properties in ordinary least squares (OLS) regressions obtain by respecifying the model and re-estimating it. Confidence in such textbook econometrics, however, is as illusory now as it was in the 1930s. Neither Frisch's nor Keynes's essentially methodological concerns have been addressed. Accordingly, few (if any) economic disputes have been resolved by appeal to the data.

The Pricing Literature

The above discussion can be exemplified in the case of the pricing literature. From the outset econometrics has experienced problems in distinguishing, at the level of predictions, core neoclassical pricing theory from other pricing theories consistent both with the core of Post Keynesian pricing theory and with other optimizing theories. This applies even in testing the theories on the same data set.

For example, Neild (1963) examined British manufacturing prices from 1950 to 1960 for all manufacturing, food manufacturing, and the chemical, textiles and paper industries. His basic rationale was to provide a 'dynamic interpretation of "full cost pricing"' (Neild, 1963: 4). To test for the presence of demand effects on prices, as implied by neoclassical theory, Neild used a cumulative measure of excess demand based on the rationale that, as price changes are governed by the level of excess demand, the level of prices would be influenced by the summation of excess demands. Neild's basic conclusion was that the terms added nothing to the model as the coefficient signs were negative and only significant in the sample period that included disturbances due to the Korean war. His preferred equation was consistent with full-cost pricing and, by implication, Post Keynesian pricing and non-core neoclassical pricing theory.

In contrast, McCallum (1970), *using Neild's data*, estimated a solely competitive pricing model consistent with the core of neoclassical pricing theory. In this model price changes are related to future and current excess demands. McCallum (1970: 147) concluded that 'the "pure excess demand" hypothesis is shown to accord very well with the empirical evidence utilised by both Neild and Rushdy and Lund'. Downward (2002) has offered some resolution of this debate using modern econometric methods. However, discussion of theoretical properties of the models was also required. As Downward (1995, 1999) shows, moreover, this lack of decisiveness has persisted with the econometrics of pricing. For example, Sawyer (1983) shows how a whole set of different structural pricing models can share support from the same basic reduced-form equation. Geroski (1991) specifically shows how his reduced-form equation is consistent with both 'backward-looking' normal-cost pricing and 'forward-looking' rational expectations price smoothing hypotheses. Further, there would be little to choose, in terms of pricing predictions, between Kalecki's non-optimizing formulation of pricing decisions, essential to the core of Post Keynesian pricing theory, and Cowling and Waterson's (1976) optimizing 'reinterpretation'. This has found much favour in the industrial organization literature that, as noted above, is typically interpreted as neoclassical.

Notwithstanding these cross-paradigm comparisons, the implications of defining 'core' Post Keynesian pricing theory in the realist manner of Downward (2000) noted above is that similar problems of identification would also arise, as the components of the core Post Keynesian account of pricing have their basis in a *variety* of pricing theories. One could argue that 'Kaleckian' pricing could be distinguished from 'full/normal-cost' pricing on the basis that a 'longer' lag of costs would be appropriate in the latter context. Establishing precisely what this longer set of costs should be, however, would be a highly artificial exercise. Moreover, if one accepts that Post Keynesian pricing theories are behaviourally defined, and hence literally stated as 'reduced-form' equations, little meaningful scope for identifying 'correct structural forms' exists. It is clear, therefore, that the role that econometrics can play in such circumstances has to be modified from one of assuming that the 'correct' view of pricing can be established by econometric means. Of course, the basic 'practical' problems associated with this specific context fundamentally stem from the methodological problem of applying a closed form of reasoning to an open-system context.

In general, the results of econometric work imply that some forms of cost are ubiquitous as significant determinants of pricing behaviour. However, there is also evidence, of a less clear-cut nature, that demand also has a (weaker) role to play. The problem associated with this complex state of affairs is that there has been 'selective' reporting of results, whether deliberately or not. This has occurred particularly along a simple empirical divide. For example, Dorward (1987) interprets the econometric evidence as broadly pro-neoclassical, in that evidence exists that demand affects prices as well as costs. Reynolds (1987), on the other hand, suggests that the results confirm the Post Keynesian position that costs determine prices in the short run. Clearly, both of these conclusions are misleading.

Such a 'selective reporting strategy' is, of course, not necessary. A precise counter-rationale can be located in the possible solutions to this problem of the inability of econometrics to discriminate between economic theories. Three alternative courses of action are available to Post Keynesians (and, indeed, other economists).[11] First, one can retreat from econometric work altogether. Secondly, one can hope that eventually the traditional approach to econometrics, or even recent developments in econometric methods, will eventually *settle* debates. Finally, one can provide some modified interpretation of the role of econometrics in producing economic knowledge. It is a central contention of this chapter that the methodological emphasis on realism noted earlier permits a feasible path ahead in the third course of action by taking into account recent developments in econometrics (see also Downward and Mearman (forthcoming)).

Recent Econometric Developments

As Pagan (1987) points out, three distinct schools of thought have emerged in econometrics as a means of explicitly addressing the problems with applied econometrics. These are the Hendry/LSE approach, the Leamer/Bayesian approach and the Sims/atheoretical approach. All of these approaches share the agenda of starting econometric analysis from some general representation of the data and then following some criteria for model simplification. To greater or lesser degrees, each approach explores the relative importance of 'subjective priors' and 'objective factors' in econometric inference.

The Hendry approach is presented as involving a continual interaction between theory (or subjective priors) and data (or objective facts). However, no hard-and-fast governing lines of demarcation exist in model appraisal. Hendry (1995: 1633–4) writes:

> The best is that theory delivers a model which happens to capture structure after appropriate estimation . . . However structure potentially can be learned from empirical evidence without prior knowledge as to what exists to be discovered . . . Nevertheless, economic theory is likely to prove a productive companion in empirical econometrics . . . although how one discovers useful knowledge remains an art rather than a science.

Knowledge, for Hendry, thus appears to derive from a complex interaction between deduction and induction. The basic strategy appears to follow these stages. A general model should be formulated. This is then reparameterized to obtain nearly orthogonal explanatory variables. The next stage is to simplify the model to the smallest version compatible with the data, and the final stage is to evaluate the model by extensive testing. The general procedure appears to be that theory determines which variables should go into the model and the data determine how to characterize the relationship.

A central emphasis of Hendry's work is that structural relations remain a part of the analysis. Accordingly, via 'encompassing' tests – attempting to account for the results of rival models – some notion of critical theoretical evaluation is established. Hendry (1993) likens the notion of encompassing to a Lakatosian progressive research strategy. It is not immediately clear that this corresponds to a notion of falsification. Moreover, the critical emphasis appears to stem largely from statistical criteria, although reparameterizations have interpretability as one of their goals.

Unlike Hendry, Leamer's approach is Bayesian. It asserts the primacy of subjective factors in all reasoning. It argues that traditional econometrics has degenerated into an approach that effectively employs misspecification errors as a 'protective belt' preventing the testing of the 'hard-core' propositions of economic theory. The reason for this lies in the official rhetoric of econometrics that appeals to the 'false idol of objectivity'. As a Bayesian, Leamer argues that it is the job of the econometrician to be 'up front' about the role of priors when engaging in econometrics. In particular, econometricians must recognize not only that economic data is non-experimental but that 'the misspecification matrix M is therefore a pure prior concept. One must decide independent of the data how good the nonexperiment is' (Leamer, 1983: 33).[12] This is because econometrics employs priors not only in establishing the (conditional) sampling function, but also in establishing the marginal or prior probability density function. Leamer's *modus operandi* is to formulate a general family of models, decide what inferences are of importance, express these in terms of parameters and form prior distributions summarizing any information not in the data set. The sensitivity of inferences to a particular choice of distributions should be analysed to explore their 'fragility'.

In fact, as Pagan (1987) points out, the sensitivity analysis recommended by Leamer is implied in the Hendry approach in testing from a general to a specific model. Where the two approaches part company is in Hendry's recommendation that inference concerning point estimates should proceed from the general model if the data indicate the complete set of variables are significant. Leamer appears to stress the fact that this is problematic simply because there are conflicting (prior) grounds for inference. There is a clash of interest because the weight placed on the role of the data rather than prior judgment in critical evaluation is different from Hendry's approach.

Sims's approach to econometrics (see, for example, Sims, 1980) has probably received the worst publicity of the attempts to rectify the problems with applied econometrics. Sims's approach essentially rejects the possibility of exogeneity and identification and is confined to the analysis of reduced forms in a simultaneous or 'vector autoregressive' context. Vector autoregressions consist of regressions of each variable of interest on lagged values of itself and the other variables under scrutiny. The largest lag structure possible is started with and then subsequently simplified in much the same manner as Hendry's approach. The objective of the Sims methodology is to provide structure-free conclusions.

It is this claim that leads to criticism of the approach as purely atheoretical. For example, Darnell and Evans (1990: 126) suggest that 'VAR has no role whatsoever in the hypothetico-deductive method of economic science ... [and] ... appears to be an example of extreme inductivism ... that fails utterly to discriminate between competing explanations.' To the extent that Sims's approach makes claims for a theory-free econometrics, this position would find little support. It has to be said, however, that Sims's concern with reduced forms does not of necessity make the approach theory-free. Its intention is to avoid problems of identification and theory choice by emphasizing data description. The approach could thus be reasonably defended as providing potential support for a set of possible economic relationships. These criticisms can be overemphasized and have no necessary foundation. Significantly, as Darnell and Evans (1990: 129) argue, the approach may have meaningful content '[in] the case that there may be some empirical regularities (economic phenomena) deserving of further study ... [despite] ... VAR itself [contributing] nothing with regard to the scientific method of economics nor, surprisingly, do its proponents pretend anything different'.

It would appear, therefore, that Darnell and Evans suggest a potential role for such techniques in an approach rejecting the hypothetico-deductive methodology that they ascribe to science *per se*! It is on this subject that attention is now focused.

Towards a Rationale for Econometrics

The above discussion offers some common themes that can be drawn upon to assert the validity of econometric practice in realist research. The starting point is to note that, while it is quite clear that realists could not justifiably invoke the extrinsic condition for closure as a defence of econometric analysis, they could nonetheless reasonably invoke the intrinsic condition. Generally speaking, the ontology of open systems entails that stable underlying processes cause events. More specifically, in the context of pricing, this is implied in the core of Post Keynesian pricing theory identified earlier. Using econometrics to partially elaborate upon these processes, in a suitably qualified way, thus seems both possible and legitimate. Because realists would reject the extrinsic condition for closure, moreover, it follows that qualifications to the use of econometrics should follow from this proposition. In particular, dualistic appeals to statistical criteria without some explicit reference to theoretical priors should be avoided. A combination of prior theoretical insight and statistical analysis, *firmly grounded in a particular context*, provides a use of econometrics that would also be in keeping with a realist methodological position that ontological boldness should be matched with epistemic caution in a social, open-system, context (Bhaskar, 1989).

Crucially, support for this proposition also follows from Keynes's epistemology, which is consistent with an open-system ontology, as implied above in his reference to Tinbergen's work. As Dow (1996a) and Lawson (1987) note, knowledge, for Keynes, derives from direct and indirect sources. The former refer to objects with which we are directly aquainted. Keynes (CW VIII: 12), for example, refers to sensory experience as a basis of direct knowledge. As Lawson (1987) argues, however, one can view Keynes's position as consistent with provisionally held prior starting points for further research. The latter is concerned with arguments constructed on the basis of direct knowledge. Theorizing falls into this category. The degree of belief in a proposition – or its probability – is then a logical relationship between types of evidence. That is, once given, direct knowledge provides a basis for a degree of belief in further, indirect, knowledge. In general, degrees of belief can only apply in the absence of certainty. In this respect Keynes emphasizes the importance of rational belief in argument rather than knowledge (Keynes, CW VIII: 10).

In general, therefore, for Keynes, uncertain ordinal probabilities may be defined and held, depending on the weight of evidence attached to propositions. Probabilities may not be comparable if the propositions to which they are attached are heterogeneous. Weight, or the amount of relevant evidence, is distinct from probability. As Keynes writes, 'The weight, to speak metaphorically, measures the *sum* of the favourable and unfavourable evidence, the probability measures the difference' (Keynes, CW VIII: 84; original emphasis). Both the weight of evidence and, hence, probability hinge on the relevance of evidence. For Keynes, this ultimately resides in *logical* justification, though there is a relative/absolute dimension to this. For

example, evidence is intrinsically defined in terms of the theoretical concepts it purports to measure. So probability is, on the one hand, *relative* to
given evidence. In this sense no probability is absolute. However, once given
a body of evidence or initial proposition, probabilities concerning subsequent propositions are *absolute* or *objective*. For Keynes, this is because
they are concerned with the degree of belief that it is rational for a person
to entertain about the proposition, given the initial evidence, knowledge
and so on. Accordingly, the relevance of evidence is not independent of the
theoretical specification involved. As noted below, it also follows from this
perspective that spreading belief is as much to do with persuasion as formal
demonstration *per se*.

On a related point, it follows from Keynes's epistemology that relevant
evidence is ascertained through a process of negative analogy. To avoid the
problem of induction, Keynes argued that one should examine a particular phenomenon in different contexts. He writes: 'There is no process of
reasoning, which from one instance draws a conclusion different from that
which it infers from a hundred instances, if the latter are known to be in *no*
way different from the former' (Keynes, CW VIII: 243; original emphasis).
If a phenomenon appears to be a common element in various contexts then
it is this commonality that indicates the relevance of a particular phenomenon. Its relevance thus adds weight to a particular account of that phenomenon. If the different contexts reveal non-common elements, then the
weight of an argument will decrease, revealing our ignorance. In short, such
'an inductive argument affirms, not that a certain matter of fact *is* so, but
that *relevant to certain evidence* there is probability in its favour' (Keynes,
CW VIII: 245; original emphasis).

As Dow writes, therefore,

> to construct and make sense of negative analogy, it is helpful to have knowledge
> of the institutional structure of, and history behind, each circumstance in which
> the common element is being observed. There is no need for economists' knowl-
> edge of institutions and economic history to be 'vague and scanty'. (Dow, 1996:
> 727)

The importance of this line of reasoning is that, if the weight of 'qualitative' evidence suggests that a particular process underlies events, this would,
prima facie, provide support – as a form of direct knowledge – for an econometric representation of that process. Of course this would be on the
understanding that the econometric method, as indeed with all methods of
data analysis, would only partially reveal these processes and that they
should be continually critically evaluated.

Quite clearly, therefore, Keynes's epistemology, which is consistent with
a realist ontology (see also Lawson, 1985a, 1989a), suggests that, with suffi-

cient prior justification, econometrics can be a useful tool, but, moreover, that its application cannot proceed independently of that prior justification because of the ubiquitous open-system nature of the economy. This implies that data analysis in itself is not sufficient as a basis of theory choice. Some of the more ambitious claims of the Hendry methodology are thus not sustainable because of this Leamer-style qualification. It remains the case that attempts to utilize Sims's approach in an 'atheoretical' way are also unsustainable. On the contrary, the *interaction* of theory and evidence should form the basis of the use of econometrics in an appropriate manner given the *particular* context.

In any econometric study, theory, and particularly prior (qualitative) analysis, should indicate the validity of econometric investigation. In particular, it should spell out the implied intrinsic conditions of closure, that is outline the nature of the real causal mechanism asserted to exist. This stage of analysis will, of course, also indicate the variables of interest, and the context of the relationship between the variables, for example their 'reduced form' or 'structural status', in the study. Recognizing the lack of applicability of the extrinsic condition for closure, the general interaction between these variables should then be examined using a broad set of specifications. These specifications should then be appraised. It is important to note that this may, but need not, involve model simplification by appeal both to theory, prior qualitative analysis and statistical criteria. Crucially, some form of 'sensitivity' analysis can then be conducted *in the context of the phenomenon under investigation*. Conclusions can thus be offered with critical reference to this set of specifications and any previous insights into the phenomenon of interest. Econometricians should, therefore, recognize that open systems do not legitimize claims to falsification but should show that econometric evidence may add weight to certain knowledge claims in the manner implied by Keynes.

These arguments suggest that econometric descriptions of data can only capture surface manifestations of the true dynamics at play. Thus, in general, one should recognize that econometrics can produce tentative evidence or demi-regularities requiring further investigation in a necessarily ongoing, and context-specific, realist research programme. This programme's essential aim should be to identify and elaborate upon the structures and mechanisms that underlie the phenomena of interest. In this respect, to explain any concrete phenomenon of interest requires drawing upon antecedent knowledge of structures and investigating their joint articulation in the production of the event in question. This is the import of Keynes's stress on the need for qualitative analysis prior to formal analysis.

Further Empirical Consequences

It is also clear from the above discussion that non-econometric means of analysis will be necessary to elaborate on the causal mechanisms underlying events. Importantly, as implied earlier, in defining the core of Post Keynesian pricing theory, such literature has been readily cited particularly by Post Keynesians, albeit in a confused methodological way (see Downward, 1994). This is not to imply that a single real explanation of events can be discovered by these means. One of the central features of a realist interpretation of economics is that, while an objective real world may be said to exist, its interpretation and explanation will be socially and individually constructed, for example, through the use of rhetoric or metaphor (see, for example, Mäki, 1988). This is despite the claims, or official rhetoric, of positivists (see, for example, the work of McCloskey, 1983, 1986; Klamer *et al.*, 1988). Of relevance to note here is McCloskey's (1983, 1986) work which argues that such an approach would only really make explicit what economists are already doing unofficially. In other words it would bring into official recognition the role that introspection, analogy and 'theoretical plausibility' are already playing in economic argument and persuasion. This is also consistent with the underlying implications of Keynes's epistemology.

Econometrics and Pricing

By way of illustration, it is worth noting that the above ideas on econometrics were explicitly employed in Downward (1995) to reinvestigate the stylized facts of pricing, and the core Post Keynesian account of pricing, on quarterly data for UK manufacturing between 1984 (Q1) and 1991 (Q4). Specifically, ideas from the Hendry and Sims approaches to econometrics were employed. Time-series techniques and in particular the 'vector autoregressive approach' were adopted to review the issue of whether prices are cost- or demand-determined in UK manufacturing. The approach was adopted as it emphasizes reduced forms consistent with the behavioural core, that is, the set of theoretical priors, of Post Keynesian pricing theory emphasizing that firms set prices by marking up some measure of average costs. Reference to the whole panorama of existing Post Keynesian research into pricing behaviour, it is argued, gives sufficient grounds to assert that the intrinsic condition for closure is reasonably satisfied in this context. By implication, the predictions of this core are that prices will change more readily following cost changes rather than demand changes. Such predictions are also consistent with optimizing accounts of pricing (for example, Cowling and Waterson, 1976, noted above) that, as a result, share neoclassical characteristics.

In deference to Hendry's work, but also to the literature on spurious regression, some notion of encompassing was possible in this context. This could occur in checking the order of integration of each variable prior to running regressions. Checking the order of integration of the price variable provides an indirect test of the excess demand/core-pricing hypothesis of neoclassical economics. It also helps in the selection of the proxy used for demand pressure on pricing. Non-optimizing, Post Keynesian pricing theory, but also many optimizing models of pricing (c.f. Cowling and Waterson), both suggest that levels of demand rather than excess demand should be associated with levels of prices.

The results suggested a unit root on the level of manufacturing prices, and even a possibility of this on the first difference of manufacturing prices. A unit root on the level of manufacturing prices would seem to rule out an excess demand 'explanation' of pricing consistent with core/perfectly competitive neoclassical pricing theory. This is because implied differences in demand and supply of manufacturing output potentially exhibit infinite persistence. Accordingly, in econometric terms the level of output seems to be the most appropriate proxy for demand pressure on prices.

Results also suggested that both last quarter's costs and demand are significant and direct determinants of manufacturing prices, with the cost effect being about three times as strong as the demand effect, but that the effects are in general small. Behaviourally, therefore, the results imply that last period's prices are carried forward to the current period – as historic reference points – with small adjustments made in the light of changes in costs and demand. These findings are entirely consistent with the behavioural emphasis of core Post Keynesian pricing theory and the predictions of optimizing, but non-core, neoclassical models. This is not the case with the core of neoclassical pricing theory. The results are thus problematic for neoclassicals, exemplifying the issues raised by Dow (1994b) noted earlier. In the spirit of Keynes, however, and with reference to the voluminous and diverse Post Keynesian literature on pricing, they are constructive in adding weight to the Post Keynesian account.

V CONCLUSIONS

This chapter suggests that fundamental problems of identification, of an ontological origin, will exist in econometrics given its closed-system emphasis and open-system application. This makes it inherently difficult to discriminate between theories. These issues are illustrated with reference to the literature on pricing. It is argued in this context that econometrics cannot be expected to discriminate between theories with essentially the same behavioural core, or sharing parametric predictions, though some comparisons can be made. It is suggested that, allied to an existing body of research of a more diverse empirical character, in the spirit of realist claims, econometrics can have a critical and constructive role to play in economics. By itself, econometrics will only problematically underpin knowledge claims. This should be of concern to neoclassical economists.

NOTES

1. With his customary insight, and in the context of evaluating econometric methods, Keynes (1939: 556) warns of the dangers of being 'more interested in getting on with the job than in spending time in deciding whether the job is worth getting on with . . . [preferring] . . . the mazes of arithmetic to the mazes of logic'. This contrasts with Pagan's (1987: 3) assessment of econometrics that, 'sound methodology was not a necessary condition for the practice of sound methods. "Get on with the job" seems the appropriate message'.
2. My definition of mainstream or neoclassical economics is a methodological one and is taken from Hodgson (1988) as discussed in this chapter.
3. Post Keynesian economics is explicitly concerned with the real world (unlike the 'ideal' states it is implied are envisaged by neoclassical theory. The basis, and implications, of claims to support a realist approach are discussed in the chapter.
4. Ontology is concerned with statements about the 'being', 'essence' or 'nature' of things. As such, it is closely allied to notions of vision. Epistemology is concerned with statements concerning 'knowledge' or 'discoursing'. Substantive dimensions of theory appraisal are epistemological categories, yet have an ontological rationale.
5. Note that this can apply deterministically or probabilistically.
6. This discussion is central to repudiating claims attacking the invocation of realist precepts in economics. Parsons (1995a) argues that the tenets of Post Keynesian methodology, realism, organicism, anti-dualism and anti-Cartesianism, are inconsistent. He argues, for example, that the form of realism just discussed advances structure/event, subject/object and theory/reality duals. The argument in these paragraphs clearly undermines these claims. Moreover, Parsons (1995b, 1996) argues that the Post Keynesian invocation of realism is flawed because it is not compatible with individual autonomy. His reasoning is as follows: (1) according to realists all events are governed by a mechanism or mechanisms; (2) any human action is an event; (3) therefore all human action is governed by some mechanism or mechanisms; (4) therefore no human action is free. This is simply wrong. Human action can represent a process as well as an event, or outcome. It is clear that the human action of walking is a causal means of transferring the human body spatially (independently of the reason for walking). Walking can be conceptualized as a causal process. This is different from the 'event' of arriving at a particular destination. Paradoxically, by describing all human action as an event, Parsons emulates, in a philosophical discourse, what neoclassicals imply in their theory, which is to reduce human endeavour to an essentially static context by emphasizing a single point in time. Making a decision (or a series of similar decisions) and carrying it (or them) out in uncertain conditions are two conceptually distinct aspects of human action. Further, as Hodgson (1988) clearly articulates, in an open-system context there may be unintended systemic causation at work that the individual is unaware of. Parsons's thesis conflates these causal notions in embracing an atomistic, reductionist notion of causation analogous to neoclassical economics. In general, therefore, it is in recognizing that humans are intentional that the purported 'duality' of realist analysis is undermined. Uncertain human endeavour provides the manifold between events or outcomes of decisions and the processes that led to their being so.

7. There is too little space here to explore the interaction between various theoretical developments in Post Keynesian pricing analysis and its commonality with research into actual price formation.

8. By 'regularity' is meant an enduring phenomenon effectively setting the parameters upon which knowledge can be said to be based or to represent through conceptual expression: that is, theory. Understanding presupposes the endurability of phenomena because knowledge has, as its basis, a requirement that data be organized meaningfully and conceptually as information (see Hodgson, 1988: 6).

9. Of course, a degree of instrumentalism affects all empirical work. As Bhaskar writes, 'The applied scientist must be adept at analysing a situation as a whole, of thinking at several different levels at once, recognising clues, piecing together diverse bits of information and assessing the likely outcomes of various courses of action. The pure scientist, on the other hand, deliberately excludes, whereas the applied scientist seeks always to accommodate, the effects of intervening levels of reality. Though he is unafraid of flights of daring (always risky for the practical man), he holds fast to his chosen objects of inquiry. The applied scientist is an instrumentalist and a conservative, the pure scientist is a realist and (at the highest level) a revolutionary. Keynes had the rare gift among economists of knowing both how to make money and how money is made' (Bhaskar, 1978: 120).

10. These terms generalize on 'internal' and 'external' conditions by not being tied to spatial characteristics.

11. This issue is even more critical for neoclassical economists, given their view of economic science outlined earlier in the chapter.

12. The distinction between experimental and non-experimental data is not crucial to Leamer's arguments. Experiments can also, through design or failure to produce closure, involve bias.

11. Keynes, Post Keynesians and methodology

Sheila C. Dow

I INTRODUCTION

The purpose of this chapter is to address the judgment expressed by some that, while Keynes made valuable contributions to the development of economic theory, those contributions are subsumed in more technically advanced modern theory. In comparison, Keynes's economic theory is limited by the narrower range of theoretical techniques available at the time. This judgment tends to be embedded in the broader methodological position that economics, by and large, progresses over time, and technical advance is part of that process. The implication is, therefore, not only that subsequent theoretical developments are an improvement on Keynes, but that not much will be gained by considering earlier (by definition less developed) stages of thought. This chapter questions the argument that, in itself, technical advance has allowed macroeconomic theory to supersede the economics of Keynes. It is argued that such a judgment should address the methodological shift which has occurred in macroeconomics, along with technical change, from an open-system approach to a closed-system approach. The logic of Keynes's methodology, which is carried forward in Post Keynesian economics, requires that the scope of application of formal techniques in general, and the choice of a closed-system methodology in particular, be justified in terms of the nature of the subject matter.

   The focus of the chapter is thus to question the notion that technical progress in economics is methodologically neutral. The argument rests on an understanding of Keynes's methodology as differing from the methodology underlying many of those theories presented as technical advances on Keynes. By methodology is meant, not the range of available methods, but the criteria for selection of methods, the way in which they are employed and combined, the way in which results are interpreted, and the criteria for theory appraisal. Once the possibility is raised of more than one methodology, we are no longer able to make comparisons between theories other than from the basis of one methodology. An argument for theoretical advance thus must consider whether any change has at the same time occurred in the methodological framework.

There is no question that the technical capacity of economics has advanced tremendously in the last sixty years. This has transformed the range of methods open to economists for expressing theory, deriving results and testing them empirically. It is often taken for granted that such technical advance is part of the inexorable march of progress in economics, by which we build up an ever-better set of models which conform ever more closely to our observation of the real world. This view is given detailed expression by Lucas (1980) in his analysis of developments in business cycle theory: 'technical advances in statistical and economic theory occurred, which transformed "Keynesian economics" into something very different from, and much more fruitful than, anything Keynes himself had foreseen' (Lucas, 1980: 701). This perception of a 'transformation' of Keynes's theory carries the suggestion of methodological change as well as changes in methods. Lucas explicitly specifies his preferred methodology, which might be classified as instrumentalist. The object of theory is to create 'a mechanical, imitation economy' which 'mimics the answers actual economies give to simple questions'. 'Any model that is well enough articulated to give clear answers to the questions we put to it will necessarily be artificial, abstract, patently "unreal"' (Lucas, 1980: 696–7). Lucas welcomes the increased range of techniques since Keynes's day as assisting the construction of better analogue models, presumably ones which predict better. The transformation, as he sees it, is away from the alternative aim he identifies in Keynes of generating 'better verbal descriptions of the world' (Lucas, 1980: 700).

Lucas is unusual in making explicit reference to Keynes, and the implications of technical advance since his day. Textbooks presenting Keynesian theory in terms of IS–LM analysis, without reference to Keynes, are accepting at face value Hicks's (1937) view that the apparatus offers only a slight extension of Keynes's theory. (See Young, 1987, for a full account of the evolution of the IS–LM apparatus.) Even much of New Keynesian theory is presented without explicit reference to Keynes. An exception is Greenwald and Stiglitz (1993), who differentiate New Keynesian economics from 'old Keynesian' economics by the use made of developments in microfoundations not available in the 1950s and 1960s. No hint is given of the methodological implications of the use made of the microfoundations, or their nature.

In spite of technical advances, it is not the case that all are in fact agreed on the criteria for advance in economics. It was clear from the reaction to Friedman's (1953) statement of instrumentalism that many economists found successful prediction an inadequate criterion for theory choice.

Indeed, the ensuing debate made it clear that it was inappropriate to represent instrumentalism and descriptivism as a (mutually exclusive) dual. Successful prediction requires an understanding of the structure of the economy, so that the analogue model is capable of capturing structural change, while pure description without theoretical abstraction is impossible (see Caldwell, 1984). So Lucas's presumption of methodological advance from descriptivism needs further probing, as indeed does his characterization of Keynes's methodology as descriptivism.

A notable feature of developments within the field of methodology itself is that there is now a widespread recognition that there are currently no absolute criteria by which to identify methodological advance, other than from the point of view of any one methodology. (There is a range of views over whether or not agreement on absolute criteria is in principle achievable; see Backhouse, 1994: ch. 1; Dow, 1997a.) This new understanding implies that Lucas's assessment of the superiority of general equilibrium theory over Keynes's theory must be understood in relative terms; that is, that general equilibrium theory is superior, given the methodological principles embodied in it. Statements by New Keynesians about their advance on Keynes must be understood in similar terms. There is nothing intrinsically wrong with forming such judgments; the point is that such judgments do not carry the weight of any absolute methodological criteria.

Keynes is a particularly interesting case study, since his philosophical foundations were extensive, and have been the subject of much scholarship over the last fifteen years. We are thus in a better position with Keynes than with many other great economists to identify his methodological position on economics, and to extrapolate it for application to modern theory. We can then assess whether the transformation of Keynesian economics to which Lucas refers would have been seen by Keynes as being 'much more fruitful' than anything he had himself foreseen.

The interpretation of Keynes's methodology to be employed here is the Post Keynesian one. Indeed, one way of defining Post Keynesianism as a school of thought is by its set of methodological principles. In interpreting Keynes's methodological principles, the focus here is on interpretation with relevance to modern economics rather than on interpretation for its own sake. This exercise is thus in the spirit of hermeneutics advocated by Gerrard (1991).

An account is offered in the next section of the foundation of Keynes's economic methodology in his earlier work in philosophy and mathematics, and, in the third section, of his economic methodology. Keynes's argument is highlighted that, while the application of mathematical argument to social systems may significantly increase knowledge in particular circumstances, its application nevertheless requires justification in terms of those circumstances. Whether or not mathematical argument is appropriate is a matter of logic. Thus advance in techniques *per se* is not a sufficient condition for theoretical advance; reference must be made to the sphere of application. The corollary is that suggestions are flawed, that modern economic theory can be regarded as an advance on Keynes *simply because* it employs more advanced techniques. If it is accepted that what was involved was also a methodological shift (changing the sphere of application of mathematical argument) then the case for advance must also refer to this shift in methodology. Post Keynesian methodology is discussed in the third section as an example of this reading of Keynes's methodology applied to theorizing in the 1990s.

II KEYNES'S LOGIC

Keynes developed his logic, prior to his involvement in economics, in *A Treatise on Probability* (Keynes, 1921). He was grappling with how in practice people overcome the problem of induction; that is, the problem that past observations are never sufficient to establish the truth of a proposition, as future observations may show it to be false. Keynes was thus concerned with how reasonable grounds for belief may be established in such circumstances, as the basis for action.

For Keynes, demonstrative argument, where propositions could be proved to be true or false, were not problematic. Rather, Keynes was concerned with non-demonstrative argument:

> In most branches of academic logic . . . all the arguments aim at demonstrative certainty. They claim to be *conclusive*. But many other arguments are rational and claim some weight without pretending to be certain. In metaphysics, in science, and in conduct, most of the arguments, upon which we habitually base our rational beliefs, are admitted to be inconclusive in a greater or less degree. (Keynes, 1921: 3)

Keynes developed a general theory of probability which encompassed quantitative probability as a special case. Keynes's probability is a logical relation based on available, relevant evidence which in general is incomplete. Probability may be quantifiable, non-quantifiable but amenable to ranking, or non-quantifiable and not amenable to ranking (see Carabelli, 1995). Further, it is the nature of the subject matter which determines whether probability may be quantified and/or ranked; quantified probability is only discernible (in principle or in practice) where the subject matter allows. Each judgment as to probability in turn is held with greater or lesser confidence depending on the weight of evidence. The weight attached to any judgment as to probability is greater the greater the degree of relevant evidence; but more evidence may either increase or decrease probability (see O'Donnell, 1989; Runde, 1990). Where there is no basis for forming a judgment as to probability, there may be no basis for action in reason; but action may still be justified on grounds of intuition (see O'Donnell, 1989; Dow, 1991).

Keynes's logic thus differs from the demonstrative certainty of classical logic. He later adopted Ramsey's term 'human logic' to classify his schema for reasoned argument in the absence of demonstrative certainty. There are two particular issues with this logic which are of importance for Keynes's subsequent economic methodology.

First, *how extensive is the domain of demonstrative logic relative to non-demonstrative logic?* Keynes saw non-demonstrative logic as the general case, and demonstrative logic as the particular case. His emphasis was on requiring scientists to justify the use of classical (demonstrative) logic by demonstrating that probabilities could be quantified in this domain. This required that events be replicable in order to generate frequency distributions. This in turn required that the system under study be finite, and that the elements of the relations under study be atomic:

> The system of the material universe must consist . . . of bodies which we may term . . . *legal atoms*, such that each of them exercises its own, separate, independent, and invariable effect, a change of the total state being compounded of a number of separate changes each of which is solely due to a separate portion of the preceding state. (Keynes, 1921: 276–7)

An organic system, in contrast, may be defined as one in which relations between ultimate real entities are internal rather than external (see Winslow, 1989). Organic complexity is characterized by attributes which are 'qualitative, non-homogeneous, synthetic, transitory, unique and time-irreversible, not liable to be reduced to numerical magnitudes' (Carabelli, 1988: 271).

Only if the system could be shown to be finite and atomic would the application of mathematics be justified. Contrary to popular misconceptions (encouraged, for example, by Stone, 1978) Keynes did not argue against the use of mathematics *per se*. He favoured mathematical argument where appropriate to the subject matter. But its use could not be universally justified, and care should therefore be taken to distinguish those contexts in which it was justified from those in which it was not justified. For Keynes, this was a matter of logic. (See Dennis, 1995, for a modern statement of a logical analysis of the role of mathematics in economics.) Where systems are organic, rather than atomic, qualitative analysis is more appropriate. As O'Donnell puts it:

Constitutive of Keynes's philosophy is a crucial principle that flows unabated through all his writings. It is the proposition that qualitative logical analysis (i) *precedes* quantitative or mathematical analysis, and (ii) *determines the scope* of its application. Translated into a slogan, it becomes 'first logic, then mathematics if appropriate'. (O'Donnell, 1990: 35)

The second issue is *how far is non-demonstrative logic amenable to formal representation?* Developments in logic in the 1950s and 1960s demonstrated that internal relations are irreducible to external relations (see Carabelli, 1992). This would imply that logic which was non-demonstrative because it referred to organic relations would not be amenable to formal representation.

However, Ramsey's (1931) subjectivist treatment of probability offered the possibility of a mathematical representation of expectations, by focusing on subjective expectations rather than the underlying objective conditions. Indeed, Ramsey directly criticized Keynes's apparently objectivist theory of probability as put forward in the *Treatise on Probability*.

Keynes accepted Ramsey's criticism of his objective probabilities up to a point:

> Ramsey argues, as against the view which I put forward, that probability is concerned not with objective relations between propositions but (in some sense) with degrees of belief, and he succeeds in showing that the calculus of probabilities simply amounts to a set of rules for ensuring that the system of degrees of belief which we hold shall be a consistent system. Thus the calculus of probabilities belongs to formal logic. But the basis of our degrees of belief – or the *a priori* probabilities, as they used to be called – is part of our human outfit, perhaps given us merely by natural selection, analogous to our perceptions and our memories rather than to formal logic. So far I yield to Ramsey – I think he is right. (Keynes, CW X: 338–9)

This passage has been taken as evidence of a radical shift in Keynes's thinking (see, for example, Bateman, 1987). But it is notable that Keynes did not endorse Ramsey's development of a mathematical treatment of expectations. Keynes's agreement with Ramsey that probabilities stem from belief rather than formal logic (as opposed to human logic) was in accord with Keynes's move away from rationalism towards a cognitive theory of probability. But this agreement 'so far' did not alter his fundamental argument about the limitations on the scope for quantifiable probability estimates. Keynes's theory of probability is a general theory of logical relations; that is, of cause. The mathematical theory of chance applied by Ramsey to expectations applies only to that subset of situations where there is no knowledge of causal relations at all. (See Carabelli, 1988: ch. 6; O'Donnell, 1989: ch. 7; Gerrard, 1992.)

When considering technical advances in economics since his time, therefore, Keynes would have considered not only the content of the advances
but also their realm of application. The increased application of formalization in economics would, according to Keynes, require justification that the
subject matter was indeed close to being finite and atomic, yielding quantifiable probability estimates. Further, where probability is understood as a
degree of belief, there is the requirement that economic agents believe that
the subject matter is close to being finite and atomic. What Lucas classified
as description in Keynes was what Keynes would have classified as qualitative analysis, as required by his logic.

III   KEYNES'S ECONOMIC METHODOLOGY

When, as an economist, Keynes turned his attention to social systems, he
argued that, in general, these systems were organic rather than atomic (see
Keynes, CW X: 262; CW XIV: 286). While specific elements of the subject
matter might be close enough to being atomic for formal analysis to be an
adequate basis for knowledge, in general formal analysis was inadequate.
In organic systems, internal relations are complex and in general unquan-
itifiable; not all influences on particular variables are knowable *a priori.*
Further, relations evolve over time as knowledge, behaviour and institutions evolve, so that processes are, in general, irreversible. Indeed, where the
economy is understood to be an open system, the appropriate theoretical
framework is itself an open system.

Keynes therefore eschewed a general, all-encompassing methodology of
closed, formal systems, built on axioms defining the rational choices of atomistic individuals. Rather, he positively embraced a methodology which
employed a range of methods (of which formal analysis was only one) in
order to build up knowledge as to causal relations in the economy (see
Chick, 1983; Harcourt, 1987). Further, Keynes understood well what
McCloskey (1983, 1986) has shown is the actual practice of economists,
regardless of their professed methodology: that persuasion is a central
element in the advance of economic knowledge, and formal analysis is only
one element in that persuasion (see Dow, 1988). Arguments are accordingly
quite deliberately constructed using different methods throughout Keynes's
work, and even within works, in order to persuade in different contexts.
Thus, for example, Keynes starts the *General Theory* with only slight
changes to the marginalist model in order to demonstrate how little it
would take to generate an unemployment equilibrium result from closed-
system theory, before proceeding to develop his own general, open-system,
theory.

The most direct connection between Keynes's logic and the content of his economic theory is his use of the concept of uncertainty. (See Lawson, 1988, for an account of the connection between Keynes's theories of probability, uncertainty and expectations.) This was drawn out most clearly in his restatement of the *General Theory* in 1937 (Keynes, CW XIV: 109–23). Uncertainty plays its most active role in the theory of investment (see Lawson, 1995b) and of money (see Runde, 1994a). Applying Keynes's theory of probability to long-term expectations of returns from investment generates the conclusion that these expectations are not amenable to mathematical formulation. In the absence of adequate frequency distribution evidence, these expectations rely, of necessity, on qualitative judgment, convention and intuition. Contrary to Coddington's (1982) argument, the absence of a formal rational foundation for long-term expectations does not lead to nihilism; rather, it focuses attention on those (non-formalizable) elements which provide the basis for action.

Keynes's monetary theory seems to allow more formal treatment. Keynes argued that the rate of interest is a monetary variable, determined by liquidity preference. He expressed a key element of liquidity preference, speculative demand, in a manner which emphasizes subjective expectations: speculative demand arises from expectations with respect to future bond prices which are held *as if* speculators are certain. But Keynes's approach is quite different from the subjective expected utility approach. This approach, based on Ramsey's logic, involves agents making (subjective) probability estimates on all (but the most trivial) choice occasions. Yet Keynes's theory of liquidity preference derives fundamentally from a perception of the importance of situations in which agents refuse to make such estimates; that is, they refuse to place bets (see Runde, 1995). Where confidence is low in expectations as to asset prices, both speculative demand and precautionary demand for money will rise, raising interest rates *ceteris paribus*.

The theory Keynes built up in the *General Theory*, while only partially formal, can by no means be characterized as descriptivist. Indeed, Keynes embraced the inevitability of abstraction in theory. What he was concerned with was the nature of the abstraction, the relations between formal and informal abstraction, and the steps required to derive policy conclusions from them (see O'Donnell, 1989: ch. 10).

Contrary to the instrumentalism of Friedman and Lucas, Keynes was concerned that assumptions, while simplifications of reality, should not be fictions. Thus, for example, he argued that theory should start with a monetary production economy rather than a real exchange economy, because of the difficulty of incorporating money later in the analysis:

The idea that it is comparatively easy to adapt the hypothetical conclusions of a real wage economics to the real world of monetary economics is a mistake. It is extraordinarily difficult to make the adaptation, and perhaps impossible without the aid of a developed theory of monetary economics . . . Now the conditions required for the 'neutrality' of money . . . are, I suspect, precisely the same as those which will insure that crises *do not occur*. If this is true, the real-exchange economics, on which most of us have been brought up . . ., though a valuable abstraction in itself and perfectly valid as an intellectual conception, is a singularly blunt weapon for dealing with the problem of booms and depressions. For it has assumed away the very matter under investigation. (Keynes, CW XIII: 410–11)

Having established assumptions which would later allow theory to be applied most easily to policy questions, Keynes favoured the construction of simplified theoretical argument to abstract from 'the extreme complexity of the actual course of events' (Keynes, CW XIV: 249). But more formal theoretical argument needs to be combined with more qualitative argument. While application of 'practical intuition' to theoretical argument is a necessary feature of translating theory into policy prescription (Keynes, 1936: 249), it is also necessary *as a part of* theoretical argument itself:

The object of our analysis is, not to provide a machine, or method of blind manipulation, which will furnish an infallible answer, but to provide ourselves with an organised and orderly method of thinking out particular problems; and, after we have reached a provisional conclusion by isolating the complicating factors one by one, we then have to go back on ourselves and allow, as well as we can, for the probable interactions of the factors amongst themselves . . . Any other way of applying our formal principles (without which, however, we shall be lost in the wood) will lead us into error. It is a grave fault of symbolic pseudo-mathematical methods of formalising a system of economic analysis . . . that they expressly assume strict independence between the factors involved and lose all their cogency and authority if this hypothesis is disallowed; whereas, in ordinary discourse, where we are not blindly manipulating but know all the time what we are doing and what the words mean, we can keep 'at the back of our heads' the necessary reserves and qualifications and the adjustments which we shall have to make later on, in a way in which we cannot keep complicated partial differentials 'at the back' of several pages of algebra which assume that they all vanish. Too large a proportion of recent 'mathematical' economics are merely concoctions, as imprecise as the initial assumptions they rest on, which allow the author to lose sight of the complexities and interdependencies of the real world in a maze of pretentious and unhelpful symbols. (Keynes, 1936: 297–8)

We find evidence in this passage of the foundation of Keynes's argument in the logic entailed by organicism. But, at the same time, Keynes clearly sees an essential role for formalism. In order to theorize at all, some segmentation of the economic system is required; that is, subsystems must be presumed (albeit for the time being) to be finite and atomic. Keynes used formal mathematical reasoning at times, and treated some relations as stable. Indeed, identifying relations which are stable *in spite of* irreversible evolutionary processes and discrete shifts in other variables was an important aspect of Keynes's theorizing (as in the consumption function). But he continually justified the assumption of atomism when he applied it in particular cases, and (as in the consumption function) was careful to specify factors which might be expected to disturb the presumably stable relation.

The identification of stable empirical relationships was one of the key contributions of the emerging field of econometrics. Keynes applied his logic of probability also to econometrics, most notably in his critique of Tinbergen's multiple correlation analysis (Keynes, CW XIV: 308–20). Again his argument was that the (atomistic) assumption of constant structural relationships which underpinned such analysis required justification on a case-by-case basis. Keynes did not make any general argument against econometrics. Indeed, he actively encouraged the development of statistical analysis where appropriate, just as he actively encouraged the use of mathematics where appropriate (see O'Donnell, 1989: ch. 9). But he placed the *onus* on the econometrician to justify the assumption of constant structure in particular subsystems, given the generally organic nature of the economic system.

Thus Keynes was not what we might call a 'pure' organicist, in that he did advocate formal mathematical argument and statistical estimation as an aid to understanding particular subsystems which were approximately finite and atomic (see Davis, 1989). Indeed, it is entailed in his logic that Keynes should avoid dualism (all-encompassing, mutually exclusive categories with fixed meaning; see Dow, 1990a). This was equally evident in Keynes's exchange with Ramsey, where it was clear that Keynes could not be classified either as a 'pure' objectivist or a 'pure' subjectivist (see Carabelli, 1988, for the fullest articulation of this general argument).

Keynes would therefore have welcomed advances in mathematical and statistical techniques in economics. In particular, he would have welcomed advances which allowed economists to address the complexities of an organic system. But we cannot be sanguine that all advances have taken account of Keynes's underlying belief that the economic system is organic. Not only has the import of his logic not been addressed directly, but also the most notable advances picked out by Lucas (1980) have moved economics in a direction which Keynes had argued was ruled out by organicness. Lucas highlighted the description of the economy as a system of stochastically disturbed difference equations, the development of a formal general equilibrium model and the development of disequilibrium analysis to explain business cycles. Thus much of the technical advance has been in extending the scope of mathematical formalism within a closed, axiomatic system, where expectations conform to quantifiable probability distributions. For Keynes, these advances all involve assumptions so at variance with his understanding of the organicism of economic relations that he would have doubted how far it would be possible to adapt conclusions in order to address policy issues.

Rather than speculating further on how Keynes would have regarded this form of technical progress in economics, let us turn to consider Post Keynesian methodology, which is a modern application of Keynes's methodology.

IV   POST KEYNESIAN METHODOLOGY

Post Keynesian economics involves a re-reading of Keynes along the lines defined by Coddington (1976) as 'fundamentalist Keynesianism'. The origins of this approach in Keynes's logic are evident in the central importance given to the concept of uncertainty. But, more generally, Post Keynesianism may be defined methodologically as being based on a vision of the economy as being organic, requiring an emphasis on (irreversibly) evolving institutions, behaviour and knowledge (see Dow, 1998). The explicit derivation from Keynes's logic has only recently been articulated, with the explosion of the Keynes philosophy literature in the late 1980s and 1990s. This articulation, and the surrounding debates, are themselves inspiring new developments in Post Keynesian economics. But Post Keynesianism can be understood as always having taken a methodological position consistent with that of Keynes. This is evident, for example, in the emphasis placed by Davidson (1972) and Chick (1983) on the methodological consequences of building theory to encompass uncertainty (as non-quantifiable risk), irreversible historical time, and money as an integral factor in capitalist economies.

In the past, Post Keynesian methodological discussion was given focus by the common judgment that axiomatic, closed-system theorizing ruled out the possibility of incorporating uncertainty, irreversible historical time and money as an integral part of the economic process. Mainstream economic theory has made great progress in attempting to overcome these limitations, and to do so with formalist techniques. But the formalization of uncertainty has ruled out consideration of uncertainty which is not even in principle reducible, has required irreversible evolutionary processes to be treated as deterministic (with stochastic variation) and eradicates the rationale for money as the refuge for uncertainty (see Davidson, 1972). Technical advance has thus occurred which has broadened the scope of mainstream economics, but it has done so by extending the coverage of theory suited to a subject matter which is close to being finite and atomistic, or of which the subjective perception is that it is finite and atomistic.

The significance for methodology of the nature of the subject matter of economics has been the focus of a recent development in thinking within Post Keynesianism: critical realism (see Lawson, 1994a). This approach focuses on the ontological level in a way which holds much in common with Keynes's logic (although the major philosophical influence is Bhaskar, 1975). The subject matter of economics is understood to have objective existence, and to be organic. This organicness places inevitable limits on knowledge, allowing different understandings. The aim of economic theory is seen as the identification of the underlying causal processes which generate the 'surface' outcomes which are the conventional subject matter of economics. The appropriate methodology is an open-system methodology, where assumptions are simplifications rather than abstractions, and where a range of (often incommensurate) methods are employed in order to build up knowledge of the complexity of the economic system. Critical realism has been identified by Lawson (1994b) as articulating the philosophical foundations of Post Keynesianism; this view finds support in Arestis (1992) and Lavoie (1992b).

Post Keynesian methodology has often been characterized in terms of its diversity of method (see, for example, Hamouda and Harcourt, 1988). From the perspective of the methodology of mainstream economics, which favours an axiomatic, closed-system approach, such diversity has appeared to lack coherence. Since dualism is part of that closed-system approach, there has been a tendency to regard the lack of a closed system as a non-system, or what we might call 'pure' pluralism, or eclecticism. Thus Caldwell (1989) advocated the moulding of the diversity of Post Keynesian methods into a coherent methodology, not realizing that diversity of method was the positive outcome of an open system methodology. The coherence of this methodology arises from the underlying vision of reality; thus neo-Austrian economics, for example, which also has an open-system methodology, employs a different range of methods from Post Keynesianism, according to a different vision of reality (see Dow, 1990b). This modified form of pluralism follows logically from the vision of reality as in general organic, and the consequent open-system theory of knowledge and open-system methodology. It is a methodology which lies outside the dual of the monism of closed-system theorizing on the one hand and the pure pluralism of postmodernism on the other (see Dow, 2001).

Formalism has its place in Post Keynesianism along with other methods. Partial arguments are constructed mathematically (see, for example, Arestis, 1992; Lavoie, 1992b) and tendencies are identified econometrically (see Lawson, 1989). But neither is treated as demonstrative in itself.

Knowledge of underlying processes requires a range of methods, many of which may not be capable of being formalized, in particular qualitative argument. Post Keynesianism may thus be characterized as having attempted to take Keynes's ideas forward, employing new formal techniques as appropriate, but ever-conscious of Keynes's arguments about the logical limits of formalism.

V   CONCLUSION

Just as neo-Austrianism and Post Keynesianism may be distinguished by the logical consequences of their different vision of reality, so also may axiomatic, closed-system theorizing be distinguished from Post Keynesianism in terms of vision of reality. Axiomatic, closed-system theorizing follows logically from an understanding of reality (on the part of economists and economic agents alike) as being finite and atomic. The sum total of technical advances since Keynes's day may only be seen uncontroversially as representing theoretical advance if the vision of reality is of a finite, atomic system.

Yet it is not altogether clear that this is the vision which predominates in economics; to the extent that there is a disparity between a predominantly organicist vision of reality and a predominantly atomistic theoretical structure, there is a logical problem to be addressed. The diversity of methods of persuasion which McCloskey (1983) had identified as being general in economics is given explicit recognition by Blanchard and Fischer (1989): 'Often the economist will use a simple ad hoc model, where an ad hoc model is one that emphasises one aspect of reality and ignores others, in order to fit the purpose for which it is being used' (Blanchard and Fischer, 1989: 505). But, in contrast to Keynes's, and Post Keynesians', logical justification for partial analyses and a range of (incommensurate) methods, Blanchard and Fischer express their methodological discomfort:

> Although it is widely adopted and almost as widely espoused, the eclectic position is not logically comfortable. It would be better for economists to have an all-purpose model, derived explicitly from microfoundations and embodying all relevant imperfections, to analyse all issues in macroeconomics (or perhaps all issues in economics). We are not quite there yet. And if we ever were, we would in all likelihood have little understanding of the mechanisms at work behind the results of simulations. Thus we have no choice but to be eclectic. (Blanchard and Fischer, 1989: 505)

Keynes's rationale for open-system theorizing, for choosing partial (as opposed to simply *ad hoc*) models, does provide for logical comfort. But it also raises questions about the type of formalism which is appropriate for particular circumstances, how it should be combined with other methods in order to yield useful policy conclusions, and therefore about what is the proper scope of formalism in economics.

This is not to say that no technical advance is welcome from the perspective of Keynes's logic – far from it. Technical advance is welcome from Keynes's perspective if it formalizes those elements closest to being atomic which previously had to be kept 'at the back of the head'. But the scope for such advances and how far they meet Keynes's logical requirements is something which has yet to be addressed head on. The case for demonstrating that theoretical advance has resulted from technical advance thus requires an explicit argument, either that technical advance is appropriate to a primarily open, organic subject matter, or alternatively that the subject matter is primarily finite and atomic.

12. How do economic theorists use empirical evidence? Two case studies

Roger E. Backhouse[1]

I THE PROBLEM

The main objective of this chapter is to compare the role played by empirical evidence in Post Keynesian and mainstream economics. Given the methodological claims often made by Post Keynesian economics, one would expect to find significant differences. This objective is approached through an analysis of the way empirical evidence is used in two textbooks: *Lectures on Macroeconomics*, by Olivier Blanchard and Stanley Fischer (1989), and *The Post Keynesian Approach to Economics*, by Philip Arestis (1992). What these books have in common is that they are graduate-level texts on economic theory. As such, their main concern is with basic conceptual issues that affect the way economic phenomena are conceived: they are not concerned with phenomena relevant only to a specific time and place. Empirical evidence, therefore, is introduced only where it is considered relevant to more general conceptual issues. Thus Blanchard and Fischer (1989: xi) write that the goals of their book are (a) to present the conceptual framework and set of models 'used and agreed upon by the large majority of macroeconomists' and (b) to show the directions in which researchers are currently working. A further characteristic shared by the two books is that their authors are well known for their applied econometric research. One would expect them, therefore, to be well aware of the potential importance of empirical evidence and to use it wherever relevant.

The background to this study is a broader concern with the role of empirical evidence in economics more generally, for, despite extensive discussion of the problem in the methodological literature, it is an issue that is far from thoroughly understood. It is widely believed that empirical evidence plays a comparatively minor role in economic theory.[2] However, diagnoses of the problem differ. Leontief (1971) blamed it on the structure of incentives in the profession causing economists to develop a theoretical superstructure more elaborate than can be supported by the available data; Blaug (1992) blames it on a failure to pursue falsificationism; Rosenberg (1992) suggests that it may be because economics is not a science at all, but a branch of political philosophy; Hausman (1992) argues that it is often a rational response to poor-quality data, given that theories are normally based on postulates which there are good reasons to accept; Fisher (1989) has blamed economists for constructing 'exemplifying' rather than 'generalizing' theories; McCloskey (1986, 1991) argues that it is because economists are in the business of persuading, and persuasion involves using a range of rhetorical devices, not simply confronting theories with empirical evidence.

At the same time, there is widespread scepticism about what econometrics has managed to achieve, for whilst empirical evidence has undoubtedly played an important role in parts of economics (albeit not the dominant one), the crucial evidence has not, by and large, been formal econometric tests or estimates of coefficients. Equally important has been informal empirical evidence. Summers (1989) has suggested that this is because informal methods (such as used by Friedman and Schwartz, 1963) involve a greater variety of evidence, the results are more robust than those derived using formal econometric methods, and they produce evidence (stylized facts rather than parameter estimates) that conforms better to the nature of economic theory and is more suggestive of new lines of inquiry.

This scepticism about the importance of econometrics in influencing the course of economic theory is reinforced by doubts about econometricians' practices. Replication, even in the limited sense of reproducing other economists' results using the same data sets that they used, many critics argue, is difficult to achieve and is rarely undertaken (Dewald *et al.*, 1986). As before, there is disagreement over the significance to be attached to this. A common view is that such replication ought to be more frequent than it is and that the incentives faced by economists and the institutions of the profession should be changed so as to encourage it (Mayer, 1993; Mirowski and Sklivas, 1991). Mirowski (1994) has pointed to the absence of mechanisms analogous to those that exist in several of the natural sciences to produce agreement: economists, he claims, do not agree on the values of important coefficients because the mechanisms needed to produce agreement do not exist. On the other side, it has been argued that most scientific work (not just in economics) is never cited by anyone, and that work that matters is probably checked by other scientists (Collins, 1991).[3]

Before turning to the two case studies, it is worth noting that there are different types of empirical evidence, and that it can be used in a variety of ways.[4] Empirical evidence can be divided into four categories:[5]

- stylized facts or generalizations – trends or correlations,
- numerical estimates of coefficients,
- historical examples,
- non-numerical institutional details.

In addition, there is the role played by the evidence in the exposition of the theory. Empirical evidence can be used for four main purposes:

- testing implications of theories,
- evidence for the assumptions made in theories,
- illustrations of theories,
- disproving rival theories.[6]

II   OLIVIER BLANCHARD AND STANLEY FISCHER, *LECTURES ON MACROECONOMICS*

To illustrate the way empirical evidence is used in this book, two chapters will be considered. These are ones in which empirical evidence is most prominent: the introduction (Chapter 1) and a chapter interestingly enti-tled 'Some useful models' (Chapter 10). The use of empirical evidence in other chapters is *much* less.

The main function of the introductory chapter is to 'introduce the major issues of macroeconomics by characterizing the basic facts that call for explanation' (Blanchard and Fischer, 1989: 1). The basic facts to which attention is drawn are the following. The first is the growth of output and its decomposition into the contributions of various factors (the 'Solow' decomposition). Madison and Solow are cited, but the 'stylized facts' about growth are taken as well-established, and supported by the authors' own calculations. Denison is cited, but simply to make the point that, despite his work, little is known about the sources of the residual.

Second is Okun's Law that a 1 per cent decrease in the unemployment rate is associated with a 3 per cent increase in output. The author empha-size Okun's methods, pointing out that other economists have followed the same techniques, all reaching the conclusion that trend growth was lower in the 1970s and 1980s than before. Two examples of such work are cited, though the precise numbers obtained are not given. Blanchard and Fischer then estimate such a decomposition themselves, giving the equation they obtained. However, their emphasis is not on the magnitude of the coeffi-cient in Okun's Law, but on the size of the residual variance in output. They describe it (1 per cent) as 'large' (Blanchard and Fischer, 1989: 10).

Blanchard and Fischer then present an analysis of output based on the assumption that all shocks have permanent effects, and that it makes no sense to look at the gap between output and a smooth trend. They cite two papers which found evidence that GDP could be described by a particular ARIMA process, whereupon they estimate such a process themselves, finding that the residual variance is similar to that derived using the technique described above. However, the significance of both this and the previous decomposition are then questioned when Blanchard and Fischer point out that it has been shown that there will in general be an infinite number of decompositions into cycle and trend.

A third method for separating trend from cycle is to analyse the joint behaviour of output and unemployment. Two papers on this are cited, and Blanchard and Fischer provide results based on their own calculations. The conclusions reached in the cited papers are not discussed.

Next, evidence is presented on co-movements in GNP and some of its components. It is concluded that the elasticity of consumption to GNP is 35 per cent ('much smaller than 1') and that 'in those periods after 1948 when GNP declines relative to a deterministic trend, the average share of the fall attributable to a decline in inventory investment is about 50%' (Blanchard and Fischer, 1989: 16). Another work is cited as evidence that, if the calculation is performed slightly differently, the latter figure would be 68 per cent.

Co-movements between GNP and certain relative prices are analysed in detail. The conclusion that there is little correlation between real wages and output is supported by six other studies, dating from 1938 to 1988, and using three different types of data (on the economy, industries and individual firms).

Finally, in discussing co-movements between GNP and nominal magnitudes, Blanchard and Fischer's own conclusions are supported by two other studies that found that, 'given nominal money, there is a positive correlation between innovations in interest rates and future innovations in GNP' (Blanchard and Fischer, 1989: 32).

In Chapter 10, the focus is primarily on theory, but an interesting range of empirical evidence is cited.

- A standard CAPM (capital asset pricing model) describes asset returns less well than the consumption CAPM, even though the latter is theoretically superior. One reference is cited.
- The Lucas asset-pricing model cannot explain both the riskless discount rate and the equity premium. Two studies are cited.
- Studies of hyperinflation (of which two, one of which has Fischer as a co-author, are cited) often stress the role of the budget deficit, which means that it is a puzzle that no correlation can be found

between deficits and inflation. This is presented as a generally accepted empirical finding.

- The tax cuts in 1981 were deflationary (backed up by two sources). A macroeconometric model (the MPS model) is cited as evidence that the transmission Blanchard and Fischer have described can be used in empirical work, though no conclusions reached with the econometric model are mentioned.
- The coefficient on expected inflation in the Phillips curve is argued to have been estimated, in the early 1970s, at between 0.4 and 0.8. This is presented as a generally accepted conclusion.
- The Layard and Nickell (1987) model of inflation and unemployment is discussed in detail: the econometric equations are presented, and short- and long-run elasticities of demand for labour are calculated. The factors Layard and Nickell see as having caused rises in the actual and equilibrium unemployment rates are listed. From all this, Blanchard and Fischer draw the conclusion that the causes affecting unemployment are complex.

The first conclusion to be drawn from these examples is that the main role of empirical evidence is to suggest problems to be solved. In the main, these are stylized facts about the economy. Some of these are regarded as well-established, though in several cases Blanchard and Fischer see the key issue as the techniques by which facts are established in particular cases. Once the techniques are established (for example, for disentangling trend and cycle) applying them is seen as routine. A second conclusion is that, although the interest is primarily in explaining stylized facts at a general level, Blanchard and Fischer *do* pay attention to precise numbers, though these rarely play an important role, except in establishing broad magnitudes (usually whether a parameter is either significantly larger than zero, or whether it is close to unity). The examples of elasticities of consumption and investment to GNP were cited above. Another example, from elsewhere in the book, is the elasticity of substitution of leisure across different periods (vital to equilibrium business cycle theories) where they cite a survey as finding 'most estimates' to be between 0 and 0.45, only to qualify this by citing another survey which argued that it could be anywhere between *minus* 0.3 and 14.

This point leads on to a third characteristic of the way Blanchard and Fischer use empirical evidence. It is frequently used to undermine simple models – to suggest doubts, and to stop students being misled regarding hypotheses that emerge from models as certainties. There is no formal testing of opponents' theories, but there is a clear element of falsificationism involved. Perhaps even more significantly, they emphasize their commitment to the view that the causes, even of trends in macroeconomic time series, are complex.

> The reader should remember the major correlations and conclude that *no simple monocausal theory can easily explain them*. Equilibrium theories based on supply shocks have to confront the weak correlations between real wages and GNP, as well as the positive relation between nominal variables and activity. Theories in which the cycle is driven by demand shocks have to give convincing explanations for the behaviour of real wages. Theories that emphasise money shocks have to confront the correlations among interest rates, money, and output. (Blanchard and Fischer, 1989: 20, emphasis added)

The inadequacy of monocausal theories is almost completely unhedged. Though their methods are very different from his, this view is reminiscent of Mitchell's attitude towards explaining the business cycle.

Finally, the emphasis in the book (perhaps in part, though not entirely, because it is a textbook) is on economic models as tools. The macroeconomic models used in the book are presented as being simplifications of reality. Some simplifications (such as the neglect of imperfect competition in considering optimal growth and the Ramsey model) are presented as being harmless. Despite all the simplifications involved, the Ramsey model is argued to be 'more than a benchmark' in that it can provide useful analysis of a small open economy (Blanchard and Fischer, 1989: 21). When it comes to considering fluctuations in output, however, the situation is different:

> We are sure that incomplete markets and imperfect competition are needed to account for the main characteristics of actual fluctuations. We also believe that such nonneoclassical constructs as bounded rationality . . . or interdependent utility functions . . . may be needed to understand important aspects of financial and labor markets. (Blanchard and Fischer, 1989: 27)

With business cycles, their defence of competitive equilibrium theorizing is that it provides a well-understood benchmark, from which deviations can be analysed.

This emphasis on models as tools comes out very clearly in Chapter 10. Blanchard and Fischer argue that, though the models developed in previous chapters can be used to clarify conceptual issues, to explain current events and to help in policy design, 'almost all economists' are eclectic when considering real-world issues. Models often have to be developed in a particular direction to suit the question in hand.[7]

> Often the economist will use a simple *ad hoc* model, where an ad hoc model is one that emphasizes one aspect of reality and ignores others, in order to fit the purpose for which it is being used.

> Although it is widely adopted and almost as widely espoused, the eclectic position is not logically comfortable. It would be better for economists to have an all-purpose model, derived explicitly from microfoundations and embodying all relevant imperfections, to analyse all issues in macroeconomics (or perhaps all issues in economics). We are not quite[!!] there yet. And if we ever were, we would in all likelihood have little understanding of the mechanisms at work behind the results of simulations. Thus we have no choice but to be eclectic. (Blanchard and Fischer, 1989: 505)

They go on to argue that the selection of suitable assumptions is an 'art'. The good economist is one who can know which unrealistic assumptions are peripheral to a particular problem, and which are crucial. There is a trade-off between the tractability of *ad hoc* models and the insights that can be obtained from starting with first principles. Interestingly, a footnote in which they cite Friedman's essay on methodology suggests that they may have 'gone further into methodology than might be wise' (Blanchard and Fischer, 1989: 558, n.3). This belief that economics is an art, in which theoretical tools are used creatively by the economist, is the way they maintain the claim that the goal of economics is empirical, whilst keeping the link between empirical evidence and their theorizing extremely loose.

III   PHILIP ARESTIS, *THE POST-KEYNESIAN APPROACH TO ECONOMICS*

Though written from a completely different perspective from *Lectures in Macroeconomics*, *The Post-Keynesian Approach to Economics* (Arestis, 1992) is similar in its use of empirical evidence, which is concentrated in a few chapters: the critique of 'Grand Neoclassical Synthesis' (GNS) economics (Chapter 3); the theory of money, credit and finance (Chapter 8); and economic policy implications (Chapter 10).[8] There is also an interesting exposition of a Post Keynesian model at the end of Chapter 4.

In criticizing GNS economics, Arestis adduces the following empirical evidence:

- evidence for systematic errors in expectations. This is reinforced by evidence on the failure of models testing rational expectations (p.73);
- persistent high unemployment in the 1930s and in Europe since the late 1970s (pp.74–5). This is clearly too well-known and uncontentious to need documenting;
- econometric work by a wide range of economists undermining Barro's work supporting the new classical theory. The results are cited, but the details are not given (pp.75–6);

- microeconomic evidence that (a) costs do not rise with output and (b) industrial prices are 'completely' insensitive to demand conditions. Two studies are cited for the former; four for the latter (p.81);
- the interest inelasticity of business investment is supported by three references, one by Arestis himself (p.83).

In Chapter 10, the following pieces of empirical evidence are cited:

- unspecified evidence that markets are important in perpetuating inequality. A survey by Sawyer is cited, but no indication is provided of the nature or strength of the evidence (p.241);
- the effects of price controls are sporadic and temporary (p.258);
- tax increases are passed on by firms. One source is cited as arguing that two-thirds of tax increases are passed on within three years, whilst another suggests tax increases are passed on in full (p.258);
- four studies are cited to argue that there is a catching-up effect that undermines attempts to use incomes policy to reduce inflation (p.260);
- unemployment is lower in countries such as Sweden, where a consensus has been worked out covering trade unions, industry and the state (p.267);
- the evidence that the performance of firms with 'worker participation' policies is superior to that of other firms is described as 'overwhelming' (p.268). The reader is referred to a survey for further information.

Finally, there is the empirical evidence cited in Chapter 8, on the banking and monetary system. This stands apart from the other chapters discussed so far, in that the empirical evidence is *far* more thoroughly integrated into the account:

- commercial banks can be regarded as oligopolists, with liability management being important (pp.186–7);
- empirical evidence is reported as being unclear as to whether cost or transactions variables are superior in explaining bank lending, three studies being cited (pp.191–2);
- considerable evidence is cited on the behaviour of bank lending to industry: its low interest elasticity and its size relative to overall bank lending to the private sector (pp.192–3);
- historical evidence is used to support the argument that UK monetary policy has favoured city interests (pp.194–5);
- the proportion of income spent on services more than doubles for those on above-average incomes when incomes double (p.199);

184 Post Keynesian econometrics, microeconomics and the theory of the firm

- there is discussion of institutional features of UK, US and European banking systems, and a discussion of the implications of the 1981 Civil Service strike for cash flows (p.202).

The differences between the empirical evidence used in Chapter 8 and elsewhere include the fact that evidence is used to establish institutional features of the banking system, and that it concerns assumptions that are claimed to be central to the theory being developed. This contrasts with the (inevitably) purely negative use of empirical evidence in Chapter 3, to undermine a competing theory, and the substantially negative use of such evidence in Chapter 10 (several of the points listed are used to rule out possibilities, not to provide the basis for positive conclusions). Much of the other evidence does not relate directly to the formal modelling in the book.

The end of Chapter 4 contains a section entitled 'The Post-Keynesian model', the core of which is an equation-by-equation description of the model (Table 4.1), plus a flow diagram showing the relationship between the various blocks of the model (Figure 4.1). Though parameters are not specified (general functional forms are used), this is a model designed for empirical work, and Arestis provides references to articles where readers can look up the empirical results. This discussion is interesting, methodologically, because it raises, quite clearly, some problems involved in defining what counts as empirical evidence. Does a model such as this count as empirical evidence? A possible answer is 'No', on the grounds that the model, as it stands, is a theoretical model: though it can be (and has been) used to generate empirical evidence, it is not in itself evidence.[9] On the other hand, though they are theoretical equations, it is likely that the model evolved in the course of the empirical work, which means that the form of the equations (the variables included and the signs of coefficients) will reflect not simply theoretical considerations, but also data on the UK economy. Thus, though the model is described as resulting from a series of 'theoretical constructs', it is more than simply a theoretical model. One might also argue that the fact that such a model can be fitted to UK data is in itself a form of empirical evidence.

Arestis's attitude towards evidence is summed up in a methodological discussion in Chapter 4, just before he discusses a complete Post Keynesian model. Several methodological premises are highlighted (Arestis, 1992: 94–7):

- theories 'should represent economic reality as accurately as possible' – the 'primary objective' of Post Keynesian theory is 'an explanation of the real world as observed';
- theories should be context-specific, requiring repeated reappraisal;

- theories should build on 'realistic abstractions', not 'imaginary models';
- theorizing is about open systems, and thus means that many different, equally valid, approaches to the same phenomenon may be required;[10]
- explanation is more important than prediction, the aim of theory being to reveal the generative structures and causal mechanisms that govern events;[11]
- stylised facts are available, and important, but these are interpreted as 'rough and ready generalizations', not stable relationships that can be pinned down precisely using econometric techniques;
- an organic approach is adopted towards economic processes, not an atomistic one.

IV SIMILARITIES

Any generalizations based on these case studies must be treated with great caution. The sample is extremely small. In addition, empirical evidence is not defined formally (though most instances would, I conjecture, be fairly uncontroversial) and it may not always have been identified correctly (sometimes it is not clear from the text, or from the titles of the cited works, whether the evidence is empirical or not). The two case studies do, however, suggest some significant conclusions.

The first major similarity is that replication is something to which economic theorists pay some attention.[12] Reference is often made to several studies that can be regarded as replicating each other. This conclusion is, however, subject to two important qualifications. The first is that this process is very informal. There is no systematic attempt to verify empirical results: the authors simply compare a range of studies that bear on the question in hand. This contrasts with the systematic attempts that are made to replicate empirical results in experimental sciences (including experimental economics). The second qualification is that replication can, and frequently is, only partial. By and large, it is the more general statements that economists wish to test, not the precise numbers.

The second main similarity is the absence of any systematic attempt to use empirical evidence either to support the assumptions made in theoretical models or to test the conclusions in any formal way. Some instances can be found, but they are few. The reasons for this are presumably the difficulty in finding evidence for the core theoretical assumptions. Blanchard and Fischer clearly accept the assumptions – primarily rationality and equilibrium – that underlie their work. Arestis takes for granted the premises that he sees as underlying Post Keynesian economics, notably the fundamental one that 'the free market economic process is inherently unstable and generates forces from within the system that are responsible for the instability and fluctuations in economic activity' (Arestis, 1992: 94). Both books adduce some evidence in support of their theories, but with the exception of Arestis's Chapter 8, it is far from systematic.

A third similarity is the virtually complete absence of formal econometric models and test statistics from both books. One, partial exception is Arestis's statement of a Post Keynesian model in Chapter 4. The exception is partial because it is presented as a theoretical model, and because no details of the econometrics are provided. Another, even more partial, exception is Blanchard and Fischer's discussion of the Layard–Nickell model. Why is there not more discussion of econometric results? There are at least five possible answers to this question.

1. Readers would not understand such material.
2. Where factual claims are made on the basis of evidence from more than one study, citing one particular set of results would not be appropriate.
3. It is taken for granted that results would be cited only where there is a good statistical fit. Readers trust the judgment of the books' authors.
4. Formal econometric results, and statistical tests, are not persuasive in establishing the existence of empirical regularities.[13]
5. Precise results do not matter for the purposes of constructing theories.[14]

The first answer is unconvincing. Anyone who can make sense of the discussion of co-movements in Blanchard and Fischer is certain to be familiar with significance tests, and should be able to interpret econometric results. Similarly, it seems unlikely that Arestis's readers would be unable to cope with such material. The second answer has, perhaps, more force, but it raises the problem of why ways are not found to summarize the results of different studies, for independent studies that supported each other would appear to be strong evidence. The third answer raises the question of why the same assumption cannot be made about proofs of theories. Another answer might be the division of labour: economics textbooks are aimed at training readers in economic theory, and interpreting econometric results is regarded as a separate task, to be left to econometrics textbooks. Alternatively, the interpretation of econometric results might be regarded as a more routine activity, in which training is less important. This leaves the last two explanations. One puzzle is why Blanchard and Fischer chose to discuss the Layard and Nickell model in detail (albeit without discussing statistical tests), when they did not do so for other models.

The fourth similarity is that, in both books, empirical evidence is, for the most part, used for two main purposes: to establish the facts that economic theories should explain; and to undermine competing theories. The first purpose is particularly strong in Blanchard and Fischer: considerable attention is paid to establishing the basic facts that theories are to explain. They use facts to undermine competing theories, though their emphasis is as much on showing that simple theories are inadequate as on showing the superiority of the theories that they put forward. In contrast, Arestis does not provide a comparable discussion of the basic statistical regularities to be explained. It may be that he is taking it for granted that the main facts to be explained are known to his readers – most of his readers will, perhaps, already have learned such facts from neoclassical texts. But the major reason will be his explicit scepticism about whether any more than 'rough and ready generalisations' can be found, which casts doubt on the value of detailed statistical information. His main use of empirical evidence, apart from that in the chapter on money, is to undermine alternative theories.

V   CONTRASTS

Whilst both texts place great importance on stylized facts, there are differences in the nature of the facts to which they attach importance, and in what they try to establish using empirical evidence. The stylized facts to which Blanchard and Fischer attach importance are Okun's Law; the elasticity of consumption with respect to income; the importance of investment; the coefficient on expected inflation in the Phillips curve; and the intertemporal elasticity of substitution. Empirical evidence is used to establish that these effects are significant. Numerical estimates are used, not because the precise values matter, but as a rhetorical device for persuading the reader that the effects concerned must be taken seriously. Significance is, *contra* McCloskey and Ziliak (1996), an economic concept, for which formal tests are not used. The same is true for Arestis. There remains a difference, however, in that the stylized facts cited by Arestis are much more frequently qualitative and institutional. Most commonly, he is concerned to establish that coefficients are approximately zero, rather than that they are significantly different from zero, examples including the interest elasticity of investment and the elasticity of the price level with respect to aggregate demand. (Two exceptions where he is concerned to establish that values are non-zero are the proportion of tax increases that are passed on in prices and the proportion of income spent on services.) The reason is perhaps that establishing a generalization that can form the basis for theorizing requires more evidence than simply a statistically significant coefficient in a regression equation.

A second contrast is that, whereas Blanchard and Fischer do compare predictions with empirical evidence, either explicitly or implicitly (if only by presenting the theories as explaining the empirical facts listed in Chapter 1), Arestis is much more concerned to establish that the assumptions he is making are realistic. This is related to his concern with institutional details. Arestis's attitude towards economic theory is most clearly illustrated by his chapter on money. The reason why theory and evidence are so inseparable in this chapter is that his monetary economics is related, to an extent not matched elsewhere, to specific institutional structures, and to establish these he needs to turn to empirical evidence. When discussing general macroeconomics, Arestis makes use of generalizations about the nature of industry, firms' pricing policies and so on. There is, however, often an ambiguity concerning whether such generalizations should be regarded as facts or as theoretical statements that might, or might not, be supported with empirical evidence.[15] In contrast, the varied nature of financial systems means that evidence on institutional detail is almost mandatory.

The contrast in the way in which empirical evidence is used in these two books arises from their very different attitudes towards economic theory. For Arestis, theory is based on specific assumptions about economic institutions and human motives. Because he has confidence that the assumptions describe the economies with which he is dealing, he has considerable confidence in the theory. On the other hand, in that it is tied to specific institutions, it is less general than much mainstream theory. The theory is also, by the standards of neoclassical theory, fairly informal, in that Arestis does not feel constrained to confine his attention to what can be proved to follow from fully-specified, formal mathematical models. In contrast, Blanchard and Fischer work with a much tighter core of economic theory, where the key assumptions appear not to require empirical support.[16] However, such models are only tools, and informality enters in at the level of the link between models and reality. Being mathematical theorems, the implications of their theories are true, the issue being whether or not they apply to the world. Thus a certain informality enters into both theories, but it comes in at different places: for Arestis it enters into the theory, whereas Blanchard and Fischer keep the theory very formal, at the expense of the theory having a somewhat looser relationship with the real world.

VI   CONCLUSIONS

This investigation of the way empirical evidence is used in two graduate textbooks reveals significant differences, as well as some remarkable similarities. Methodological differences *do* matter. Substantive differences in the content are accompanied by very different styles. Yet, though that of Blanchard and Fischer is possibly slightly simpler (the distinction between theory and facts is sharper, stylized facts are more precisely defined), in neither case is the methodology pursued completely straightforward.[17] Empirical evidence plays an important role in both books, but it is used in a great variety of ways.[18]

NOTES

1. I am grateful to Philip Arestis for detailed and helpful comments on a draft of this chapter. The usual disclaimer applies.
2. Klamer and Colander (1990) argue, on the basis of a survey of students in leading US universities, that graduate students soon become aware of this.
3. There are, of course, controversies within econometrics concerning the methods to be used. See, for example, Granger (1990).
4. Evidence could also be classified according to the reasons why it is believed: results that have been replicated; facts that are believed because they accord with common sense, or are thought obvious; and facts that are too unimportant for it to be worth questioning them. The issue of replication is considered in detail in Backhouse (1997a).
5. The distinctions are not always absolutely clear-cut, but they are workable.
6. This chapter is concerned with the role of empirical evidence in economic theory. Before going any further, it is important to emphasize that economic theory is not synonymous with economics as a whole. Though economic theorists speak as though it were the case, and though some philosophers have adopted a similar line (Rosenberg, 1992; Hausman, 1992), economics involves many activities that do not depend on economic theory in the sense in which theory is commonly understood by economists. The use of Box–Jenkins methods to forecast industrial production, inflation or the FTSE 100 share index, or research on trends in the distribution of income, whether between factors of production or individuals, does not rely on specific economic theories. It would be very wrong, however, to suggest that such activities were not a part of economics.
7. Though Blanchard and Fischer may be eclectic when compared with many mainstream theorists, however, most heterodox economists would no doubt see their eclecticism as constrained within fairly strict bounds. Eclecticism is something that looks very different from different perspectives.
8. Of the other clear-cut references to empirical evidence, several concern the labour market, such as the reference to the inconclusive nature of the evidence for a long-run Phillips curve trade-off (Arestis, 1992: 17) or the references to evidence concerning the importance (or lack of it) of factors such as search, long-term unemployment or capacity scrapping for the labour market (Arestis, 1992: 172, 174).
9. This is the way I read this section when I wrote the first draft of this chapter. Support for this view is provided by Arestis's introduction to the model: 'When all these theoretical constructs are brought together we arrive at the full model summarized in Table 4.1' (Arestis, 1992: 110).
10. Babylonian methodology advocated by Dow (1985) is cited here.
11. Lawson's critical realism is cited here.
12. I develop this point further in Backhouse (1997a).
13. In the sense argued by Summers (1989).
14. They may, of course, be very important for other purposes, such as providing detailed policy advice in specific circumstances.
15. This is related to the problem of defining empirical evidence discussed above. It is, of

course, well established in the philosophy of science literature that there is no clear-cut dividing line to be drawn between theoretical and evidential propositions.

16. It is likely that the basic assumption of rationality is regarded as corroborated by the large number of other theories that rely on it.

17. A similar conclusion is reached in Backhouse (1997b).

18. By leaving the argument here, I may be accused of ducking the question, 'Which is better?' This, however, is a very big question. Blanchard and Fischer's more formal, though eclectic, approach is valuable for isolating mechanisms and for testing claims about possible causal mechanisms operating. Arestis's 'realistic' method keeps in closer touch with the real world, and permits him to discuss issues that cannot be tackled within formal mathematical models. To evaluate them we would need to consider wider issues such as how theories are used in practice.

13. Conflict in wage and unemployment determination in the UK

Philip Arestis and Iris Biefang-Frisancho Mariscal[1]

I INTRODUCTION

This chapter presents a theoretical model of wage and unemployment determination in which historical and ideological elements, as well as conventional economic factors, play a role. The model is based on the view that labour productivity is not given by the existing technology alone but also by various socioeconomic determinants and in particular the real wage rate (Bowles and Boyer, 1988). Furthermore, the model illustrates the battle over the distribution of income (Rowthorn, 1977, 1995). It also follows the tradition of Keynes, in that workers bring with them not only labour power but also their past history and norms of justice in the workplace, which are more important in determining their relative and average wage level than purely market forces of supply and demand (Keynes, 1936).

Having established the theoretical model in section II, we then go on to estimate the model in section III, using quarterly data for the UK over the period from 1966 until 1994. Section IV concludes.

II THE WAGE MODEL

The model is summarized in Figure 13.1. Conflict arises over labour productivity and the real wage (block I). The only means workers have to enforce wage claims is the threat of a reduction in productivity or a complete withdrawal of labour. The only means employers have to discipline wage demands is the threat of dismissal, which is only effective if workers suffer a non-negligible cost of job loss. This cost is determined by workers' income from present and alternative work, as well as by the probability of becoming unemployed and receiving social security benefits. Workers' decisions on the

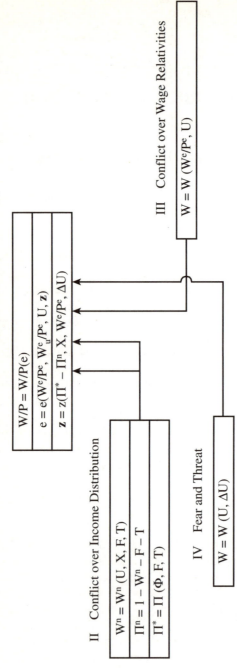

I   Conflict over Real Wages and Labour Productivity

$W/P = W/P(e)$

$e = e(W^e/P^e, W^e_u/P^e, U, z)$

$z = z(\Pi^* - \Pi^n, X, W^e/P^e, \Delta U)$

II   Conflict over Income Distribution

$W^n = W^n(U, X, F, T)$

$\Pi^n = 1 - W^n - F - T$

$\Pi^* = \Pi(\Phi, F, T)$

III   Conflict over Wage Relativities

$W = W(W^e/P^e, U)$

IV   Fear and Threat

$W = W(U, \Delta U)$

V   Model

$W_{t+1} = P^e g(W^e/P^e, W^e_u/P^e, U, \Delta U, F^e, T^e, \Pi^*, \Pi^n, X)$

Figure 13.1   Wage Determination in the UK

degree of work intensity depends on the *shape and position of the workers' effort function*. The effort function is determined by the cost of job loss, but perhaps even more importantly, by social, ideological and political factors (Arestis and Skott, 1993; Skott, 1991). Wages are negotiated and negotiations determine the nominal wage on the basis of price expectations and real wage expectations, so that we may write the negotiated wage W_{t+1} as:

$$W_{t+1} = P^e f(W^e/P^e, W^e_u/P^e, U, \mathbf{z})$$
$$df/d[(W^e/P^e)] > 0 \ df/d[(W^e_u/P^e)] > 0 \ df/dU < 0, \qquad (13.1)$$

where the variable (W^e/P^e) is the expected real wage which serves as a guideline for wage comparisons, as neither workers nor employers have complete information over wage relativities. The variable (W^e_u/P^e) stands for expected real unemployment compensation, as an alternative to income out of work, (U) is the unemployment rate, which reflects the chance of re-employment in case of job loss, and $\mathbf{z}$ comprises the degree of class conflict, worker militancy, customs and ideas on fairness, as well as changes in demand for labour. Higher real wage expectations or higher real unemployment benefits increase pressure on wage demands. Improved unemployment compensation changes the income distribution between those receiving income from work and those receiving income from unemployment by favouring the latter. In order to preserve the prevailing income structure, pressure on wage demands increases. Falling unemployment rates increase the probability of finding alternative employment and strengthen workers' power in the labour market, again increasing pressure on wage demands.

We turn our attention next to discussing the effect of the individual elements of vector $\mathbf{z}$, namely class struggle, worker aggressiveness, notions of pay norms and fairness, and the growth rate of unemployment on work intensity and ultimately on wage setting. Firstly, we turn to block II in order to discuss the conflict over the distribution of income between workers and employers, and to workers' aggressiveness in response to disappointed wage aspirations (Rowthorn, 1977, 1995).

Wages are negotiated in a decentralized bargaining process and provide workers with a negotiated wage share, which, after the claims of the government (T) and foreign sectors (F) are satisfied, provides firms with a residual negotiated profit share (Π^n). After the wage settlement, employers set prices as a mark-up over costs in order to achieve their target profit share (Π^*). Since wage and price setting are not centrally coordinated, there is no mechanism that ensures that the conflicting claims of the private sector are reconciled. The aspiration gap $(\Pi^* - \Pi^n)$ measures the extent to which actual real wages differ from target real wages and thus measures the degree of conflict between workers and employers over income distribution. The aspiration gap is determined by workers' and employers' power and their willingness to use it in the labour market and the product market, respectively. Workers are the more successful in wage claims, the lower is the rate of unemployment (U) and the more aggressive they are (x). Workers' bargaining power lies in their ability to withdraw labour; that is, they may threaten industrial action or, alternatively, they may reduce work effort in a less dramatic way.

The third element in vector **z** introduces the notion of fairness (block III). Although the struggle over income shares may be based on views of what workers and employers consider 'fair' income shares, here we are concerned with the wage structure, where workers resist money wage cuts for fear of a decline in their relative position in the wage hierarchy (Keynes, 1936). The importance of preserving the existing wage structure may be explained by the notion of fairness (Hicks, 1975). A wage system with well-established wage differentials is regarded as fair: 'it has the sanction of custom. It then becomes what is expected; and (admittedly on a low level of fairness) what is expected is fair' (Hicks, 1975: 65). The real expected wage (W^e/P^e) is understood in this context as the historical element that affects the effort function and the negotiated (real) wage.

So far we have emphasized the role that unemployment plays in mitigating wage demands. Turning to the fourth element of vector **z**, namely the growth of the unemployment rate, we will be more specific in discussing the effect of the unemployment rate on the effort function (block IV). Even when the level of unemployment is very high, there is little pressure on unions to sacrifice wage increases for the hope of a better employment outlook. In contrast, when the unemployment rate is *rising*, employed workers fear losing jobs and the faster unemployment rises, the more threatened workers feel and so may give in on wage objectives. The mechanism of unemployment as a disciplinary device in wage demands requires not only the existence of high unemployment, but, more importantly, a rising flow into unemployment which is a threat to those still employed (Boddy and Crotty, 1975). Changes in the unemployment rate (ΔU) is an additional variable in the wage equation, capturing the effect of threat and fear in wage settlements.

We may summarize that the cost of job loss, wage aspirations, militancy, pay norms, and the growth of unemployment affect workers' effort function and the negotiated wage as follows:

$$W_{t+1} = P^e g(W^e/P^e, W^e_u/P^e, U, \Delta U, F^e, T^e, \Pi^*, \Pi^n, X)$$
$$dg/d[(W^e/P^e)] > 0 \ \ dg/d[(W^e_u/P^e)] > 0 \ \ dg/dU < 0$$
$$dg/d\Delta U < 0 \ \ dg/dF^e > 0 \ \ dg/dT^e > 0 \quad\quad (13.2)$$
$$dg/d\Pi^* > 0 \ \ dg/d\Pi^n < 0 \ \ dg/dX > 0,$$

where F and T account for claims of the foreign and government sectors, respectively, on the output of the private sector.

We assume that the variables in equation (13.2) are additively separable and loglinear, so that we may write:

$$
\begin{aligned}
w_{t+1} = p^e &+ \alpha_1(w_u^e - p^e) + \alpha_2(w^e - p^e) \\
&+ \alpha_3[p^e - w^e + lp^e + \Phi^e] - \alpha_4[p - w + lp] \\
&+ \alpha_5 x - \alpha_6 u - \alpha_7 \Delta u + \alpha_8 \mathbf{ti} + \alpha_9 \mathbf{ti}^e,
\end{aligned} \tag{13.3}
$$

where lower-case letters denote logarithms and where all coefficients are greater than zero. The vector **ti** stands for the claims of the foreign and government sectors on private output and contains real import costs and tax variables. If the claims of the government and foreign sector increase, there is less output available for distribution of income between employers and workers, and conflict arises over who will bear the costs. The rise in conflict increases wage inflation. The expressions in square brackets describe the aspiration gap as discussed above, but without the tax and import cost variables, as they are already included in vector **ti**.[2] The first square bracket describes the target profit share as a mark-up over real wage costs in dependence of the demand conditions in the product market, proxied by capacity utilization Φ. Excess capacity limits employers' ability to raise prices. Capacity utilization is itself explained by capital stock and output, where the latter indicates the level of economic activity which is proxied by the unemployment rate (Rowthorn, 1995).

The preceding equation implies:

$$
\begin{aligned}
w_{t+1} - w = (1 &- \alpha_1 - \alpha_2 + \alpha_3)(p^e - p) \\
&+ \alpha_1(w_u^e - w_u) + (\alpha_2 - \alpha_3)(w^e - w) + \alpha_3(lp^e - lp) \\
&+ (\alpha_2 - 1)(w - p) + \alpha_1(w_u - p) + (\alpha_3 - \alpha_4)(p + lp - w) \\
&+ \alpha_5 x - \alpha_6 u - \alpha_3 \theta_2 u^e - \alpha_7 \Delta u - \alpha_3 \theta_1 k^e.
\end{aligned} \tag{13.4}
$$

We assume that expectations are formed in the following way (Nickell, 1990):

$$
s^e = s + \Delta s_t, \tag{13.5}
$$

where s stands for any variable. Taking into account the formation of expectations, equation (13.4) can be rewritten as:

$$
\begin{aligned}
\Delta\Delta w = (\alpha_2 &- \alpha_3 + \alpha_4 - 1)(w - p) + (\alpha_2 - \alpha_3 - 1)\Delta(w - p) + \alpha_1(w_u - p) \\
&+ \alpha_1\Delta(w_u - p) + (\alpha_3 - \alpha_4)lp + \alpha_3\Delta lp + \alpha_5 x \\
&- (\alpha_6 + \alpha_3\theta_2)u - (\alpha_7 + \alpha_3\theta_2)\Delta u + (\alpha_8 + \alpha_9)\mathbf{ti} + \alpha_9\Delta\mathbf{ti} \\
&- \alpha_3\theta_1 k - \alpha_3\theta_1\Delta k.
\end{aligned} \tag{13.6}
$$

The relationship in equation (13.6) can be described as follows: nominal wage acceleration depends on real wages, productivity, unemployment, real benefits, tax and import costs, capital stock, the expected changes in these variables and a variable capturing militancy. Most of the variables included are standard (Wren-Lewis, 1990; Hall and Henry, 1987; Layard et al., 1991), except for the capital stock. The capital stock alters in response to prolonged shocks such as the oil price shocks in the 1970s and 1980s (Rowthorn, 1995). These shocks induced inflationary pressure, so that demand was curbed, unemployment rose and, in response to the decline in demand, capital was scrapped. When oil prices fell, demand recovered and unemployment fell, but not as low as before the shocks, owing to the loss in capital stock. As a result, economies may operate with a higher level of unemployment, a lower level of capital and normal capacity utilization. The implications are obvious: government spending policies of direct investment should be introduced and accompanied by an expansion of markets for consumption goods. In order to promote expenditure in consumption goods, a redistributive incomes policy would be needed that would rely on the continuous increase in the minimum wage relative to the average level of wages. If the government fails to intervene, there is no reason why the market should recover through its own forces and that unemployment should fall to the level before the shocks.

We turn now to the long-run real wage equation, assuming productivity neutrality with respect to unemployment, which implies that shifts towards higher productivity growth increase demand and output in line, leaving the level of unemployment unchanged (Blanchard, 1988). This is an assumption that is widely backed by empirical results. Furthermore, in the long run, we expect that $\Delta(w-p)$, $\Delta(w_u-p)$, Δlp, $\Delta \mathbf{ti}$, Δu and Δk are stationary, so that we may derive the following long-run wage equation:

$$(w-p-lp)=\beta_1(w_u-p)+\beta_2 x-\beta_3 u+\beta_4 \mathbf{ti}+\beta_5 k \qquad (13.7)$$

with

$$\sigma=(1-\alpha_2+\alpha_3-\alpha_4)\ \beta_1=\frac{\alpha_1}{\sigma}\ \beta_2=\frac{\alpha_5}{\sigma}$$

$$\beta_3=\frac{\alpha_6+\alpha_3\theta_2}{\sigma}\ \beta_4=\frac{\alpha_8+\alpha_9}{\sigma}\ \beta_5=\frac{\alpha_3\theta_1}{\sigma}.$$

When the target and the negotiated profit shares are equal, where the latter is derived as a residual in the bargaining process, unanticipated inflation is zero and the 'equilibrium' unemployment rate can be derived (Rowthorn, 1977). Assuming that firms mark up prices over labour costs, an aspiration gap of zero implies that the real wages (per unit of output) that firms offer in view of their target profits are equal to the bargained real wage share. If we equate firms' target (feasible) real wage share with the real bargained wage share, the unemployment function may be derived as follows:

$$u = \gamma_1(w_u - p) + \gamma_2 x + \gamma_3 \mathbf{ti} - \gamma_4 k \qquad (13.8)$$

with

$$\lambda = \theta_2 + \beta_3 \quad \gamma_1 = \frac{\beta_1}{\lambda} \quad \gamma_2 = \frac{\beta_2}{\lambda}$$

$$\gamma_3 = \frac{\beta_3 + \theta_3}{\lambda} \quad \gamma_4 = \frac{\theta_1 - \beta_5}{\lambda}.$$

Long-run unemployment is an increasing function of real benefits, tax and import costs, and worker militancy, and declines with the increase in the capital stock. A positive relationship between real wages and unemployment insurance implies that a fall in the latter results in a decline in unemployment, due to its labour cost-reducing impact. However, a cut in wage compensation may have other effects that outweigh the favourable cost effects. In response to a fall in real benefits, the unemployed may reduce searching time, and they may have to accept jobs for which they are less suitably qualified than they would have accepted if the cost of search had been less. The consequent inefficiencies in the labour market may have an adverse effect on the unemployment rate and it may be an empirical question as to which of the effects is more important. We return to that discussion in the next section. An increase in taxes or import costs will, under given demand conditions, increase conflict over income shares and will raise inflationary pressure. The more wage earners resist a fall in their income share, the lower are the tax and import effects on the long-run unemployment rate. Worker militancy affects the bargained real wage and *ceteris paribus* income distribution, where the latter determines the level of employment through its supply and demand side effects.

III   THE EMPIRICAL MODEL

The data is seasonally adjusted and the estimation period is from 1966(Q1) until 1994(Q4). The definition and source of the variables are provided in the appendix. It is notoriously difficult, and admittedly an unsolved problem, to capture militancy. We chose the number of strikes, although knowing that strikes are only a fraction of all wage fights and that only a fraction of these conflicts are actually registered in the statistics, while the theoretical model incorporates both types of conflict. In the interpretation of the results we assume that the relationship between registered strikes, the actual number of strikes and smaller conflicts is constant (Paldam, 1989).

We estimate a vector autoregressive regression (VAR) model for the determination of real wages and unemployment as described by equations (13.7) and (13.8), applying Johansen's (1988) maximum likelihood test and estimation procedures.[3] The Akaike Information Criterion and the Schwarz–Bayesian Criterion suggest that the optimal lag length for the VAR is two. The likelihood ratio test of the deletion of the deterministic trend and a dummy for the first quarter of 1975, where real wages were exceptionally high, rejects the null hypothesis with a CHSQ(10)=43.91. The restriction of proportionality between real wages and productivity was tested and accepted with a CHSQ(2)=2.50. When we incorporated this restriction into the VAR model, we found two cointegrating vectors for the VAR with the variables $(w-p-lp)$, u, x and k. The results of the maximal eigenvalue test reject the null hypothesis of no and at least one cointegrating vector with 36.23 (27.07; 24.73) and 20.72 (20.96; 18.60). The hypothesis of at least two cointegrating vectors is not rejected by the maximal eigenvalue test with 15.29 (20.97; 18.60). The values in brackets are the critical values at the 5 per cent and 10 per cent significance level. The results of the trace test are 69.04 (47.21; 43.95), 32.81 (29.68; 26.79) and 28.73 (29.68; 26.79), suggesting two cointegrating vectors, and, at the 10 per cent significance level, a possible third cointegrating vector. As the evidence of a third cointegrating vector is not very strong, we turn to the identification of the two cointegrating vectors applying the Pesaran and Shin (1994) approach, which relies on imposing non-homogeneous restrictions on the two cointegrating vectors. The result is the following cointegrating relationships:

$$(w-p-lp) = -0.095u + 0.079x + 0.090k \qquad (13.9a)$$
$$ (na) \qquad (0.02) \qquad (na)$$

$$u = 0.305x - 2.308k \qquad (13.9b)$$
$$ (0.14) \qquad (0.76),$$

where the values in brackets denote the standard errors. The likelihood ratio test for the validity for the overidentifying restriction is CHSQ(1)=0.007 with a significance level of 0.94, denoting the validity of the restricted system. Both equations are economically sensible in the sense that the coefficients are correctly signed and significant. The result that rises in labour productivity lead to proportional rises in real wages supports our suggestion that there is a direct relationship between the real wage and productivity (block I). Our empirical result, which is a special case of this suggestion, implies that in the long run unemployment is not affected by productivity growth, and that increases in labour productivity are absorbed fully by rises in real wages. Unemployment has a moderating effect on wage claims, and militancy may in the long run increase the wage share. Unemployment falls dramatically with increases in capital stock and rises with rising militancy. Militancy affects unemployment in that it enhances the conflict over income shares, causing pressure on inflation. In order to contain inflation, demand has to be reduced and unemployment rises. The effect of the capital stock on unemployment has been discussed in section II.

When we compare the empirical results with our theoretical proposition, a number of variables such as the tax and import wedge, as well as real benefits, do not play any role in the determination of the long-run wage and unemployment rates. The lack of empirical evidence of tax and import effects is due to their being more likely short- or medium-run effects. For example, an increase in import cost in relation to the domestic price level improves competitiveness and raises wage pressure by making consumption goods more expensive relative to value added output. If a rise in competitiveness enables firms to mark up prices to compensate for the higher cost in the long run, this would imply that they could increase their domestic profit share indefinitely (Layard *et al.*, 1991). Equally, a permanent effect of competitiveness on wage setting implies that workers can resist a decline in real wages indefinitely. A similar argument would apply to increases in taxation.

We argued above that workers' effort function is also determined by the cost of job loss, where the latter is itself partly explained by real unemployment compensation. Although we could find a correctly signed and sensible coefficient of real unemployment benefit in the wage equation, for the unemployment equation the variable was negatively signed and implausibly high. The negative sign might, as we suggested before, account for inefficiencies in the labour market. However, in view of an extremely high elasticity of about twenty, and previous results (for example, Arestis and Biefang-Frisancho Mariscal, 1994), we estimated both equations without real unemployment benefits.

We turn to the empirical result of nominal wage acceleration as described by equation (13.6), considering, however, that the test for the long-run equation suggested that there is proportionality between real wages and productivity:

$$\Delta\Delta(w-lp)=0.460-0.115\ ecm_{t-1}-0.765\Delta(w-p-lp)_{t-1}+0.190\Delta\mathbf{ti}_{t-3}$$
$$(2.46)\quad(2.44)\qquad(8.21)\qquad\qquad(2.19)$$
$$+\,0.052\Delta(w_u-p)_{t-2}+0.092\Delta(w_u-p)_{t-4}-0.068\Delta u_{t-1}$$
$$(1.84)\qquad\qquad(3.45)\qquad\qquad(1.69)\qquad\qquad(13.10)$$

$$+0.093\Delta u_{t-2}-0.103\Delta u_{t-5}+0.460\Delta lp_{t-1}$$
$$(2.22)\qquad (3.69)\qquad (3.03)$$
$$+0.0004trend+0.046D75.1.$$
$$(2.07)\qquad (3.63)$$

$R^2=0.67$ se$=0.011397$ AR$(4,92)=1.4$ RESET$(1,95)=0.2$ NORM$(2)=$ 3.6 HET$(1,106)=2.2$

The disturbances were tested for fourth-order autocorrelation (AR), heteroscedasticity (HET), functional form misspecification (RESET) and normality (NORM) and none of the tests was significant at the usual 5 per cent significance level.

We find that real wage growth, productivity growth, real unemployment benefit growth, unemployment growth, as well as the growth of taxes and import cost, affect nominal wage acceleration, as discussed regarding equation (13.6). The error correction term (*ecm*) shows that the adjustment process towards equilibrium is completed after slightly more than two years. A 1 per cent growth of unemployment reduces wage acceleration by about 0.08 per cent. In contrast to the long-run relationship, we find wage resistance in view of changes in import and tax costs.

Equation (13.9b) implies the following short-run unemployment relationship:

$$\Delta u=1.516-0.035ecm2(-3)-0.217ecm(-4)+0.811\Delta u_{t-1}$$
$$(5.32)\ (2.32)\qquad (3.40)\qquad (14.75)$$
$$-0.126\Delta\Delta u_{t-4}-0.184\Delta k_{t-3}+0.002trend+0.144D74.1\quad(13.11)$$
$$(1.65)\qquad (2.05)\qquad (4.21)\qquad (5.15)$$

$R^2=0.81$ se$=0.025981$ AR$(4,96)=1.9$ RESET$(1,99)=0.8$ Norm$(2)=2.0$ HET$(1,106)=1.7$

All variables are correctly signed and significant at the 5 per cent significance level, except for acceleration in unemployment ($\Delta\Delta u$), which is significant at the 10 per cent level. The other diagnostics suggest that the disturbances are white noise and that there is no functional form misspecification. The variable *ecm2* is the error correction term derived from equation (13.9b) and shows that the adjustment towards the relationship in (13.9b) is very sluggish indeed, a result which is in line with other empirical studies. The significance of the *ecm* term from the wage equation in the short-run unemployment relationship suggests that disequilibrium errors in the wage equation are also corrected for in the unemployment relationship. In view of our discussion on the importance of the capital stock in wage and unemployment determination, it should be noted that this variable is also significant in the short-run equation, suggesting its importance under more general conditions than in (13.9b). The variable $D74.1$ captures an outlier due to the three-day week in the first quarter in 1974.

IV CONCLUDING REMARKS

The problem of unemployment is ultimately one of investment, and a substantial increase in capacity-creating investment is needed. Active government policies are needed to promote investment and at the same time an active expansion of markets for consumption goods is necessary. If the market is left to the forces of demand and supply, high unemployment rates are inevitable. Without government intervention it would be difficult to see how the economy would move towards a full employment situation.

NOTES

1. We are grateful for comments to the participants of the Leeds conference, '*Keynes, Knowledge and Uncertainty*'; also, to Victoria Chick, Bernard Corry, Peter Howells, Malcolm Sawyer and Peter Skott.
2. It is of course possible to write out the tax variables individually; however, the algebra becomes tedious and does not add to the argument.
3. The results of the Dickey–Fuller tests suggest that all variables are integrated of order one. The test results can be provided by the authors on request.

APPENDIX

All the data are from the NIESR, except for the following variables: the number of strikes comes from the *Employment Gazette*, and the gross domestic capital stock variable comes from *Economic Trends*. The data are seasonally adjusted and cover the period 1966Q1 to 1994Q4.

$\Delta x_t = x_t - x_{t-1}$
   u = log of unemployment rate
   lp = labour productivity
   w = average wages and salaries
   x = number of strikes
   w_u = unemployment benefits
   p = consumer price deflator
   k = gross domestic capital stock
   ti = direct taxes as a proportion of the wage bill + employer's tax rate
       + logarithm of consumer price index − logarithm of GDP price
       index
D74.1 = 1 for the first quarter in 1974 and 0 otherwise
D75.1 = 1 for the first quarter in 1975 and 0 otherwise

Bibliography

Aharoni, Y. (1966), *The Foreign Investment Decision Process*, Boston MA: Graduate School of Business Administration, Harvard University.

Akyüz, Y. (1994), 'Taming international finance', in J. Michie and J. Grieve Smith (eds) (1995), *Managing the Global Economy*, Oxford: Oxford University Press.

Akyüz, Y. and A. Cornford (1995), 'International capital movements: some proposals for reform', in J. Michie and J. Grieve Smith (eds), *Managing the Global Economy*, Oxford: Oxford University Press.

Allais, M. (1953), 'Le Comportement de l'Homme Rationnel devant le Risque: Critique des Postulats et Axiomes de l'Ecole Americaine', *Econometrica*, **21** (4), 503–46.

Allen, W. (1965), 'Introduction' in W. Allen (ed.), *International Trade Theory: Hume to Ohlin*, New York: Random House.

Allsopp, V. (1995), *Understanding Economics*, London and New York: Routledge.

Amariglio, J. (1988), 'The body, economic discourse, and power: an economist's introduction to Foucault', *History of Political Economy*, **20**, 583–613.

Amariglio, J. and D. Ruccio (1995), 'Keynes, postmodernism, uncertainty', in S. Dow and J. Hillard (1995).

Anderson, B. (1991), *Imagined Communities*, London: Verso.

Angell, J.W. (1926), *The Theory of International Prices*, Cambridge, MA: Harvard University Press.

Angell, N. (1911), *The Great Illusion*, New York: G.P. Putnam's Sons.

Arbejderbevægelsens Erhvervsråd (1996), *Economic Trends*, Copenhagen: eget forlag.

Arblaster, A. (1984), *The Rise and Decline of Western Liberalism*, Oxford: Blackwell.

Arestis, P. (1988), 'Post Keynesian theory of money, credit and finance', in P. Arestis (ed.), *Post-Keynesian Monetary Economics: New Approaches to Financial Modelling*, Aldershot, UK and Brookfield, US: Edward Elgar.

Arestis, P. (1992), *The Post-Keynesian Approach to Economics: An Alternative Analysis of Economic Theory and Policy*, Aldershot, UK and Brookfield, US: Edward Elgar.

Arestis, P. and I. Biefang-Frisancho Mariscal (1994), 'Wage determination in the UK: further empirical results using cointegration', *Applied Economics*, 365–86.

Arestis, P. and P. Howells (1996), 'Theoretical reflection on endogenous money: the problem with convenience lending', *Cambridge Journal of Economics*, **20**, 539–51.

Arestis, P. and E. Paliginis (1995), 'Fordism, Post-Fordism and gender', *Économie Appliquée*, **48** (1), 89–108.

Arestis, P. and M. Sawyer (1993), 'Political economy: an editorial manifesto', *International Papers in Political Economy*, **1**.

Arestis, P. and P. Skott (1993), 'Conflict, wage relativities and hysteresis in UK wage determination', *Journal of Post Keynesian Economics*, 365–86.

Arestis, P., S.P. Dunn and M. Sawyer (1999a), 'Post Keynesian economics and its critics', *Journal of Post Keynesian Economics*, **21**, Summer, 527–49.

Arestis, P., S.P. Dunn and M. Sawyer (1999b), 'On the coherence of Post Keynesian economics: a comment upon Walters and Young', *Scottish Journal of Political Economy*, **46** (3), 339–45.

Armstrong, P., A. Glyn and J. Harrison (1984), *Capitalism Since World War Two*, London: Fontana.

Arrow, K.J. (1951), *Social Choice and Individual Values*, New York: Wiley.

Arrow, K.J. (1974a), 'Limited knowledge and economic analysis', *American Economic Review*, **64**, 1–10.

Arrow, K.J. (1974b), *The Limits of Organization*, New York and London: Norton & Co.

Arrow, K.J. (1982), 'Risk perception in psychology and economics', *Economic Inquiry*, **20**, 1–9.

Arrow, K.J. (1985), 'Informational structure of the firm', *American Economic Review: AEA Papers and Proceedings*, **75**, May, 303–7.

Arrow, K.J. and F. Hahn (1971), *General Competitive Analysis*, Edinburgh: Oliver and Boyd.

Asimakopulos, A. (1971), 'The determination of investment in Keynes's model', *Canadian Journal of Economics*, 382–8.

Aston, T. and C. Philpin (eds) (1985), *The Brenner Debate*, Cambridge: Cambridge University Press.

Atkinson, A.C. (1985), *Plots, Transformations and Regressions*, Oxford Scientific Publications.

Aumann R. (1962), 'Utility theory without the completeness axiom', *Econometrica*, **30**, 445–62.

Axelrod, R. (1984), *The Evolution of Cooperation*, New York: Basic Books.

Backhouse, R.E. (1985), *A History of Modern Economic Analysis*, Oxford: Blackwell.

Backhouse, R.E. (ed.) (1994), *New Directions in Economic Methodology*, London: Routledge.

Backhouse, R.E. (1997a), *Truth and Progress in Economic Knowledge*, Cheltenham, UK and Lyme, US: Edward Elgar.

Backhouse, R.E. (1997b), 'Rhetoric and Methodology in modern macro-economics', in B. Snowdon and H. Vane (eds), *Reflections on the Development of Modern Macroeconomics*, Cheltenham, UK and Lyme, US: Edward Elgar.

Banerjee, A., J.J. Dolado, J.W. Galbraith and D.F. Hendry (1993), *Co-intergration, Error Correction and the Econometric Analysis of Non-Stationary Data*, Oxford: Oxford University Press.

Bank for International Settlements (1993), *Central Bank Survey of Foreign Exchange Market Activity in April 1992*, Basle: BIS Monetary and Economic Department.

Bank of England (1996), 'Recent price shocks', *Inflation Report*, August 7–8, London: Bank of England.

Banks, J. and E. Hanushek (eds) (1995), *Modern Political Economy*, Cambridge: Cambridge University Press.

Baran, P.A. and P.M. Sweezy (1966), *Monopoly Capital: An essay on the American economic and social order*, Harmondsworth: Penguin.

Barry, N. (1981), *An Introduction to Modern Political Theory*, London: Macmillan.

Basili, M. and A. Vercelli (1998), 'Environmental option values, uncertainty aversion and learning', in G. Chichilnisky, G. Heal and A. Vercelli (eds), *Sustainability: Dynamics and Uncertainty*, Amsterdam: Martin Kluwer.

Bateman, B.W. (1987), 'Keynes's changing conception of probability', *Economics and Philosophy*, **3**, 97–119.

Bateman, B. (1989), '"Human Logic" and Keynes's economics: a comment', *Eastern Economic Journal*, **15**, 63–67.

Bateman, B.W. and J.B. Davis (eds) (1991), *Keynes and Philosophy: Essays on the Origin of Keynes's Thought*, Aldershot, UK and Brookfield, US: Edward Elgar.

Baumol, W.J. (1982), 'Contestable markets: an uprising in the theory of industry structure', *American Economic Review*, **72**, 1–15.

Begg, D.K.H. (1982), *The Rational Expectations Revolution in Macroeconomics*, Oxford: Philip Allan.

Bell, D. (1978), *The Cultural Contradictions of Capitalism*, New York: Basic Books.

Belman, D. (1992), 'Unions, the quality of labor relations and firm performance', in L. Mishel and P.B. Voos (eds), *Unions and Economic Competitiveness,* New York: M. E. Sharpe.

Bhaskar, R. (1975), *A Realist Theory of Science*, Leeds: Harvester.

Bhaskar, R. (1978), *A Realist Theory of Science*, Brighton: Harvester Press.

Bhaskar, R. (1989a), *Reclaiming Reality*, London: Verso.

Bhaskar, R. (1989b), *The Possibility of Naturalism*, 2nd edition, Hemel Hempstead: Harvester Wheatsheaf.

Bhaskar, R. (1993), *Dialectic: The Pulse of Freedom*, London: Verso.

Binmore K.G. (1986), 'Remodelled rational players', discussion paper, London School of Economics, London.

Blanchard, O.J. (1988), 'Comment on Nickell: the supply side and macro-economic modelling', in R.C. Bryant *et al.* (eds), *Empirical Economics for Independent Economies*, Washington: Brookings Institution.

Blanchard, O.J. and S. Fischer (1989), *Lectures on Macroeconomics*, Cambridge, MA and London: MIT Press.

Blanchard, O.J. and D. Quah (1989), 'The dynamic effects of aggregate demand and supply disturbances', *American Economic Review*, **79**, 655–73.

Blaug, M. (1980), *The Methodology of Economics: How Economists Explain*, Cambridge: Cambridge University Press.

Blaug, M. (1985), *Economic Theory in Retrospect*, Cambridge: Cambridge University Press.

Blaug, M. (1992), *The Methodology of Economics: How Economists Explain*, revised edition, Cambridge: Cambridge University Press.

Blecker, R. (1991), 'Low saving rates and the "Twin Deficits": confusing the symptoms and causes of economic decline', in P. Davidson and J. Kregel (eds), *Economic Problems of the 1990s*, Aldershot, UK and Brookfield, US: Edward Elgar.

Blinder, A.S. (1991), 'Why are prices sticky? Preliminary results from an interview study', *American Economic Association Papers and Proceedings*, May.

Bliss, C. (1975), *Capital Theory and the Distribution of Income*, Amsterdam: North-Holland.

Boddy, R. and J. Crotty (1975), 'Class conflict and macro-policy: the political business cycle', *Review of Radical and Political Economics*, 1–19.

Boland, L.A. (1979), 'A critique of Friedman's critics', *Journal of Economic Literature*, **17**, 503–22.

Boland, L.A. (1981), 'On the futility of criticizing the neoclassical maximization hypothesis', *American Economic Review*, **71**, 1031–36.

Bonner, J. (1986), *An Introduction to the Theory of Social Choice*, Baltimore: Johns Hopkins.

Booth, A.L. (1995), *The Economics of the Union*, Cambridge: Cambridge University Press.

Bowles, S. and R. Boyer (1988), 'Labour discipline and aggregate demand: a macroeconomic model', *American Economic Review*, **74** (3), 395–400.

Bowles, S. and H. Gintis (1993), 'The revenge of homo economicus: contested exchange and the revivial of political economy', *Journal of Economic Perspectives*, **7** (1), 83–102.

Brady, M.E. (1987), 'J.M. Keynes' Theory of Evidential Weight: its relation to information processing theory and application in The General Theory', *Synthese*, **71**, 37–59.

Brady, M. and H.B. Lee (1989), 'Dynamics of choice behaviour: the logical relation between linear objective probability and non linear subjective probability', *Psychological Reports*, **64**, 91–7.

Braverman, H. (1974), *Labour and Monopoly Capital: The organisation of work in the twentieth century,* New York: Monthly Review Press.

Bray, J., S. Hall, A. Kuleshov, J. Nixon and P. Westaway (1995), 'The interfaces between policy makers, markets and modellers', *Economic Journal,* **105**, 989–1000.

Bray, M. (1982), 'Learning, estimation, and the stability of rational expectations equilibria', *Journal of Economic Theory*, **26**, 313–17.

Bray, M., and N.E. Savin (1986), 'Rational expectations equilibria, learning and model specification', *Econometrica*, **54**, 1129–60.

Brenner, R. (1986), 'The social basis of economic development', in J. Roemer (ed.) (1986), 23–53.

Broomhead, D.S. and G.P. King (1986), 'Extracting qualitative dynamics from experimental data', *Physica,* **20D**.

Brown-Collier, E. (1985), 'Keynes's view of an organic universe: the implications', *Review of Social Economy*, **43**, 14–23.

Buckley, P.J. and M. Carter (1966), 'The economics of business process design', *International Journal of the Economics of Business*, **3** (1), 5–25.

Buckley, P.J. and M. Carter (1997), 'The economics of business process design in multinational firms', in M. Ricketts and R. Mudambi (eds), *The Organization of the Firm: International Business Perspectives*, London: Routledge.

Buckley, P.J. and M. Casson (1976), *The Future of the Multinational Enterprise*, London: Macmillan.

Buckley, P.J. and M. Casson (1981), 'The optimal timing of a foreign direct investment', *Economic Journal*, **92** (361), March, 75–87.

Buckley, P.J. and M. Casson (1988), 'A theory of co-operation in international business', in F. Contractor and P. Lorange (eds), *Co-operative Strategies in International Business*, Lexington, MA: Lexington Books.

Buckley, P.J. and M. Casson (1991), *The Future of the Multinational Enterprise* (2nd edition), London: Macmillan.

Buckley, P.J. and M. Casson (1992), 'Organizing for Innovation: The multinational enterprise in the twenty-first century', in P.J. Buckley and M. Casson (eds), *Multinational Enterprises in the World Economy: Essays in Honour of John Dunning*, Aldershot, UK and Brookfield, US: Edward Elgar.

Buckley, P.J. and M. Casson (1993), 'Economics as an imperialist social science', *Human Relations*, **46** (9), September, 1035–52.

Buckley, P.J. and M. Casson (1996), 'An economic model of international joint ventures', *Journal of International Business Studies*, **27** (5), 849–76.

Buckley, P.J. and M. Chapman (1996a), 'Economics and social anthropology – reconciling differences', *Human Relations*, **49** (9), 1123–50.

Buckley, P.J. and M. Chapman (1996b), 'Wise before the event: the creation of corporate fulfilment', *Management International Review*, **36** (1), Special Issue, 95–110.

Buckley, P.J. and M. Chapman (1996c), 'Theory and method in international business research', *International Business Review*, **5** (3), 233–45.

Buckley, P.J. and M. Chapman (1997), 'The measurement and perception of transaction costs', *Cambridge Journal of Economics*, **21** (2), March, 127–45.

Buckley, P.J. and M. Chapman (1998), 'The management of co-operative strategies in R&D and innovation programmes', *International Journal of the Economics of Business*, **5** (3), November, 369–81.

Buckley, P.J., Z. Berkova and G.D. Newbould (1983), *Direct Investment in the UK by Smaller European Firms*, London: Macmillan.

Buckley, P.J., C.L. Pass and K. Prescott (1988), 'Measures of international competitiveness: a critical survey', *Journal of Marketing Management*, **4** (2), Winter, 175–200.

Bull, H. (1977), *The Anarchical Society*, London: Macmillan.

Caldwell, B.J. (ed.) (1984), *Appraisal and Criticism in Economics,* London: Allen and Unwin.

Caldwell, B.J. (1989), 'Post Keynesian methodology: an assessment', *Review of Political Economy*, **1**, 41–64.

Caldwell, B.J. and A.W. Coats (1984), 'The rhetoric of economics: a comment on McCloskey', *Journal of Economic Literature*, **22**, 575–78.

Camerer, C. (1989), 'Bubbles and fads in asset prices', *Journal of Economic Surveys*, **3**, 3–43.

Campbell, J.Y. and K. Froot (1994), 'International experiences with security transaction taxes', in J. Frankel (ed.), *The Internationalization of Equity Markets*, Chicago: University of Chicago Press.

Cannan, E. (1921), 'The meaning of bank deposits', *Economica*, **1** (new series), 28–36.

Capponi, O. (1992), 'Keynesian equilibrium and the inducement to invest,' in M. Sebastiani (ed.), *The Notion of Equilibrium in the Keynesian Theory*, London: Macmillan, pp. 46–60.

Carabelli, A.M. (1985), 'Cause, chance and possibility', in T. Lawson and H. Pesaran (eds), *Keynes's Economics: Methodological Issues*, London: Croom Helm.

Carabelli, A.M. (1988), *On Keynes's Method*, London: Macmillan.

Carabelli, A.M. (1991), 'The methodology of the critique of the classical theory: Keynes on organic interdependence', in B. Bateman and J. Davis (eds), *Keynes and Philosophy*, Aldershot, UK and Brookfield, US: Edward Elgar.

Carabelli A.M. (1992), 'Organic interdependence and the choice of units in the General Theory', in B. Gerrard and J.V. Hillard (eds), *The Philosophy and Economics of J.M. Keynes*, Aldershot, UK and Brookfield, US: Edward Elgar.

Carabelli, A.M. (1994), 'Keynes on mensuration and comparison', in K. Vaughn (ed.), *Perspectives on the History of Economic Thought*, Volume X, Aldershot, UK and Brookfield, US: Edward Elgar.

Carabelli, A.M. (1995), 'Uncertainty and measurement in Keynes: probability and organicness', in S. Dow and J.V. Hillard (eds), *Keynes, Knowledge and Uncertainty*, Aldershot, UK and Brookfield, US: Edward Elgar.

Card, D. and A.B. Krueger (1995), *Myth and Measurement: the New Economics of the Minimum Wage*, Princeton: Princeton University Press.

Carrier, J.G. (1997), 'Introduction', in J.G. Carrier (ed.), *Meanings of the Market*, Berg: Oxford.

Cartwright, B. and R. Warner (1976), 'The medium is not the message' in Loubser *et al.* (1976), 639–59.

Carvalho, F. (1983–4), 'On the concept of time in Shaklean and Sraffian economics', *Journal of Post Keynesian Economics*, **6** (2), 265–80.

Casson, M. (1981), 'Foreword', in A.M. Rugman, *Inside the Multinational*, London: Croome Helm.

Casson, M. (1991), *The Economics of Business Culture: Game Theory, Transactions Costs and Economic Performance*, Oxford: Clarendon Press.

Casson, M. (1995), *Entrepreneurship and Business Culture Studies in the Economics of Trust, Volume One*, Aldershot, UK and Brookfield, US: Edward Elgar.

Chapman, M. and P.J. Buckley (1997), 'Markets, transaction costs, economists and social anthropologists', in J.G. Carrier (ed.), *Meanings of the Market*, Oxford: Berg.

Chatfield, C. (1995), 'Model uncertainty, data mining and statistical inference', *Journal of the Royal Statistical Society,* A, **158**, 419–66.

Chick, V. (1983), *Macroeconomics After Keynes: A Reconsideration of the General Theory*, Oxford: Philip Allan.

Chick, V. (1992), 'The small firm under uncertainty: a puzzle of the General Theory', in B. Gerrard and J. Hillard (eds), *The Philosophy and Economics of J.M. Keynes*, Aldershot, UK and Brookfield, US: Edward Elgar.

Chick, V. (1995), 'Is there a case for Post-Keynesian economics?', *Scottish Journal of Political Economy*, **42** (1), 20–36.

Chick, V. and M. Caserta (1996), 'Provisional equilibrium and macroeconomic theory', in P. Arestis and M. Sawyer (eds), *Markets, Unemployment and Economic Policy: Essays in Honour of G.C. Harcourt*, vol 2, London: Routlege.

Choquet, G. (1955), 'Theory of capacities', *Annales de l'Institut Fourier*, **5**, 131–295.

Church, K.B., P.R. Mitchell, P.N. Smith and K.F. Wallis (1993), 'Comparative properties of models of the UK economy', *National Institute Economic Review,* **3** (145), 87–107.

Clarke, P. (1988), *The Keynesian Revolution in the Making, 1924–1936*, Oxford: Clarendon.

Clegg, H.A., A. Fox and A.F. Thompson (1964), *A History of British Trade Unions Since 1889. Volume 1: 1889–1910*, Oxford: Clarendon.

Clements, M.P. (1995), 'Rationality and the role of judgement in macroeconomic forecasting', *Economic Journal,* **105**, 410–20.

Clements, M.P. and D.F. Hendry (1995), 'Macroeconomic forecasting and modelling, *Economic Journal,* **105**, 1000–13.

Clower, R. (1969), 'Introduction', in R. Clower (ed.), *Monetary Theory*, Harmondsworth: Penguin.

Coase, R.H. (1937), 'The nature of the firm', *Economica*, **4** (new series), 386–405 reprinted in G.J. Stigler and K.E. Boulding (eds) (1953), *Readings in Price Theory: Selected by a committee of the American Economic Association*, London: George Allen and Unwin Ltd.

Coase, R.H. (1960), 'The problem of social cost', *Journal of Law and Economics*, **3**, 1–44.

Coase, R.H. (1988[1946]), 'The marginal cost controversy', *Economica*, **13** (new series), references are to the reprint in Coase (1988a).

Coase, R.H. (1988a), *The Firm, the Market, and the Law*, Chicago: University of Chicago Press.

Coase, R.H. (1988b), 'The firm, the market, and the law', in Coase 1988a, pp. 1–31.

Coase, R.H. (1988c), 'How should economists choose?', in *Ideas, Their Origins, and Their Consequences*, Washington DC: American Enterprise Institute, pp. 63–79.

Coase, R.H. (1993[1992]), 'The institutional structure of production', *American Economic Review*, **82**, references are to the reprint in O.E. Williamson and S.G. Winter (eds) (1993), 227–35.

Coase, R.H. (1993a), 'The nature of the firm: Origin', in O.E. Williamson and S.G. Winter (eds) (1993), pp. 34–47.

Coase, R.H. (1993b), 'The nature of the firm: Meaning', in O.E. Williamson and S.G. Winter (eds) (1993), pp. 48–60.

Coase, R.H. (1993c), 'The nature of the firm: Influence', in O.E. Williamson and S.G. Winter (eds) (1993), pp. 61–74.

Coddington, A. (1976), 'Keynesian economics: the search for first principles', *Journal of Economic Literature*, **72**, 480–87.

Coddington, A. (1982), 'Deficient foresight: a troublesome theme in Keynesian economics', *American Economic Review,* **72**, 480–87.

Coddington, A. (1983), *Keynesian Economics: The Search for First Principles*, London: Allen and Unwin.

Cohen, G. (1978), *Karl Marx's Theory of History: A Defence*, Oxford: Oxford University Press.

Cohen, J. (1989), *An Introduction to the Philosophy of Induction and Probability,* Oxford: Oxford University Press.

Colander, D. and A. Klamer (1987), 'The making of an economist,' *Journal of Economic Literature*, **22**, 575–78.

Coleman, J. (1990), *Foundations of Social Theory*, London: Prentice-Hall.

Collins, H. (1991), 'The meaning of replication and the science of economics', *History of Political Economy,* **23**, 123–42.

Connolly, B. (1994), *The Rotten Heart of Europe: The Dirty War for Europe's Money*, London: Faber.

Cornwall, J. (1994), *Economic Breakdown and Recovery: Theory and Policy*, Armonk, NY: M.E. Sharpe.

Cottrell, A.F. (1993), 'Keynes's Theory of Probability and its relevance to economics: three theses', *Economics and Philosophy*, **9**, 25–51.

Cowling, K. and R. Sugden (1987), *Transnational Monopoly Capitalism*, Brighton: Wheatsheaf.

Cowling, K. and R. Sugden (1993), 'Control, markets and firms', in C. Pitelis (ed.), *Transaction costs, markets and hierarchies*, Oxford: Basil Blackwell.

Cowling, K. and R. Sugden (1998), 'The essence of the modern corporation: markets, strategic decision-making and the theory of the firm', *The Manchester School*, **66** (1), 59–86.

Cowling, K. and M. Waterson (1976), 'Price–cost margins and market structure', *Economica*, **43**.

Cross, R. (1982), 'The Duhem-Quine thesis, Lakotos, and the appraisal of theories in macroeconomics', *Economic Journal*, **92**, 320–40.

Cruise O'Brien, R. (1995), 'Is trust a calculable asset in the firm?', *Business Strategy Review*, Winter, 39–54.

Curley, S.P. and J.F. Yates (1985), 'The center and the range of the probability interval as factors affecting ambiguity preferences', *Organizational Behavior and Human Decision Processes*, **36**, 273–87.

Curley, S.P., J.F. Yates and R.A. Abrams (1986), 'Psychological sources of ambiguity avoidance', *Organizational Behavior and Human Decision Processes*, **38**, 230–56.

Curley, S.P. and J.F. Yates (1989), 'An empirical evaluation of descriptive models of ambiguity reactions in choice situations', *Journal of Mathematical Psychology*, **33**, 397–427.

D'Souza, D. (1991), *Illiberal Education*, New York: Free Press.

D'Souza, D. (1995), *The End of Racism: Principles for a Multiracial Society*, New York: Free Press.

Dahl, R. (1984), *Modern Political Analysis*, Englewood Cliffs: Prentice-Hall.

Dahlman, C.J. (1979), 'The problem of externality', *Journal of Law and Economics*, **22** (1), 141–62.

Dalziel, P. (1995), 'Inflation and endogenous money: a process analysis', paper presented to the 24th Conference of Economists, Adelaide: University of Adelaide, September.

Danziger, S. and P. Gottschalk (1988–9), 'Increasing inequality in the United States: what we know and what we don't', *Journal of Post Keynesian Economics*, **11** (2), Winter, 174–95.

Darnell, A.C. and J.L. Evans (1990), *The Limits of Econometrics*, Aldershot, UK and Brookfield, US: Edward Elgar.

Dasgupta, P. (1988), 'Trust as a commodity', in D. Gambetta (ed.), *Trust; Making and Breaking of Cooperative Relations*, Oxford: Basil Blackwell.

Davidson, P. (1972), *Money and the Real World*, London: Macmillan.

Davidson, P. (1977), 'Money and general equilibrium', reprinted in *Money and Employment: The collected writings of Paul Davidson, Volume 1*, London: Macmillan, 1990.

Davidson, P. (1978), *Money and the Real World*, 2nd edition, London: Macmillan.

Davidson, P. (1981), 'Post Keynesian economics', in D. Bell and I. Kristol (eds), *The Crisis in Economic Theory*, New York: Basic Books.

Davidson, P. (1982–3), 'Rational expectations: a fallacious foundation for studying crucial decision-making processes', *Journal of Post Keynesian Economics*, **5**, 182–97.

Davidson, P. (1983), 'The marginal product curve is not the demand curve for labor and Lucas's labor supply function is not the supply curve for labor in the real world', *Journal of Post Keynesian Economics*, **6** (1), Fall, 105–17.

Davidson, P. (1988), 'A technical definition of uncertainty and the long-run non-neutrality of money', *Cambridge Journal of Economics*, **12**.

Davidson, P. (1989), 'On the endogeneity of money once more', *Journal of Post Keynesian Economics*, **11**, 488–91.

Davidson, P. (1991), 'Is Probability Theory relevant for uncertainty? A Post Keynesian perspective', *Journal of Economic Perspectives*, **5** (1), 129–43.

Davidson, P. (1992), 'Eichner's approach to money and macroeconomics', in W. Milberg (ed.), *The Megacorp and Macrodynamics*, New York: M.E. Sharpe.

Davidson, P. (1992–3), 'Reforming the world's money', *Journal of Post Keynesian Economics*, **15** (2) Winter, 153–80.

Davidson, P. (1994), *Post Keynesian Macroeconomic Theory: A Foundation for Successful Economic Policies for the Twenty First Century,* Aldershot, UK and Brookfield, US: Edward Elgar.

Davidson, P. (1996a), 'Are grains of sand in the wheels of international finance sufficient to do the job when boulders are often required?', mimeo, University of Tennessee, Knoxville, June.

Davidson, P. (1996b), 'Reality and economic theory', *Journal of Post Keynesian Economics*, **18**, 479–508.

Davidson, P. and G.S. Davidson (1984), 'Financial Markets and Williamson's Theory of Governance: Efficiency versus concentration versus power', reprinted in *Money and Employment: The Collected Writings of Paul Davidson, Volume 1*, London: Macmillan, 1990.

Davidson, P. and J. Kregel (1980), 'Keynes's paradigm: a theoretical framework for monetary analysis', in E. Nell (ed.), *Growth Profits and Property*, Cambridge: Cambridge University Press.

Davies, J.E. and F.S. Lee (1988), 'A Post Keynesian appraisal of the contestability criterion', *Journal of Post Keynesian Economics*, **11**, 3–24.

Davis, J.B. (1989), 'Keynes on atomism and organicism', *Economic Journal*, **99**, 1159–72.

Davis, J.B. (1989/90), 'Keynes and organicism', *Journal of Post Keynesian Economics*, **12**, 308–15.

Davis, J.B. (1990), 'Rorty's contribution to McCloskey's understanding of conversation as the methodology of economics', *Research in the History of Thought and Methodology*, **7**, 73–85.

Davis, J.B. (1994), *Keynes's Philosophical Development*, Cambridge: Cambridge University Press.

Davis, J.B. (1995), *Keynes's Philosophical Development*, Cambridge: Cambridge University Press.

De Bondt, W. and R. Thaler (1985), 'Does the stock market over-react?', *The Journal of Finance*, **XI**, 793–808.

DeCanio, S.J. (1979), 'Rational expectations and learning from experience', *Quarterly Journal of Economics*, **93**, 47–58.

De Finetti, B. (1937), 'La Prévision: ses lois logiques, ses sources Subjectives', *Annales de l'Institut Henry Poincaré*, **7**, 1–68; English translation: 'Foresight: its logical laws, its subjective sources', in H.E. Kyburg and H.E. Smokler (eds) (1964), *Studies in Subjective Probabilities*, New York: Wiley, pp. 93–158.

De Marchi, N. and C. Gilbert (1989) (eds), special edition on econometrics, *Oxford Economic Papers*, **41**.

De Wolff, P. (1965), *Wages and Labour Mobility*, Paris: OECD.

Debreu, G. (1959), *Theory of Value*, New Haven: Yale University Press.

Deleplace, G. and E. Nell (eds) (1996), *Money in Motion*, London: Macmillan.

Dempster, A.P. (1968), 'A generalisation of Bayesian inference', *Journal of the Royal Statistical Society*, Series B (Methodological), **30** (2), 205–47.

Dennis, K. (1995), 'A logical critique of mathematical formalism in economics', *Journal of Economic Methodology*, **2**, 181–200.

Derrida, J. (1974), *Of Grammatology*, trans. G. Spivak, Baltimore: Johns Hopkins University Press.

Derrida, J. (1978a), 'Freud and the scene of writing', in *Writing and Difference*, trans. Allan Bass, London: Routledge and Kegan Paul.

Derrida, J. (1978b), 'Structure, sign and play in the discourse of the human sciences', in *Writing and Difference*, trans. Allan Bass, London: Routledge and Kegan Paul.

Derrida, J. (1981a), 'Plato's pharmacy', in *Dissemination*, trans. Barbara Johnson, London: Athlone Press.

Derrida, J. (1981b), *Positions*, trans. Allan Bass, London: Athlone Press.

Derrida, J. (1982), '*Ousia* and *Grammē*', in *Margins of Philosophy*, trans. Allan Bass, Chicago: University of Chicago Press.

Derrida, J. (1984), 'Deconstruction and the other', in R. Kearney (ed.), *Dialogues with Contemporary Continental Thinkers*, Manchester: Manchester University Press.

Desai, M. (1995), 'The ties that bind', *The Times Higher Education Supplement*, 27 October.

Dewald, W.G., J.G. Thursby and R.G. Anderson (1986), 'Replication of empirical economics: the *Journal of Money, Credit and Banking* project', *American Economic Review*, **76**, 587–603.

Dews, P. (1987), *Logics of Disintegration: Post-structuralist Thought and the Claims of Critical Theory*, London: Verso.

Diaconis, P. and D. Freedman (1986), 'On the consistency of Bayes estimates', *The Annals of Statistics*, **14** (1), 1–26.

Diamond, P.A. (1994), *On Time: Lectures on Models of Equilibrium*, Cambridge: Cambridge University Press.

Dickens, D. and A. Fontana (eds) (1994), *Postmodernism and Social Inquiry*, London: University College of London Press.

Dillard, D. (1984), 'Keynes and Marx: a centennial appraisal', *Journal of Post Keynesian Economics*, **6**, 421–32.

Dixon, H. and N. Rankin (1994), 'Imperfect competition and macroeconomics: a survey', *Oxford Economic Papers*, **46**; reprinted in Dixon and Rankin (eds) (1995) (page references refer to the latter).

Dixon, H. and N. Rankin (eds) (1995), *The New Macroeconomics*, Cambridge: Cambridge University Press.

Dobbs, I.M. (1991), 'A Bayesian approach to decision-making under ambiguity', *Economica*, New Series, **58** (232), 417–40.

Dornbusch, R. (1976), 'Expectations and exchange rate dynamics', *Journal of Political Economy*, **84**.

D'Orville, H. and D. Najman (1995), *Towards a New Multilateralism: Funding Global Priorities*, New York: United Nations.

Dorward, N. (1987), *The Pricing Decision: Economic Theory and Business Practice*, London: Harper and Row.

Dosi, G. *et al.* (1992), 'Towards a theory of corporate coherence', in G. Dosi, G. Giannetti and P. Toninelli (eds), *Technology and Enterprise in a Historical Perspective*, Oxford: Clarendon Press.

Dosi, G., K. Pavitt and L. Soete (1990), *The Economics of Technical Change and International Trade*, New York: NYU Press.

Douma, S. and H. Scheider (1991), *Economic Approaches to Organizations*, New York: Prentice Hall.

Dow, A.C. and S.C. Dow (1989), 'Endogenous money creations and idle balances', in J. Pheby (ed.), *New Directions in Post-Keynesian Economics*, Aldershot, UK and Brookfield, US: Edward Elgar, pp. 147–64.

Dow, J. and S.J. Werlang (1992a), 'Excess volatility of stock prices and Knightian uncertainty', *European Economic Review*, **36**, 631–8.

Dow, J. and S.J. Werlang (1992b), 'Uncertainty aversion, risk aversion, and the optimal choice of portfolio', *Econometrica*, **60**, 197–204.

Dow, S.C. (1985), *Macroeconomic Thought: A Methodological Approach*, Oxford: Basil Blackwell.

Dow, S.C. (1988), 'What happened to Keynes's economics?', in O.F. Hamouda and J. Smithin (eds), *Keynes and Public Policy After Fifty Years, Vol. I: Economics and Policy*, pp. 101–10.

Dow, S.C. (1990a), 'Beyond dualism', *Cambridge Journal of Economics*, **19**, 143–58.

Dow, S.C. (1990b), 'Post Keynesianism as political economy: a methodological discussion', *Review of Political Economy*, **2** (3), 345–58.

Dow, S.C. (1991), 'Keynes's epistemology and economic methodology', in R.M. O'Donnell (ed.), *Keynes as Philosopher–Economist*, London: Macmillan, pp. 144–67.

Dow, S.C. (1992), 'The Post Keynesian School', in D. Mair and A. Miller (eds), *A Modern Guide to Economic Thought*, Aldershot, UK and Brookfield, US: Edward Elgar.

Dow, S.C. (1994a), 'Methodological pluralism and pluralism of method,' discussion paper, University of Stirling, May.

Dow, S.C. (1994b), 'Whither mainstream economics? A survey of economic methodology', discussion paper, University of Stirling, June.

Dow, S.C. (1996a), 'The appeal of neoclassical economics: some insights from Keynes' epistemology', *Cambridge Journal of Economics*, **19**, 715–33.

Dow, S.C. (1996b), 'Horizontalism: a critique', *Cambridge Journal of Economics*, **20**, 497–508.

Dow, S.C. (1997a), 'Mainstream economic methodology', *Cambridge Journal of Economics*, **21**, 73–93.

Dow, S.C. (1997b), 'Methodological pluralism and pluralism of method', in A. Salanti and E. Screpanti (eds), *Pluralism in Economics: Theory, History and Methodology*, Cheltenham, UK and Lyme, US: Edward Elgar, pp. 89–99.

Dow, S.C. (1998), 'Post Keynesian methodology', in J.B. Davis, D.W. Hands and U. Mäki (eds), *The Handbook of Economic Methodology*, Cheltenham, UK and Lyme, US: Edward Elgar, pp. 378–82.

Dow, S.C. (2001), 'Modernism and postmodernism: a dialectical process', in S. Cullenberg, J. Amariglio and D.F. Ruccio (eds), *Postmodernism, Economics and Knowledge*, London: Routledge.

Dow, S.C. and J.V. Hillard (eds) (1995), *Keynes, Knowledge and Uncertainty*, Aldershot, UK and Brookfield, US: Edward Elgar.

Downward, P.M. (1994), 'A reappraisal of case study evidence on business pricing: neoclassical and Post Keynesian perspectives', *British Review of Economic Issues*, **16** (39), 23–43.

Downward, P.M. (1995), 'A Post Keynesian perspective of UK manufacturing pricing', *Journal of Post Keynesian Economics*, **17**, 403–26.

Downward, P.M. (1999), *Pricing Theory in Post Keynesian Economics*, Cheltenham, UK and Northampton, MA, US: Edward Elgar.

Downward, P.M. (2000), 'A realist appraisal of Post Keynesian pricing theory', *Cambridge Journal of Economics* **24** (2), 211–24.

Downward, P.M. (2002), 'A Post Keynesian view of historical pricing dynamics in the UK', *Journal of Post Keynesian Economics*, **24** (2), 329–44.

Downward, P.M. and A. Mearman (forthcoming), 'Critical realism and econometrics: constructive dialogue with Post Keynesian economics' in

P.M. Downward (ed.), *Applied Economics and the Critical Realist Critique*, London: Routledge.

Doyle, M. (1986), 'Liberalism and world politics', *American Political Science Review*, **80**, 1151–63.

Drago, R. (1989–90), 'A simple Keynesian model of efficiency wages', *Journal of Post Keynesian Economics*, **12** (2), Winter, 171–82.

Drakopoulos, S. (1992), 'Keynes economic thought and the theory of consumer behaviour', *Scottish Journal of Political Economy*, **39**, 318–36.

Dunlop, J.T. (1944), *Wage Determination Under Trade Unions*, New York: Macmillan.

Dunn, S.P. (1996), 'A Post Keynesian contribution to the theory of the firm', *Leeds University Business School discussion paper series*, E96/18, University of Leeds.

Dunn, S.P. (1997), 'Bounded rationality, uncertainty and a Post Keynesian approach to transaction costs', *Leeds University Business School discussion paper series*, E97/08, University of Leeds.

Dunn, S.P. (1999), 'Bounded rationality, "fundamental" uncertainty and the firm in the long run', in S.C. Dow and P. Earl (eds), *Contingency, Complexity and the Theory of the Firm: Essays in Honour of Brian Loasby, Volume Two*, Cheltenham, UK and Northampton, MA, USA: Edward Elgar.

Dunn, S.P. (2000a), 'Wither Post Keynesianism?', *Journal of Post Keynesian Economics*, **22** (3), 343–64.

Dunn, S.P. (2000b), '"Fundamental" uncertainty and the firm in the long run', *Review of Political Economy*, **12** (4), 419–33.

Dunn, S.P. (2001a), 'Uncertainty, strategic decision-making and the essence of the modern corporation: extending Cowling and Sugden', *The Manchester School*, **69**, 31–41.

Dunn, S.P. (2001b). 'Galbraith, uncertainty and the modern corporation', in M. Keaney (ed.), *Economist with a public purpose: Essays in Honour of John Kenneth Galbraith*, London: Routledge.

Dunn, S.P. (forthcoming), 'Towards a Post Keynesian theory of the multi-national corporation: some Galbraithian insights' in K. Nielson (ed.), *Uncertainty and Economic Decision-Making: Ambiguity, Mental Models and Institutions*, Cheltenham, UK and Northampton, MA, US: Edward Elgar.

Dutt, A. (1992), 'Keynes, market forms and competition', in B. Gerrard and J. Hillard (eds), *The Philosophy and Economics of J.M. Keynes*, Aldershot, UK and Brookfield, US: Edward Elgar.

Edgeworth, F.Y. (1881), *Mathematical Psychics*, London: Kegan Paul.

Eichengreen, B. (1984), 'Keynes and protection', *Journal of Economic History*, **XLIV**.

Eichengreen, B. (1996), 'The Tobin tax: what have we learned?', in Haq *et al.*, pp. 273–87.

Eichengreen, B. and C. Wyplosz (1993), 'The unstable EMS', *Brookings Papers on Economic Activity*, **1**, 51–145.

Eichengreen, B. and C. Wyplosz (1996), 'Taxing international financial transactions to enhance the operation of the international monetary system', in Haq *et al.*, pp. 15–40.

Eichengreen, B., J. Tobin and G. Wyplosz (1995), 'Two cases for sand in the wheels of international finance', *Economic Journal*, **105**, 162–72.

Eichner, A.S. (1976), *The Megacorp and Oligopoly*, Cambridge: Cambridge University Press.

Eichner, A.S. (1979), 'An anthropogenic approach to labor economics', *Eastern Economic Journal*, **5** (4), October, 349–66; reprinted in A.S. Eichner (1985), *Towards a New Economics*, Armonk, NY: M.E. Sharpe, pp. 75–97.

Eichner, A.S. (1986), *Toward a New Economics: Essays in Post-Keynesian and Institutionalist Theory*, London: Macmillan.

Einhorn, H.J. and R.M. Hogarth (1985), 'Ambiguity and uncertainty in probabilistic inference', *Psychological Review*, **92**, 433–61.

Einhorn, H.J. and R.M. Hogarth (1986), 'Decision making under ambiguity', *Journal of Business*, **59**, S225–S250.

Ellsberg, D. (1961), 'Risk, ambiguity and the savage axioms', *Quarterly Journal of Economics*, **75**, November, 643–69.

Ellsberg, D. (1963), 'Reply', *Quarterly Journal of Economics*, **77**, November, 336–42.

Epstein, L., and M. Le Breton (1993), 'Dynamically consistent beliefs must be Bayesian', *Journal of Economic Theory*, **61**, 1–22.

Epstein, L.G. and T. Wang (1994), 'Intertemporal asset pricing under Knightian uncertainty', *Econometrica*, **62**, 283–322.

European Commission (1994a), *Growth, Competitiveness and Employment: Ways Forward into the Twenty-first Century*, White Paper (Delors Report II), Luxembourg: Office for Official Publications of the European Communities.

European Commission, DGXI (1994b), *The Potential Benefits of Integration of Environmental and Economic Policies: An Incentive-Based Approach to Policy Integration*, Luxembourg: Office for Official Publication of the European Communities.

European Commission, Committee for the Study of Economic and Monetary Union (1989), *Report on Economic and Monetary Union in the European Community* (Delors Report I), Luxembourg: Office for Official Publication of the European Communities.

European Commission, Directorate-General for Economic and Financial

Affairs (1990), 'One Market, One Money', *European Economy*, 44, October.

European Parliament (1994), 'The Social Consequences of the Economic and Monetary Union', *Final Report, Social Affairs Series*, 10–1994, Luxembourg.

Evans, G.W. (1983), 'The stability of rational expectations in macroeconomic models', in R. Frydman and E.S. Phelps (eds), *Individual Forecasting and Aggregate Outcomes. 'Rational' Expectations Examined*, Cambridge: Cambridge University Press.

Evans, G.W., and S. Honkapohja (1990), 'Learning, convergence, and stability with multiple rational expectations equilibria', STICERD discussion paper, London.

Fearon, J. (1995), 'Rationalist explanations for war', *International Organisation*, **49**, 79–414.

Felix, D. (1996), 'Statistical appendix' to Haq *et al.* (1996), pp. 289–300.

Felix, D. and R. Sau (1996), 'On the revenue potential and phasing in of the Tobin tax', in Haq *et al.* (1996), pp. 223–54.

Fish, S. (1994), *There's No Such Thing as Free Speech*, Oxford: Oxford University Press.

Fisher, F.M. (1989), 'Games economists play: a non-cooperative view', *Rand Journal of Economics*, **20**, 113–24.

Fisher, I. (1925), 'Our unstable dollar and the so-called business cycle', *Journal of the American Statistical Association*, **20**.

Fitzroy, F.R. and D. Mueller (1984), 'The co-operation and conflict in contractual organisations', reprinted in D. Mueller (ed.) (1986), *The Modern Corporation: Profits, Power, Growth and Performance*, London: Harvester Wheatsheaf.

Foot, M.D.K.W. (1996), 'International regulatory co-operation post-Barings', *Bank of England Quarterly Bulletin*, **36** (2).

Ford, J.L. (1994), *G.L.S. Shackle: The Dissenting Economist's Economist*. Aldershot, UK and Brookfield, US: Edward Elgar.

Förster, S. (1995), 'Dreams and nightmares: German military leadership and the images of future warfare, 1871–1914', mimeo, *Universität Bern Historisches Institut*.

Foss, N.J. (1996), 'The "alternative" theories of Knight and Coase and the modern theory of the firm', *Journal of the History of Economic Thought*, **18** (Spring), 76–95.

Foster, J. and P. Wild (1995), 'The logistic diffusion approach to econometric modelling in the presence of evolutionary change', Department of Economics, University of Queensland discussion paper no. 181.

Foucault, M. (1972), *The Archaeology of Knowledge*, trans. A. Sheridan, New York: Pantheon.

Foucault, M. (1979), *Discipline and Punish*, New York: Vintage Books.

Fourgeaud, C., C. Gourieroux and J. Pradel, (1986), 'Learning procedure and convergence to rationality', *Econometrica*, **54**, 845–68.

Fourie, F.C. v. N. (1993), 'In the beginning there were markets?', in C. Pitelis (ed.), *Transaction costs, markets and hierarchies*, Oxford: Basil Blackwell.

Frankel, J. (1996), 'How well do foreign exchange markets work: might a Tobin tax help?', in Haq *et al.* (1996), pp. 41–82.

Frankel, S.H. (1977), *Money, Two Philosophies: The Conflict of Trust and Authority*, Oxford: Basil Blackwell.

Fransman, M. (1995), *Japan's Computer and Communications Industry*, Cambridge: Cambridge University Press.

Frazer, W.J. and L.A. Boland (1983), 'An essay on the foundations of Friedman's methodology', *American Economic Review*, **73**, 129–44.

Freeman, R. and J.L. Medoff (1984), *What do Unions do?*, New York: Basic Books.

Friedman, D. (1989), *The Machinery of Freedom*, La Salle, IL: Open Court.

Friedman, G. and M. Lebard (1991), *The Coming War With Japan*, New York: St Martin's Press.

Friedman, M. (1953a), 'The case for flexible exchange rates', *Essays in Positive Economics*, Chicago: University of Chicago Press.

Friedman, M. (1953b), 'The methodology of positive economics', *Essays in Positive Economics*, Chicago: University of Chicago Press, pp. 3–43.

Friedman, M. and R. Friedman (1980), *Free to Choose*, London: Secker and Warburg.

Friedman, M. and A.J. Schwartz (1963), *A Monetary History of the United States, 1867–1960*, Chicago: University of Chicago Press.

Frisch, R. (1938), 'Statistical versus theoretical relations in economic macrodynamics', mimeo in Memorandum of 6/11/48 entitled *Autonomy of Economic Relations*, Universitets Okonomiske Institutt, Oslo.

Fukuyama, F. (1992), *The End of History and the Last Man*, New York: Free Press.

Fukuyama, F. (1995), *Trust: The Social Virtues and the Creation of Prosperity*, New York: Free Press.

Gabriel, J. (1994), *Worldviews of International Relations*, London: Macmillan.

Galbraith, J.K. (1967), *The New Industrial State*; 2nd rev. edn, Harmondsworth: Penguin, 1974.

Gamble, A. (1994), *The Free Economy and the Strong State*, London: Macmillan.

Garber, P. and M.P. Taylor (1995), 'Sand in the wheels of foreign exchange markets: a skeptical note', *The Economic Journal*, **105**.

Gärdenfors, P. and N.E. Sahlin (1982), 'Unreliable probabilities, risk taking and decision making,' *Synthèse*, **53**, 361–86.

Gärdenfors, P. and N.E. Sahlin (1988) (eds), *Decision, Probability and Utility*, Cambridge: Cambridge University Press.

Garrison, R.W. (1982), 'Austrian economics as the middle ground: comments on Loasby', in I.M. Kirzner (ed.), *Method, Process and Austrian Economics: Essays in Honor of Ludwig von Mises*, Lexington, MA: D.C. Heath.

Gasché, R. (1986), *The Tain of the Mirror: Derrida and the Philosophy of Reflection*, Cambridge, MA: Harvard University Press.

Gellner, E. (1983), *Nations and Nationalism*, Ithaca: Cornell University Press.

Geroski, P.A. (1991), 'Price dynamics in UK manufacturing: a microeconomic view', *Economica*, **59**, 403–19.

Gerrard, B. (1991), 'Keynes's *General Theory*: interpreting the interpretations', *Economic Journal*, **101**, 276–87.

Gerrard, B. (1992), 'From A Treatise on Probability to The General Theory: continuity or change in Keynes's thought?', in B. Gerrard and J. Hillard (eds), *The Philosophy and Economics of J.M. Keynes*, Aldershot, UK and Brookfield, US: Edward Elgar, pp. 80–95.

Gerrard, B. (1995), 'The scientific basis of economics: a review of the methodological debates in economics and econometrics', *Scottish Journal of Political Economy*, **42**, 221–35.

Gershenfeld, N.A. and A.S. Weigend (1993), 'The future of time series: learning and understanding', in N. A. Gershenfeld and A.S. Weigend (eds), *Time Series Prediction: Forecasting the Future and Understanding the Past,* Reading, MA: Addison-Wesley.

Ghirardato, P. (1994), 'Coping with ignorance: unforeseen contingencies and non-additive uncertainty', discussion paper, Department of Economics, Berkeley.

Giddens, A. (1987), *The Nation State and Violence*, Berkeley: University of California Press.

Gilbert, C.L. (1986), 'Professor Hendry's econometric methodology', *Oxford Bulletin of Economics and Statistics*, **48**, 283–307.

Gilbert, C.L. (1989), 'LSE and the British approach to time series econometrics', *Oxford Economic Papers*, **41**, 108–28.

Gilboa, I. (1987), 'Expected utility with purely subjective non-additive probabilities', *Journal of Mathematical Economics*, **16**, 65–8.

Gilboa, I. (1989), 'Additivizations of nonadditive measures', *Mathematics of operation research*, **4**, 1–17.

Gilboa, I. and D. Schmeidler (1989), 'Maximin expected utility with a non-unique prior', *Journal of Mathematical Economics* **18**, 141–53.

Gilboa, I. and D. Schmeidler (1993), 'Updating ambiguous beliefs', *Journal of Economic Theory*, **59**, 33–49.

Gill, J. and R. Butler (1996), 'Cycles of trust and distrust in joint-ventures', *European Management Journal*, **14** (1), February, 81–99.

Gilpin, R. (1981), *War and Change in World Politics*, Cambridge: Cambridge University Press.

Glahe, F.R. (ed.) (1991), *Keynes' The General Theory of Employment, Interest and Money*, Maryland: Rowan and Littlefield.

Godley, W. and F. Cripps (1981), *Macroeconomics*, London: Fontana Paperbacks.

Good, I.J. (1962), 'Subjective probability as the measure of a non-measurable set, in E. Nagel, P. Suppes and A. Tarski (eds), *Logic, Methodology and Philosophy of Science*, Stanford, CA: Stanford University Press, pp. 319–29.

Good I.J. (1980), 'Subjective probability as the measure of a non measurable set', in H.E. Kyburg and H.E. Smokler (eds), *Studies in Subjective Probability*, New York: Krieger.

Goodwin, C. (ed.) (1991), *Economics and National Security*, Durham, NC: Duke University Press.

Gowler, D. and K. Legge (1983), 'The meaning of management and the management of meaning: a view from social anthropology', in M.J. Earl (ed.), *Perspectives on Management*, Oxford: Oxford University Press.

Granger, C. (1990), *Modelling Economic Series*, Oxford: Oxford University Press.

Gray, J. (1993), *Beyond the New Right*, London: Routledge.

Gray, J. (1995), *Liberalism*, Minneapolis: University of Minnesota Press.

Graziani, A. (1989), 'The theory of the monetary circuit', *Thames Papers in Political Economy*, Spring, 1–26.

Graziani, A. (1994), *La teoria monetaria della produzione*, Arezzo, Banca Popolare dell'Etruria e del Lazio/Studi e Ricerche.

Graziani, A. (1996), 'Money as purchasing power and money as a stock of wealth in Keynesian economic thought', in G. Deleplace and E. Nell (eds), *Money in Motion*, London: Macmillan.

Greenaway, D. (1995), 'Policy forum: sand in the wheels of international finance, editorial note', *The Economic Journal*, **105**.

Greenwald, B. and J. Stiglitz (1993), 'New and old Keynesians', *Journal of Economic Perspectives*, **7**, 23–44.

Haavelmo, T. (1944), 'The probability approach in econometrics', *Econometrica (supplement)*, **12**, 1–118.

Habermas, J. (1990), 'Beyond the temporalized philosophy of origins: Jacques Derrida's critique of phonocentrism', in *The Philosophical Discourse of Modernity*, London: Polity.

Hahn, F. (1982), 'Reflections on the invisible hand', *Lloyds Bank Review*, **144**, 1–21.

Hahn, F. and R. Solow (1995), *A Critical Essay on Modern Macroeconomic Theory*, Cambridge, MA: MIT Press.

Hall, J. (1986), *Powers and Liberties: The Causes and Consequences of the Rise of the West*, Harmondsworth: Penguin.

Hall, R.L. and C.J. Hitch (1951), 'Price theory and business behaviour', in T. Wilson and P.W.S. Andrews (eds), *Oxford Studies in the Price Mechanism*, Oxford: Clarenden Press.

Hall, S. (1995), 'Macroeconomics and a bit more reality', *Economic Journal,* **105**, 974–88.

Hall, S.G. and S.G.B. Henry (1987), 'Wage models', *National Institute Economic Review*, 70–75.

Hamouda, O.F. and G.C. Harcourt (1988), 'Post Keynesianism: from criticism to coherence?', *Bulletin of Economic Research*, **40**, 1–34.

Hamouda, O. and J. Smithin (1988), 'Some remarks on "Uncertainty and Economic Analysis"', *Economic Journal*, **98**, 159–64.

Handelman, S. (1995), *Comrade Criminal: Russia's New Mafia*, New Haven: Yale University Press.

Haq, M.U., I. Kaul and I. Grunberg (eds) (1996), *The Tobin Tax: Coping with Financial Volatility*, Oxford: Oxford University Press.

Harcourt, G.C. (1987), 'The legacy of Keynes: theoretical methods and unfinished business', in D.A. Reese (ed.), *The Legacy of Keynes, Nobel Conference XXII*, San Francisco: Harper and Row, pp. 1–22.

Harcourt, G.C. (1995a), 'Taming speculators', in *Capitalism, Socialism and Post-Keynesianism*, Aldershot, UK and Brookfield, US: Edward Elgar.

Harcourt, G.C. (1995b), 'A "modest proposal" for taming speculators and putting the world on course to prosperity', *Capitalism, Socialism and Post-Keynesianism*, Aldershot, UK and Brookfield, US: Edward Elgar, ch. 3; originally published in *Economic and Political Weekly*, **29** (28), September 1994, 2490–92.

Harcourt, G. and P. Riach (eds) (1997), *The Second Edition of the General Theory*, London: Routledge.

Hargreaves Heap, S. (1989), *Rationality in Economics*, Oxford: Blackwell.

Hargreaves Heap, S. (1993), 'Post-modernity and new conceptions of rationality in economics', in B. Gerrard (ed.), *The Economics of Rationality*, London: Routledge.

Hargreaves Heap, S. and Y. Varoufakis (1995), *Game Theory: A Critical Introduction*, London: Routledge.

Harland, R. (1987), *Superstructuralism: the Philosophy of Structuralism and Post-Structuralism*, London and New York: Methuen.

Harris, N. (1987), *The End of the Third World*, Harmondsworth: Penguin.

Harrod, R.F. (1939), 'An essay in dynamic theory', *Economic Journal*, **49**, 14–33.

Harrod, R.F. (1951), *The Life of John Maynard Keynes*, New York: Harcourt, Brace.

Harvey, J. (1995), 'The international monetary system and exchange rate determination: 1945 to the present', *Journal of Economic Issues*, **29**.

Hausman, D.M. (1992), *The Inexact and Separate Science of Economics*, Cambridge: Cambridge University Press.

Hayek, F.A. (1931), *Prices and Production,* London: Routledge.

Hayek, F.A. (1937), 'Economics and knowledge', *Economica*, N.S., **4**, 33–54.

Hayek, F.A. (1945), 'The use of knowledge in society', *American Economic Review*, **35**.

Hayek, F.A. (1952), *The Sensory Order,* Chicago: University of Chicago Press.

Hayek, F.A. von (1988), *The Fatal Conceit*, Chicago: University of Chicago Press.

Heckscher, E. (1919), 'The effect of foreign trade on the distribution of income', *Ekonomisk Tidskrift*, **XXI**, translated by S. Laursen and reprinted in H. Ellis and L. Metzler (eds), *Readings in the Theory of International Trade*, London: George Allen and Unwin.

Heiner, R. (1983), 'The origin of predictable behavior', *American Economic Review*, **73**, 560–95.

Hendry, D.F. (1980), 'Econometrics: alchemy or science?', *Economica*, **47**, 387–406, reprinted in *Econometrics: Alchemy or Science?* (1993), Oxford: Blackwell.

Hendry, D.F. (1993), *Econometrics: Alchemy or Science?*, Oxford: Blackwell.

Hendry, D.F. (1995), *Dynamic Econometrics*, Oxford: Oxford University Press.

Hendry, D.F. and M.S. Morgan (1989), 'A re-analysis of confluence analysis', in N. De Marchi and C. Gilbert (eds), special edition on Econometrics, *Oxford Economic Papers*, **41**.

Hewitson, G. (1995), 'Post-Keynesian monetary theory: some issues', *Journal of Economic Surveys*, **9**, 285–310.

Hey, J. (ed.) (1989), *Current Issues in Microeconomics*, London: Macmillan.

Hicks, J.R. (1932), *The Theory of Wages*, London: Macmillan.

Hicks, J.R. (1937), 'Mr Keynes and the "classics": a suggested interpretation', *Econometrica*, **5**, 147–59.

Hicks, J.R. (1967), *Critical Essays in Monetary Theory*, Oxford: Clarendon Press.

Hicks, J.R. (1974), *The Crisis in Keynesian Economics*, New York: Basic Books.

Hicks, J.R. (1975), *The Crisis in Keynesian Economics*, Basil Blackwell, Oxford.

Hicks, J.R. (1979), *Causality in Economics*, New York: Basic Books.

Hicks, J.R. (1985), *Methods of Dynamic Economics*, Oxford: Clarendon Press.

Hieser, R.O. (1952), 'The degree of monopoly power', *Economic Record*, **28** (54), May, 1–12.

Hieser, R.O. (1954), 'Review of J. Steindl, *Maturity and Stagnation in American Capitalism* (1952)', *Economic Record*, **30** (58), May, 106–9.

Hieser, R.O. (1970), 'Wage determination with bilateral monopoly in the labour market', *Economic Record*, **46** (113), March, 55–72.

Hindess, B. and P. Hirst (1977), *Mode of Production and Social Formation*, London: Macmillan.

Hirsch, A. and N. de Marchi (1984), 'Methodology: a comment on Frazer and Boland, I', *American Economic Review*, **74**, 782–88.

Hirsch, F. (1976), *Social Limits to Growth*, Cambridge, MA: Harvard University Press.

Hirschman, A. (1970), *Exit, Voice and Loyalty*, Cambridge, MA: Harvard University Press.

Hirschman, A. (1982a), 'Rival interpretations of market society', *Journal of Economic Literature*, **XX**, 1463–84.

Hirschman, A. (1982b), *Shifting Involvements*, Princeton: Princeton University Press.

Hirschman, A. (1991), *The Rhetoric of Reaction*, Cambridge, MA: Harvard University Press.

Hobsbawm, E. (1990), *Nations and Nationalism Since 1780*, Cambridge: Cambridge University Press.

Hobsbawm, E. (1995), *The Age of Extremes: A History of the World, 1914–1991*, New York: Pantheon.

Hodgson, G.M. (1982), 'Theoretical and policy implications of variable productivity', *Cambridge Journal of Economics*, **6** (3), September, 213–26.

Hodgson, G.M. (1988), *Economics and Institutions: A Manifesto for a Modern Institutional Economics*, Cambridge: Polity Press.

Hodgson, G.M. (1999), *Evolution and Institutions: On Evolutionary Economics and the Evolution of Economics,* Cheltenham, UK and Northampton, MA, US: Edward Elgar.

Hofman, H. (1992), 'Kommissionen er på tynd is' (The EC Commission on shaky grounds), *Samfundsøkonomen*, **11** (3), April, 5–12, Copenhagen.

Holtham, G. (1995), 'Managing the exchange rate system', in J. Michie and

226   *Bibliography*

J. Grieve Smith (eds), *Managing the Global Economy*, Oxford: Oxford University Press.

Hoogduin, L. (1987), 'On the difference between the uncertainty and the development of a more general monetary theory', *De Economist*, **135** (1), 54–65.

Hoover, K.D. (1984), 'Methodology: a comment on Frazer and Boland, II', *American Economic Review*, **74**, 789–97.

Howard, M. (1979), *Modern Theories of Income Distribution*, London: Macmillan.

Howard, M. and J. King (1985), *The Political Economy of Marx*, Harlow: Longman.

Howard, M. and J. King (1989), *A History of Marxian Economics, Volume I, 1883–1929*, Princeton: Princeton University Press.

Howard, M. and J. King (1992), *A History of Marxian Economics, Volume II, 1929–1990*, Princeton: Princeton University Press.

Hume, D. (1740), *An Abstract of a Treatise of Human Nature; A Pamphlet Hitherto Unknown*, reprinted with an introduction by J.M. Keynes and P. Sraffa (1938), Cambridge: Cambridge University Press.

Hutton, W. (1994), *The State We're In*, London: Jonathon Cape.

Hutton, W. (1996), *The State We're In*, London: Vintage.

Isard, P. (1995), *Exchange Rate Economics*, Cambridge: Cambridge University Press.

Jensen, H. (1983), 'J.M. Keynes as a Marshallian', *Journal of Economic Issues*, **18**, 67–94.

Jespersen, J. (1994a), 'Europæisk Integration – valutarisk set', working paper, Roskilde Universitetscenter, June.

Jespersen, J. (1994b), 'Environment as a macroeconomic issue: the missing link of the Maastricht Treaty', in P.-O. Bergeron and M.-A. Gaiffe (eds), *Croissance, Compétitivité, Emploi: à la recherche d'un modèle pour l'Europe*, Brugge, Collège d'Europe.

Jespersen, J. (1995), 'The Monetary Union and the European Central Bank', in P. Arestis and V. Chick (eds), *Finance, Development and Structural Change: Post-Keynesian Perspectives*, Aldershot, UK and Brookfield, US: Edward Elgar.

Johansen, S. (1988), 'Statistical analysis of cointegration vectors', *Journal of Economic Dynamics and Control*, **12** (2), 231–54.

Johanson, J. and J.-E. Vahlne (1977), 'The internationalization process of the firm: a model of knowledge development and increasing foreign market commitments', *Journal of International Business Studies*, **8** (1), 23–32.

Johanson, J. and F. Wiedersheim-Paul (1975), 'Psychic distance and buyer–seller interaction', *Organisasjon, Marked og Samfund*, **16** (5), 308–24.

Johnson, C. (1993), *System and Writing in the Philosophy of Jacques Derrida*, Cambridge: Cambridge University Press.

Jones, R. and J. Ostroy (1984), 'Flexibility and uncertainty', *Review of Economic Studies*, **51**, 13–32.

Kahn, R.F. (1931), 'The relation of home investment to employment', *Economic Journal*, **41**, 173–98.

Kahneman, D. and A. Tversky (1973), 'On the psychology of prediction', *Psychological Review*, **80**, 237–51.

Kahneman, D., P. Slovic and A. Tversky (1982), *Judgement Under Uncertainty: Heuristics and Biases*, New York: Cambridge University Press.

Kaldor, N. (1978), *Further Essays in Economic Theory*, London: Duckworth.

Kaldor, N. (1983), 'Keynesian economics after fifty years', in D. Worswick and J. Trevithick (eds), *Keynes and the Modern World*, Cambridge: Cambridge University Press.

Kalecki, M. (1936), 'Review of Keynes's General Theory', reprinted in M. Kalecki (1990), *Collected Writings*, vol. I, (ed.) J. Osiatinski, Oxford: Clarendon.

Kalecki, M. (1941), 'The theory of long run distribution of the production industry', *Oxford Economic Papers*, June.

Kalecki, M. (1943), 'Political aspects of full employment', *Political Quarterly*, **14** (4), October–December, 322–31.

Kalecki, M. (1954), *Theory of Economic Dynamics*, London: Allen and Unwin.

Kanth, R. (1986), *Political Economy and Laissez-Faire*, New York: Rowan and Littlefield.

Kaul, I. and J. Langmore (1996), 'Potential uses of the revenue from a Tobin tax' in Haq *et al.* (1996), pp. 255–72.

Kay, N. (1984), *The Emergent Firm: Knowledge, Ignorance and Surprise in Economic Organisation*, London: Macmillan.

Kelsey, D. and J. Quiggin (1992), 'Theories of choice under ignorance and uncertainty', *Journal of Economic Surveys*, **6**, 133–53.

Kenen, P.B. (1995), 'Capital controls, the EMS and EMU', *Economic Journal*, **105**, 181–92.

Kenen, P.B. (1996), 'The feasibility of taxing foreign exchange transactions', in Haq *et al.* (1996), pp. 109–28.

Kennedy, P. (1989), *The Rise and Fall of Great Powers*, London: Fontana.

Keohane, R. (ed.) (1986), *Neorealism and its Critics*, New York: Columbia University Press.

Keynes, J.M. (1910), '8 lectures on company finance and stock exchange, lent term' (Notebook), Keynes's MSS, King's College Library, Cambridge, UA/6/3.

Keynes, J.M. (1921), *A Treatise on Probability*, London: Macmillan.

Keynes, J.M. (1925), *A Short View of Russia*, London: Leonard and Virginia Woolf.

Keynes, J.M. (1926), *The End of Laissez-Faire*, Edinburgh: Neill & Co.

Keynes, J.M. (1936), *The General Theory of Employment, Interest, and Money*, London: Macmillan and New York: Harcourt, Brace and Co.

Keynes, J.M. (1937), 'The General Theory of Employment', *Quarterly Journal of Economics*, **51**, February, 209–23, reprinted in J.M. Keynes (1971–1989), Volume XIV.

Keynes, J.M. (1939), 'Professor Tinbergen's Method', *Economic Journal*, **44**, 558–68.

Keynes, J.M. (1940), 'Comment', *Economic Journal*, **50**, 154–56.

Keynes, J.M. (1971–1989)

'Indian Currency and Finance', *The Collected Writings of John Maynard Keynes*, Volume I, London: Macmillan for the Royal Economic Society.

'The Economic Consequences of the Peace', *The Collected Writings of John Maynard Keynes*, Volume II, London: Macmillan for the Royal Economic Society.

'A Revision of the Treaty: Being a Sequel to The Economic Consequences of the Peace', *The Collected Writings of John Maynard Keynes*, Volume III, London: Macmillan for the Royal Economic Society.

'A Tract on Monetary Reform', *The Collected Writings of John Maynard Keynes*, Volume IV, London: Macmillan for the Royal Economic Society.

'A Treatise on Money: The Pure Theory of Money', *The Collected Writings of John Maynard Keynes*, Volume V, London: Macmillan for the Royal Economic Society.

'A Treatise on Money: The Applied Theory of Money', *The Collected Writings of John Maynard Keynes*, Volume VI, London: Macmillan for the Royal Economic Society.

'The General Theory of Employment, Interest and Money', *The Collected Writings of John Maynard Keynes*, Volume VII, London: Macmillan for the Royal Economic Society.

'A Treatise on Probability', *The Collected Writings of John Maynard Keynes*, Volume VIII, London: Macmillan for the Royal Economic Society.

'Essays in Persuasion', *The Collected Writings of John Maynard Keynes*, Volume IX, London: Macmillan for the Royal Economic Society.

'Essays in Biography', *The Collected Writings of John Maynard Keynes*, Volume X, London: Macmillan for the Royal Economic Society.

'Economic Articles and Correspondence', in D. Moggridge (ed.), *The*

Collected Writings of John Maynard Keynes, Volume XI, London: Macmillan for the Royal Economic Society.

'Economic Articles and Correspondence and Editorial', in D. Moggridge (ed.), *The Collected Writings of John Maynard Keynes*, Volume XII, London: Macmillan for the Royal Economic Society.

'The General Theory and After, Part I: Preparation', in D. Moggridge (ed.), *The Collected Writings of John Maynard Keynes*, Volume XIII, London: Macmillan for the Royal Economic Society.

'The General Theory and After, Part II: Defence and Development', in D. Moggridge (ed.), *The Collected Writings of John Maynard Keynes*, Volume XIV, London: Macmillan for the Royal Economic Society.

'Activities, 1906–1914: India and Cambridge', in E. Johnson (ed.), *The Collected Writings of John Maynard Keynes*, Volume XV, London: Macmillan for the Royal Economic Society.

'Activities, 1914–1919: The Treasury and Versailles', in E. Johnson (ed.), *The Collected Writings of John Maynard Keynes*, Volume XVI, London: Macmillan for the Royal Economic Society.

'Activities, 1920–1922: Treaty Revision and reconstruction', in E. Johnson (ed.), *The Collected Writings of John Maynard Keynes*, Volume XVII, London: Macmillan for the Royal Economic Society.

'Activities, 1922–1932: The End of Reparations', in E. Johnson (ed.), *The Collected Writings of John Maynard Keynes*, Volume XVIII, London: Macmillan for the Royal Economic Society.

'Activities, 1922–1929: The Return to Gold and Industrial Policy', in D. Moggridge (ed.), *The Collected Writings of John Maynard Keynes*, Volume XIX, London: Macmillan for the Royal Economic Society.

'Activities, 1929–1931: Rethinking Employment and Unemployment Policies', in D. Moggridge (ed.), *The Collected Writings of John Maynard Keynes*, Volume XX, London: Macmillan for the Royal Economic Society.

'Activities, 1931–1939: World Crises and Policies in Britain and America', in D. Moggridge (ed.), *The Collected Writings of John Maynard Keynes*, Volume XXI, London: Macmillan for the Royal Economic Society.

'Activities, 1939–1945: Internal War Finance', in D. Moggridge (ed.), *The Collected Writings of John Maynard Keynes*, Volume XXII, London: Macmillan for the Royal Economic Society.

'Activities, 1940–1943: External War Finance', in D. Moggridge (ed.), *The Collected Writings of John Maynard Keynes*, Volume XXIII, London: Macmillan for the Royal Economic Society.

'Activities, 1944–1946: The Transition to Peace', in D. Moggridge (ed.), *The Collected Writings of John Maynard Keynes*, Volume XXIV, London: Macmillan for the Royal Economic Society.

'Activities, 1940–1944: Shaping the Post-War World, the Clearing Union', in D. Moggridge (ed.), *The Collected Writings of John Maynard Keynes*, Volume XXV, London: Macmillan for the Royal Economic Society.

'Activities, 1941–1946: Shaping the Post-War World, Bretton Woods and Reparations', in D. Moggridge (ed.), *The Collected Writings of John Maynard Keynes*, Volume XXVI, London: Macmillan for the Royal Economic Society.

'Activities, 1940–1946: Shaping the Post-War World, Employment and Commodities', in D. Moggridge (ed.), *The Collected Writings of John Maynard Keynes*, Volume XXVII, London: Macmillan for the Royal Economic Society.

'Social, Political and Literary Writings', in D. Moggridge (ed.), *The Collected Writings of John Maynard Keynes*, Volume XXVIII, London: Macmillan for the Royal Economic Society.

'The General Theory and After, A Supplement', in D. Moggridge (ed.), *The Collected Writings of John Maynard Keynes*, Volume XIX, London: Macmillan for the Royal Economic Society.

'Bibliography and Index', in D. Moggridge (ed.), *The Collected Writings of John Maynard Keynes*, Volume XXX, London: Macmillan for the Royal Economic Society.

King, J.E. (1990), *Labour Economics*, 2nd edn, London: Macmillan.

King, J.E. (1995), *Conversations with Post Keynesians*, London: Macmillan.

King, J.E. (1996), 'The First Post Keynesian: Joan Robinson's "Essays in the Theory of Employment" (1937)', in P. Arestis and M.C. Sawyer (eds), *Employment, Economic Growth and the Tyranny of the Market: Essays in Honour of Paul Davidson*, Cheltenham, UK and Brookfield, US: Edward Elgar, pp. 164–84.

King, J.E., R. Rimmer, and S. Rimmer (1992), 'The law of the shrinking middle: inequality of earnings in Australia, 1975–1989', *Scottish Journal of Political Economy* **39** (4), November, 391–412.

Klamer, A.J. and D. Colander (1990), *The Making of an Economist*, Boulder, CO: Westview Press.

Klamer, A.J., D.N. McCloskey and R. Solow (eds) (1988), *The Consequences of Economic Rhetoric*, Cambridge: Cambridge University Press.

Knight, F.H. (1921), *Risk, Uncertainty and Profit*, New York: Houghton Mifflin.

Knight, F.H. (1933), *Risk Uncertainty and Profit*, 2nd edition, London: London School of Economics.

Koopman B.C. (1940), 'The axioms and algebra of intuitive probability', *Annals of Mathematics*, **41**, 269–92.

Koopmans, T. (1957), *Three Essays on the State of Economic Science*, New York: McGraw-Hill.

Kregel, J.A. (1973), 'Economic methodology in the face of uncertainty: the modelling methods of Keynes and the Post Keynesians', *Economic Journal*, **86**, 209–25.

Kregel, J.A. (1980), 'Marx, Keynes, and social change: is Post-Keynesian theory Neo-Marxist?', in E. Nell (ed.), *Growth, Profits and Property*, Cambridge: Cambridge University Press.

Kreps, D.M. (1988), *Notes on the Theory of Choice*, Boulder, CO: Westview Press.

Kreps, D.M. (1990), *A Course in Microeconomic Theory*, Princeton: Princeton University Press.

Kriesler, P. (1996), 'Microfoundations: a Kaleckian perspective', in J.E. King (ed.), *An Alternative Macroeconomic Theory: the Kaleckian Model and Post Keynesian Economics*, Boston: Kluwer, pp. 55–72.

Kristol, I. (1983), *Reflections of a Neoconservative*, New York: Basic Books.

Krugman, P. (1988), 'The persistent US trade deficit', *Australian Economic Papers*, December.

Krugman, P. (1989), 'The case for stabilizing exchange rates', *Oxford Review of Economic Policy*, **5**.

Krugman, P. (1991a), 'Myths and realities of US competitiveness', *Science Magazine*, November.

Krugman, P. (1991b), *Geography and Trade*, Cambridge, MA: MIT Press.

Krugman, P. (1994a), 'Competitiveness: a dangerous obsession', *Foreign Affairs*, March/April.

Krugman, P. (1994b), *Peddling Prosperity*, New York: Norton.

Krugman, P. (1996), 'What difference does globalization make?', *Business Economics*, January.

Krugman, P. and L. Taylor (1978), 'The contractionary effects of devaluation', *Journal of International Economics*, **8**, 445–56.

Kuhn, T.S. (1962), *The Structure of Scientific Revolutions*, Chicago: University of Chicago Press.

Kurz, M. (1991a), 'On rational belief equilibria', discussion paper, Stanford University.

Kurz, M. (1991b), 'On the structure and diversity of rational beliefs', discussion paper, Stanford University.

Kurz, M. (1993), 'Rational preferences and rational beliefs', unpublished manuscript.

Kyburg, H.E. (1992), 'Getting fancy with probability', *Synthèse*, **90**, 189–203.

Kyburg, H.E. and H.E. Smokler (eds) (1964), *Studies in Subjective Probabilities*, New York: Wiley.

Kydland, F.E. and E.C. Prescott (1982), 'Time to build and aggregate fluctuations', *Econometrica*, **50**, 1345–70.

Lachmann, L.M. (1986), *The Market as an Economic Process,* Oxford: Basil Blackwell.

Laclau, E. and C. Mouffe (1985), *Hegemony and Socialist Strategy: Towards a Radical Democratic Politics,* London and New York: Verso.

Lakatos, I. (1974), 'Falsification and the methodology of scientific research programmes' in I. Lakatos and A. Musgrave (eds), *Criticism and the Growth of Knowledge,* Cambridge: Cambridge University Press.

Langlois, R.N. (1984), 'Internal organisation in a dynamic context: some theoretical consideration', in M. Jussawalla and H. Ebenfield (eds), *Communication and Information Economics,* Amsterdam: North-Holland.

Langlois, R.N. (1988), 'Economic change and the boundaries of the firm', *Journal of Institutional and Theoretical Economics,* **144**, 635–57.

Langlois, R.N. (1992), 'Transaction cost economics in real time', *Industrial and Corporate Change,* **1**, 456–65.

Langlois, R.N. & M. Everett (1992), 'Complexity, genuine uncertainty, and the economics of organisation', *Human Systems Management,* **11**, 67–76.

Laury, J.S.E., G.R. Lewis and P.A. Ormerod (1978), 'Properties of macro-economic models of the UK economy: a comparative survey', *National Institute Economic Review,* **83**.

Lavoie, M. (1992a), 'Towards a new research programme for Post-Keynesianism and Neo-Ricardianism', *Review of Political Economy,* **4**.

Lavoie, M. (1992b), *Foundations of Post Keynesian Analysis,* Aldershot, UK and Brookfield, US: Edward Elgar.

Lavoie, M. (1995), 'Horizontalism, structuralism, liquidity preference and the principle of increasing risk', working paper no. 9513E, Ottawa, Ontario: University of Ottawa.

Lavoie, M. (1996), 'Mark up pricing versus normal cost pricing in Post Keynesian models', *Review of Political Economy,* **8**, 57–66.

Lawlor, M.S. (1994), 'The own-rates framework as an interpretation of The General Theory: a Suggestion for complicating the Keynesian theory of money', in J.B. Davis (ed.), *The State of Interpretation of Keynes,* Boston: Kluwer Academic Publishers.

Lawson, T. (1981), 'Keynesian model-building and the rational expectations critique', *Cambridge Journal of Economics,* **5**, 311–26.

Lawson, T. (1985a), 'Keynes, prediction and econometrics', in T. Lawson and H. Pesaran (eds), *Keynes' Economics: Methodological Issues,* London: Croom Helm.

Lawson, T. (1985b), 'Uncertainty and economic analysis', *Economic Journal,* **95**, 909–27.

Lawson, T. (1987), 'The relative/absolute nature of knowledge and economic analysis', *Economic Journal,* **97**, 951–70.

Lawson, T. (1988), 'Probability and uncertainty in economic analysis', *Journal of Post Keynesian Economics*, **11**, 95–70.

Lawson, T. (1989a), 'Realism and instrumentalism in the development of econometrics', *Oxford Economic Papers*, **41**, 236–58.

Lawson, T. (1989b), 'Abstractions, tendencies and stylised facts: a realist approach to economic analysis', *Cambridge Journal of Economics*, **13**, 59–78.

Lawson, T. (1994a), 'The nature of Post Keynesianism and its links to other traditions: a realist perspective', *Journal of Post Keynesian Economics*, **16**, 499–538.

Lawson, T. (1994b), 'A realist theory for economics' in R.E. Backhouse (ed.), *New Directions in Economic Methodology*, London: Routledge.

Lawson, T. (1994c), 'Methodology in economics' in P. Arestis and M. Sawyer (eds), *The Elgar Companion to Radical Political Economy*, Aldershot, UK and Brookfield, US: Edward Elgar.

Lawson, T. (1995a), 'The "Lucas Critique": A Generalisation', *Cambridge Journal of Economics*, **19**, 257–76.

Lawson, T. (1995b), in S.C. Dow and J. Hillard (eds), *Keynes, Knowledge and Uncertainty,* Aldershot, UK and Brookfield, US: Edward Elgar, pp. 77–106.

Lawson, T. (1997), *Economics and Reality*, London: Routledge.

Lawson, T., R. Tarling, and F. Wilkinson (1982), 'Charges in the inter-industry structure of wages: some theoretical positions', *Cambridge Journal of Economics*, **6** (3), September, 227–9.

Layard, R. and S. Nickell (1987), 'The labour market', in R. Dornbusch and R. Layard (eds), *The Performance of the British Economy*, Oxford: Clarendon Press.

Layard, R., S. Nickell and R. Jackman (1991), *Unemployment*, Oxford: Oxford University Press.

Leamer, E. (1983), 'Let's take the con out of econometrics', *American Economic Review*, **73**, 31–44.

Lechte, J. (1994), *Fifty key contemporary thinkers: from structuralism to postmodernity*, London and New York: Routledge.

Leibenstein, H. (1968), 'Entrepreneurship and development', *American Economic Review*.

Leibenstein, H. (1987), *Inside the Firm: the Inefficiencies of Hierarchy*, Cambridge, MA: Harvard University Press.

Leijonhufvud, A. (1969), *Keynes and the Classics*, London: Institute of Economic Affairs.

Leontief, W.A. (1971), 'Theoretical assumptions and non-observed facts', *American Economic Review,* **61**, 1–7.

Lester, R.A. (1946), 'Shortcomings of marginal analysis for wage–

employment problems', *American Economic Review*, **36** (1), March, 63–82.

Levi, I. (1974), 'On indeterminate probabilities', *Journal of Philosophy*, **71**, 391–418.

Levi, I. (1986), *Hard Choices: Decision Making Under Unresolved Conflict*, Cambridge: Cambridge University Press.

Levy, J. (1989), 'The causes of war: a review of theories and evidence', in Tetlock *et al.* (1989), 209–33.

Littleboy, B. (1990), *On Interpreting Keynes: A Study in Reconciliation*, London and New York: Routledge.

Loasby, B.J. (1976), *Choice, Complexity and Ignorance: An Enquiry into Economic Theory and Practice of Decision Making*, Cambridge: Cambridge University Press.

Loasby, B.J. (1986), 'Competition and imperfect knowledge: the contribution of G.B. Richardson', *Scottish Journal of Political Economy*, **33**, 145–58.

Loubser, J., R.C. Baum, A. Effrat and V.M. Lidz (eds) (1976), *Explorations in General Theory in Social Science, Volume Two*, New York: Free Press.

Lucas Jr, R.E. (1978), 'Asset prices in an exchange Economy', *Econometrica*, **46**, 1429–45.

Lucas Jr, R.E. (1980), 'Methods and problems in business cycle theory', *Journal of Money, Credit and Banking*, **12**, 696–715.

Lucas Jr, R.E., (1986), 'Adaptive behaviour and economic theory', *Journal of Business*, **59**, Supplement, S401–26.

Luenberger, D. (1995), *Microeconomic Theory*, New York: McGraw-Hill.

Luhmann, N. (1979), *Trust and Power*, New York: John Wiley.

Lukes, S. (1974), *Power: A Radical View*, London: Macmillan.

Machina, M.J. (1989), 'Choice under uncertainty: problems solved and unsolved' in J. Hey (ed.) (1989), pp. 12–46.

Machina, M.J. and D. Schmeidler (1992), 'A more robust definition of subjective probability, *Econometrica*, **60** (4), 745–80.

Maddison, A. (1991), *Dynamic Forces in Capitalist Development*, Oxford: Oxford University Press.

Mair, D. and A. Miller (eds) (1992), *A Modern Guide to Economic Thought*, Aldershot, UK and Brookfield, US: Edward Elgar.

Mäki, U. (1988), 'How to combine rhetoric and realism in the methodology of economics', *Economics and Philosophy*, **4**, 89–109.

Mäki, U. (1989), 'On the problem of realism in economics', *Ricerche Economiche*, **43**, 176–98, reprinted in B. Caldwell (ed.), *The Philosophy and Methodology of Economics*, Aldershot, UK and Brookfield, US: Edward Elgar.

Mäki, U. (1990), 'Scientific realism and Austrian explanation', *Review of Political Economy*, **2**, 310–44.

Mäki, U. (1992a), 'On the method of isolation in economics', in C. Dilworth (ed.), *Idealization IV: Intelligibility in Science*, special issue of *Poznan Studies in the Philosophy of The Sciences and the Humanities*, **26**, 319–54.

Mäki, U. (1992b), 'Friedman and realism', *Research in the History of Economic Thought and Methodology*, **10**, 171–95.

Mäki, U. (1992c), 'The market as an isolated causal process: a metaphysical ground for realism', in B. Caldwell and S. Boehm (eds), *Austrian Economics: Tensions and New Developments*, Dordrecht: Kluwer, pp. 35–59.

Mäki, U. (1993a), 'Isolation, idealization and truth in economics', in B. Hamminga and N. de Marchi (eds), *Idealization in Economics*, special issue of *Poznan Studies in the Philosophy of the Sciences and the Humanities*, **38**, 147–68.

Mäki, U. (1993b), 'Economics with institutions: agenda for methodological research', in U. Mäki, C. Knudsen and B. Gustafsson (eds), *Rationality, Institutions and Economic Methodology*, London: Routledge.

Mäki, U. (1994), 'Reorienting the assumptions issue', in R. Backhouse (ed.), *New Directions in Economic Methodology*, London: Routledge, pp. 236–56.

Mäki, U. (1995), 'Diagnosing McCloskey', *Journal of Economic Literature*, **33**, 1300–318.

Mäki, U. (1998a), 'Is Coase a realist?', *Philosophy of the Social Sciences*, **28**, 5–31.

Mäki, U. (1998b), 'Against Posner against Coase against theory', *Cambridge Journal of Economics*, **22**, 587–95.

Mäki, U. (1998c), 'Realisticness', in J. Davis, W. Hands and U. Mäki (eds), *Handbook of Economic Methodology*, Cheltenham, UK and Northampton, US: Edward Elgar.

Mäki, U. (1998d), 'Aspects of realism about economics', *Theoria*, **13**, 301–19.

Mäki, U. (ed.) (2001), *The Economic World View: Studies in the Ontology of Economics*, Cambridge: Cambridge University Press.

Malcolmson, D. (1984), 'Efficient labour organisations: incentives, power and the transaction cost approach', in F. Stephen (ed.), *Firm Organisations and Labour*, London: Macmillan.

Malinvaud, E. (1985), *Lectures on Microeconomic Theory*, Amsterdam: North-Holland.

Mann, M. (1986), *The Sources of Social Power, Volume I*, Cambridge: Cambridge University Press.

Mann, M. (1988), *States, War and Capitalism*, Oxford: Blackwell.

Mann, M. (1993), *The Sources of Social Power, Volume II*, Cambridge: Cambridge University Press.

Manning, A. (1995), 'How do we know that real wages are too high?', *Quarterly Journal of Economics*, **110** (4), November, 1111–25.

Marcet, A. and T.J. Sargent (1988), 'The fate of systems with "adaptive" expectations', *American Economic Review, Papers and Proceedings*, **78**, 168–72.

Marcet, A. and T.J. Sargent (1989a), 'Convergence of least squares learning mechanisms in self-referential stochastic models', *Journal of Economic Theory*, **48**, 337–68.

Marcet, A. and T.J. Sargent (1989b), 'Convergence of least squares learning in environments with hidden state variables and private information', *Journal of Political Economy*, **97**, 1306–22.

Marglin, S. (1974), 'What do bosses do? The origins and functions of hierarchy in capitalist production', *Review of Radical Political Economics*, **6**, 60–112.

Marris, R. (1964), *The Economic Theory of 'Managerial' Capitalism*, London: Macmillan.

Marris, R. (1997), in Harcourt and Riach (1997), vol 1, pp. 52–82.

Marris, R. and D. Mueller (1980), 'The Corporation, Competition and the Invisible Hand', reprinted in D. Mueller (ed.), *The Modern Corporation: Profits, Power, Growth and Performance*, London: Harvester Wheatsheaf, 1986.

Marshall, A. (1879), *The Pure Theory of Foreign Trade*, reprinted London: London School of Economics and Political Science, 1930.

Marshall, A. (1920), *Principles of Economics*, 8th edn, London: Macmillan.

Marshall, A. (1923), *Money, Credit and Commerce*, London: Macmillan.

Marshall, A. (1994), 'Ye machine', *Research in the History of Economic Thought and Methodology*, Archival Supplement 4, Greenwich, CT: JAI Press, 116–32.

Marshall, T. (1992), *Citizenship and Social Class*, London: Pluto Press.

Marx, K. (1867), *Capital, Volume I*, London: Lawrence and Wishart.

Marx, K. (1967), *Capital*, Three Volumes, Moscow: Progress Publishers.

Marx, K. (1973), *Grundrisse*, New York: Random House.

Marx, K. (1976), *Capital*, vol. 1. (translated by B. Fowkes), Harmondsworth: Penguin.

Marx, K. (1982), *The Poverty of Philosophy*, New York: International Publishers.

Mas-Colell, A., M. Whinston and J. Green (1995), *Microeconomic Theory*, New York: Oxford University Press.

Matthei, J. (1984), 'Rethinking Scarcity: Neoclassicism, NeoMalthusianism and NeoMarxism', *Review of Radical Political Economics*, **16**.

Mayer, A. (1981), *The Persistence of the Old Regime*, New York: Pantheon.

Mayer, T. (1993), *Truth versus Precision in Economics*, Aldershot, UK and Brookfield, US: Edward Elgar.

McCallum, B.T. (1970), 'The effect of demand on prices in British manufacturing: another view', *Review of Economic Studies*, **37**, 147–56.

McCann Jr, C.R. (1994), *Probability Foundations of Economic Theory*, London: Routledge.

McCloskey, D.N. (1983), 'The rhetoric of economics', *Journal of Economic Literature*, **21**, 481–517.

McCloskey, D.N. (1985), *The Rhetoric of Economics*, Madison: University of Wisconsin Press.

McCloskey, D.N. (1986), *The Rhetoric of Economics*, Brighton: Wheatsheaf.

McCloskey, D.N. (1991), *Rhetoric and Persuasion in Economics*, Cambridge: Cambridge University Press.

McCloskey, D.N. (1994), *Knowledge and Persuasion in Economics*, Cambridge: Cambridge University Press.

McCloskey, D.N. (1995), 'Modern epistemology: against analytic philosophy: a reply to Mäki', *Journal of Economic Literature*, **33**, 1319–23.

McCloskey, D.N. and S. T. Ziliak (1996), 'The standard error of regressions', *Journal of Economic Literature*, **34**, 97–114.

McConnell, C.R. and S.L. Brue (1992), *Contemporary Labor Economics*, 3rd edn, New York: McGraw-Hill.

McDonald, I.M. and R.M. Solow (1981), 'Wage bargaining and employment', *American Economic Review*, **71** (5), December, 896–908.

McNally, D. (1988), *Political Economy and the Rise of Capitalism*, Berkeley: University of California Press.

McNally, D. (1993), *Against the Market*, London: Verso.

Mearsheimer, J.J. (1990), 'Back to the future', *International Security*, **15** (1), 5–56.

Meek, R. (1971), 'Smith, Turgot and the "four stages" theory', *History of Political Economy*, **3**, 9–27.

Meek, R. (1973), *Precursors of Adam Smith*, London: Dent.

Meek, R. (1976), *Social Science and the Ignoble Savage*, Cambridge: Cambridge University Press.

Mellis, C. and R. Whittaker (1998), 'The Treasury forecasting record: some new results', *National Institute Economic Review*, **164**, 65–79.

Mendez, R.P. (1996), 'Harnessing the global foreign currency market: proposal for a foreign currency exchange (FXE)', *Review of International Political Economy*, **3**, 498–512.

Mercer, J. (1995), 'Anarchy and identity', *International Organisation*, **49**, 229–52.

Messori, M. (1985), 'Le circuit de la monnaie: acquis et problèmes non résolus', in R. Arena and A. Graziani (eds), *Production, Circulation et Monnaie*, Paris: Presses Universitaires de France, pp. 207–41.

Messori, M. and R. Tamborini (1993), 'Money, credit and finance in a sequence economy', discussion paper 20, Dipartimento di Scienze Economiche, University of Rome La Sapienza.

Milberg, W. (1996), 'Globalization and international competitiveness', paper presented at fourth Post Keynesian Workshop, University of Tennessee, Knoxville.

Milgrom, P. and J. Roberts (1992), *Economics, Organisation and Management*, Englewood Cliffs: Prentice-Hall.

Mill, J.S. (1836), 'On the definition of political economy and the method of investigation proper to it' in J.M. Robson (ed.) (1967), *Collected Works of John Stuart Mill*, vol. 4, Toronto: University of Toronto Press.

Mill, J.S. (1909), *Principles of Political Economy, with Some of their Applications to Social Philosophy*, (ed.) W.J. Ashley, London: Longmans, Green and Co.

Mini, P. (1974), *Philosophy and Economics: The Origins and Development of Economic Theory*, Gainesville: The University Presses of Florida.

Mini P. (1994), *J.M. Keynes: A Study in the Psychology of Original Work*, London: Macmillan.

Minsky, H.P. (1976), *John Maynard Keynes*, London: Macmillan.

Minsky, H.P. (1982), *Can 'It' Happen Again? Essays on Instability and Finance*, New York: M.E. Sharpe.

Mintzberg, Henry (1973), *The Nature of Management Work*, New York, Harper and Row.

Mirowski, P. (1994), 'A visible hand in the market place of ideas: precision measurement as arbitrage', *Science in Context*, **7**, 563–89.

Mirowski, P. and S. Sklivas (1991), 'Why econometricians don't replicate (although they do reproduce)?', *Review of Political Economy*, **3**, 146–63.

Mitchell, D.J.B. (1993), 'Keynesian, old Keynesian, and new Keynesian wage nominalism', *Industrial Relations* **32** (1), Winter, 1–29.

Mizon, G.E (1995), 'Progressive modelling of macroeconomic time series: the LSE methodology', *European University Institute Working paper ECO 95110,* Florence.

Modigliani, F. (1944), 'Liquidity preference and the theory of interest and money', *Econometrica*, **12**, 45–88.

Moggridge, D.E. (1992), *Maynard Keynes: An Economist's Biography*, London and New York: Routledge.

Moore, B. (1966), *Social Origins of Dictatorship and Democracy*, Harmondsworth: Penguin.

Moore, B. (1996), 'M-C-M' and sequence analysis: the central role of interest rates in a monetary theory of production', paper presented to the fourth Post Keynesian Workshop, June, California: University of California.

Moore, B.J. (1988), *Horizontalists and Verticalists: The Macroeconomics of Credit Money*, Cambridge: Cambridge University Press.

Moore, B.J. (1991), 'Money supply endogeneity: "reserve price setting", or "reserve quantity setting"?', *Journal of Post Keynesian Economics*, **13**, 404–13.

Moore, B.J. (1995), 'The exogeneity of short-term interest rates: a reply to Wray', *Journal of Post Economic Issues*, **29**, 258–66.

Moore, G.E. (1903), *Principia Ethica*, Cambridge: Cambridge University Press.

Morriss, P. (1987), *Power: A Philosophical Analysis*, Manchester: Manchester University Press.

Morrow, J. (1985), 'A continuous-outcome expected utility theory of war', *Journal of Conflict Resolution*, **29**, 473–502.

Mueller, D. (1989), *Public Choice II*, Cambridge: Cambridge University Press.

Mullin, T. (1993), 'A dynamical systems approach to time series Analysis', in T.Mullin (ed.), *The Nature of Chaos*, Oxford: Oxford Scientific Publications.

Mussa, M. (1986), 'Nominal exchange rate regimes and the behavior of real exchange rates: evidence and implications', *Carnegie–Rochester Conference Series on Public Policy*, **25**, 117–214.

Mussella, M. and C. Panico (1993), 'Kaldor on endogenous money and interest rates', in G. Mongiovi and C. Rühl (eds), *Macroeconomic Theory: Diversity and Convergence*, Aldershot, UK and Brookfield, US: Edward Elgar.

Neild, R. (1963), *Pricing and Employment in the Trade Cycle*, Cambridge: Cambridge University Press.

Nelson, J. (1996), *Feminism, Objectivity and Economics*, London: Routledge.

Nelson, R.R. and S.G. Winter (1982), *An Evolutionary Theory of Economic Change*, Cambridge, MA: Harvard University Press.

von Neumann, J. and O. Morgenstern (1944), *Theory of Games and Economic Behaviour*, Princeton: Princeton University Press.

Newbould, G.D., P.J. Buckley and J. Thurwell (1978), *Going International – The Experience of Smaller Companies Overseas*, New York: Halstead Press.

Newman, P. (1965), *The Theory of Exchange*, Englewood Cliffs: Prentice-Hall.

Nickell, S. (1990), 'Unemployment: a survey', *Economica*, 391–439.

Norris, C. (1987), *Derrida*, Hammersmith, London: Fontana Press.

North, D. (1990), *Institutions, Institutional Change and Economic Performance*, Cambridge: Cambridge University Press.

Nozick, R. (1974), *Anarchy, State and Utopia*, New York: Basic Books.

Nye, J. (1993), *Understanding International Conflicts*, New York: Harper Collins.

O'Donnell, R.M. (1982), 'Keynes, philosophy and economics: an approach to rationality and uncertainty', unpublished doctoral dissertation, Cambridge University.

O'Donnell, R.M. (1989), *Keynes's Philosophy, Economics and Politics*, London: Macmillan.

O'Donnell, R.M. (1990), 'Keynes on mathematics: philosophical applications and economic applications', *Cambridge Journal of Economics*, **14**, 29–48.

O'Donnell, R.M. (1991), 'Keynes on probability, expectations and uncertainty', in R.M. O'Donnell (ed.), *Keynes as Philosopher–Economist*, London: Macmillan, pp. 3–60.

OECD (1993), *Economic Outlook,* June, Paris.

OECD (1995), *Tax Revenue Statistics*, Paris: OECD.

Oller, L.-E. and B. Barot (1999), 'Comparing the accuracy of European GDP forecasts', National Institute of Economic Research, Stockholm, Sweden.

Olson, M. (1965), *The Logic of Collective Action*, Cambridge, MA: Harvard University Press.

Olson, M. (1982), *The Rise and Decline of Nations*, New Haven: Yale University Press.

Olson, M. (1993), 'Dictatorship, democracy and development', *American Political Science Review*, **87**, 567–76.

Ordershook, P. (1986), *Game Theory and Political Theory*, Cambridge: Cambridge University Press.

Organisation for Economic Co-operation and Development (1995), *Revenue Statistics 1995*, Paris: OECD.

Orléan, A. (1989), 'Mimetic contagion and speculative bubbles', *Theory and Decision*, **27**, 63–92.

Ormerod, P. (1994a), 'On inflation and unemployment', in J. Michie and J. Grieve-Smith (eds), *Unemployment in Europe*, New York: Academic Press, Harcourt Brace.

Ormerod, P. (1994b), *The Death of Economics*, London: Faber and Faber.

Ormerod, P. (1995), 'Local linear approximations to non-linear systems in economics', mimeo, Post-Orthodox Economics, London.

Ormerod, P. and M. Campbell (1997), 'Predictability and economic time series', in C. Heij, H. Schumacher, B. Hanzon and K. Praagam (eds), *System Dynamics in Economic and Financial Models*, New York: John Wiley.

Ormerod, P. and C. Mounfield (2000), 'Random matrix theory and the failure of macroeconomic forecasts', *Physica A*, **280**, p. 497.

Pagan, A.R. (1987), 'Three econometric methodologies: a critical appraisal', *Journal of Economic Surveys*, **1**, 3–24.

Paldam, M. (1989), 'A wage structure theory of inflation, industrial conflicts and trade unions', *Scandinavian Journal of Economics*, 63–81.

Parguez, A. (1975), *Monnaie et Macroéconomie*, Paris: Economica.

Parkin, F. (1979), *Marxism and Class Theory: A Bourgeois Critique*, London: Tavistock.

Parrinello, S. (1995), 'The efficiency wage hypothesis in the long period', in G.C. Harcourt, A. Roncaglia and R. Rowley (eds), *Income and Employment in Theory and Practice: Essays in Memory of Athanasios Asimakopulos*, London: Macmillan, pp. 167–84.

Parsons, S. (1995a), 'Saving Keynes from the Post Keynesians', paper presented at the Post Keynesian Study Group, 5 May 1995; abstract reproduced in the Post Keynesian Study Group Newsletter, September 1995.

Parsons, S. (1995b), 'Post Keynesian Realism and Keynes' General Theory', *Discussion Paper in Economics*, no. 95–04, De Montfort University, Leicester.

Parsons, S. (1996), 'Post Keynesian Realism and Keynes' General Theory', *Journal of Post Keynesian Economics*, **18**, 419–41.

Pasinetti, L.L. (1974), *Growth and Income Distribution*, Cambridge: Cambridge UniversityPress.

Penrose, E. (1995), *The Theory of the Growth of the Firm*, Oxford: Oxford University Press.

Petrella, R. (ed.) (1995), *Limits to Competition: Report of the Group of Lisbon*, Cambridge, MA: MIT Press.

Peppard, J. and P. Rowland (1995), *The Essence of Business Process Re-Engineering*, Hemel Hempstead: Prentice Hall.

Perelman, M. (1984), *Classical Political Economy: Primitive Accumulation and the Social Division of Labour*, Totowa: Rowman and Allanheld.

Pesaran, M.H. and Y. Shin (1994), 'Identification of and testing for cointegrating relations with general non-homogenous restrictions', mimeo, University of Cambridge, Department of Applied Economics.

Phelps Brown, E.H. (1972), 'The underdevelopment of economics', *Economic Journal*, **82**, 1–10.

Phelps Brown, E.H. (1977), *The Inequality of Pay*, Oxford: Oxford University Press.

Pitelis, C. (1991), *Market and Non-Market Hierarchies*, Oxford: Basil Blackwell.

Pitelis, C. and R. Sugden (1986), 'The separation of ownership and control in the theory of the firm: a reappraisal', *International Journal of Industrial Organisation*, **4**, 69–86.

Polanyi, K. (1944), *The Great Transformation*, Boston: Beacon Press.

Polanyi, M. (1967), *The Tacit Dimension*, New York: Anchor.

Polanyi, M. (1973), *Personal Knowledge*, London: Routledge.

Pollin, R. (1991), 'Two theories of money supply endogeneity: some empirical evidence', *Journal of Post Keynesian Economics*, **13**, 366–96.

Ponsard, C. (1986), 'Foundations of soft decision theory', in J. Kacprzyk and R.R. Yeger (eds), *Management Decision Support Systems Using Fuzzy Sets and Possibility Theory*, Cologne: Verlag TUV, Rheinland.

Popper, K.R. (1959), *The Logic of Scientific Discovery*, London: Hutchison.

Popper, K.R. (1963), *Conjectures and Refutations: The Growth of Scientific Knowledge*, London: Routledge and Kegan Paul.

Porter, B. (1994), *War and the Rise of the State*, New York: Free Press.

Posner, R.A. (1993), 'The new institutional economics meets law and economics', *Journal of Institutional and Theoretical Economics*, **149**, 73–87.

Potter, S.M.(1995), 'A nonlinear approach to US GNP', *Journal of Applied Econometrics*, **10**, 109–26.

Prahalad, C.K. and G. Hamel (1990), 'The core competence of the corporation', *Harvard Business Review*, **68**, 79–91.

Pratten, C. (1993), *The Stock Market*, Cambridge: Cambridge University Press.

Pressman, S. (1992), 'The trade policies of John Maynard Keynes', mimeo, Department of Economics, Monmouth College.

Przeworski, A. (1991), *Democracy and the Market*, Cambridge: Cambridge University Press.

Radice, H.K. (1988), 'Keynes and the policy of practical protectionism', in J.V. Hillard, (ed.), *J.M. Keynes in Retrospect*, Aldershot, UK and Brookfield, US: Edward Elgar.

Radner, R. (1968), 'Competitive equilibrium under uncertainty', *Econometrica*, **36** (1), 31–58.

Raeff, M. (1983), *The Well-Ordered Police State*, New Haven: Yale University Press.

Raffaelli, T. (2001), 'Marshall on mind and society: neurophysiological models applied to industrial and business organization', *European Journal of the History of Economic Thought*, **8**, 208–29.

Ramsey, F.P. (1931), *Foundations of Mathematics*, London: Routledge and Kegan Paul.

Rawls, J. (1971), *A Theory of Justice*, London: Oxford University Press.

Rebitzer, J.B. (1993), 'Radical political economy and the economics of labor markets', *Journal of Economic Literature*, **31** (3), September, 1394–1434.

Rees, R. (1989), 'Uncertainty, Information and Insurance', in Hey (ed.) (1989), 79–126.

Reich, M. (1995), 'Radical economics: successes and failures', in F. Moseley (ed.), *Heterodox Economic Theories: True or False?*, Aldershot, UK and Brookfield, US: Edward Elgar, pp. 45–70.

Resnick, S. and R. Wolff (1987), *Knowledge and Class: A Marxian Critique of Political Economy*, Chicago: University of Chicago Press.

Reynolds, L.G. (1951), *The Structure of Labor Markets*, New York: Harper.

Reynolds, P.J. (1987), *Political Economy: A Synthesis of Kaleckian and Post Keynesian Economics*, Sussex: Wheatsheaf Books.

Rhymes, T.K. (1989), *Keynes's Lectures, 1932–35: Notes of a Representative Student*, London: Macmillan in association with the Royal Economic Society.

Riach, P.A. (1976), 'The language of inflation', in E.L. Wheelwright and F. Stilwell (eds), *Readings in Political Economy, Volume 2*, Sydney: ANZ Book Co., pp. 53–60.

Riach, P.A. (1995), 'Wage–employment determination in a post Keynesian world', in P. Arestis and M. Marshall (eds), *The Political Economy of Full Employment*, Aldershot, UK and Brookfield, US: Edward Elgar, pp. 163–75.

Ricardo, D. (1951), *On the Principles of Political Economy and Taxation*, Cambridge: Cambridge University Press, first published 1817.

Richardson, G.B. (1960), *Information and Investment: A Study in the Working of the Competitive Economy*, Oxford: Oxford University Press; 2nd edn 1990.

Richardson, G.B. (1964), *Economic Theory*, London: Hutchinson.

Richardson, G.B. (1972), 'The organisation of industry', *Economic Journal*, **82**, 883–96.

Richardson, G.B. (1975), 'Adam Smith on competition and increasing returns', in A.S. Skinner and T. Wilson (eds), *Essays on Adam Smith*, Oxford: Clarendon Press, reprinted in G.B. Richardson (1998), *The Economics of Imperfect Knowledge*, Cheltenham, UK and Northampton, MA, USA: Edward Elgar, pp. 157–67.

Richardson, G.B. (1997), 'Innovation, equilibrium and welfare', Chapter 2 in S.C. Dow and J. Hillard (eds) (2002), *Post Keynesian Econometrics,*

Microeconomics and the Theory of the Firm, Cheltenham, UK and Northampton, US: Edward Elgar.

Rizvi, S. (1994), 'The microfoundations project in general equilibrium theory', *Cambridge Journal of Economics*, **18**, 357–77.

Robinson, J. (1933), *The Economics of Imperfect Competition*, London: Macmillan.

Robinson, J. (1937), *Essays in the Theory of Employment*, London: Macmillan.

Robinson, J. (1962), *Economic Philosophy*, Chicago: Aldine Publishing Co.

Robinson, J. (1964a), *Economic Philosophy*, Harmondsworth: Penguin Books Ltd.

Robinson, J. (1964b), 'Kalecki and Keynes', *Collected Economic Papers*, vol III, Oxford: Blackwell.

Robinson, J. (1969), 'Preface' to Robinson (1933), 2nd edn, v–xii.

Robinson, J. (1978), *Contributions to Modern Economics*, Oxford: Basil Blackwell.

Robinson, J. and J. Eatwell (1973), *An Introduction to Modern Economics*, London: McGraw-Hill.

Roemer, J. (ed.) (1986), *Analytical Marxism*, Cambridge: Cambridge University Press.

Rogoff, K. (1996), 'The purchasing power parity puzzle', *Journal of Economic Literature*, **34** (2), 647–68.

Rorty, R. (1982), 'Philosophy as a kind of writing', in *Consequences of Pragmatism*, Minneapolis: University of Minnesota Press.

Rorty, R. (1989), 'From ironist theory to private allusions: Derrida', in *Contingency, Irony, and Solidarity*, Cambridge: Cambridge University Press.

Rose, A. (1994), 'Are exchange rates macroeconomic phenomena?', *Federal Reserve Bank of San Francisco Review*, **1**, 19–30.

Rosecrance, R. (1986), *The Rise of the Trading State*, New York: Basic Books.

Rosenberg, A. (1992), *Economics – Mathematical Politics or Science of Diminishing Returns*, Chicago: University of Chicago Press.

Rosenberg, N. and L. Birdzell (1986), *How the West Grew Rich*, New York: Basic Books.

Ross, A.M. (1953), *Trade Union Wage Policy*, Berkeley: University of California Press.

Rothbard, M. (1973), *For a New Liberty*, New York: Collier.

Rotheim, R.J. (1988), 'Keynes and the language of probability and uncertainty', *Journal of Post Keynesian Economics*, **11**, 83–99.

Rotheim, R.J. (1989/90), 'Organicism and the role of the individual in Keynes's thought', *Journal of Post Keynesian Economics*, **12**, 316–26.

Rotheim, R.J. (1991), 'Marx, Keynes and the theory of a monetary economy', in G.A. Caravale (ed.), *Marx and Modern Economic Analysis. Volume II: The Future of Capitalism and the History of Thought*, Aldershot, UK and Brookfield, US: Edward Elgar, pp. 240–63.

Rotheim, R.J. (1992), 'Interdependence and the Cambridge economic tradition', in B. Gerrard and J.V. Hillard, (eds), *The Philosophy and Economics of J.M. Keynes*, Aldershot, UK and Brookfield, US: Edward Elgar.

Rotheim, R.J. (1995), 'Keynes on uncertainty and individual behaviour within a theory of effective demand', in S. Dow and J.V. Hillard (eds), *Keynes, Knowledge and Uncertainty*, Aldershot, UK and Brookfield, US: Edward Elgar.

Rothschild, K.W. (1942–3), 'Monopsony, buying costs, and welfare expenditure', *Review of Economic Studies*, **10** (1), 62–7.

Rothschild, K.W. (1947), 'Price theory and oligopoly', *Economic Journal*, **57** (227), September, 299–320.

Rothschild, K.W. (1954), *The Theory of Wages*, Oxford: Blackwell.

Rothschild, K.W. (1957), 'Approaches to the theory of bargaining', in J.T. Dunlop (ed.), *The Theory of Wage Determination*, London: Macmillan, pp. 281–91.

Rothschild, K.W. (1989), 'Some reflections on the growth of female labour supply and the tertiary sector', *International Review of Applied Economics*, **3** (2), June, 232–42.

Rothschild, K.W. (1993), *Employment, Wages and Income Distribution: Critical Essays in Economics*, London: Routledge.

Rothschild, K.W. (1994), 'Austro-Keynesianism reconsidered', *Contemporary Austrian Studies*, **2**, 119–29.

Rowthorn, R.E. (1977), 'Conflict, inflation and money', *Cambridge Journal of Economics*, **1**, 215–39.

Rowthorn, R.E. (1995), 'Capital formation and unemployment', *Oxford Review of Economic Policy*, **11** (1), 26–39.

Roy, S. (1989), *Philosophy of Economics: On the Scope of Reason in Economic Enquiry*, London: Routledge.

Runde, J. (1990), 'Keynesian uncertainty and the weight of arguments', *Economics and Philosophy*, **6**, 275–92.

Runde, J. (1994a), 'Keynesian uncertainty and liquidity preference', *Cambridge Journal of Economics*, **18**, 129–44.

Runde, J. (1994b), 'Keynes After Ramsey: in defence of *A Treatise on Probability*', *Studies in History and Philosophy of Science*, **25**, 97–121.

Runde, J. (1995), 'Risk, uncertainty and Bayesian decision theory: a Keynesian view', in S.C. Dow and J. Hillard (eds), *Keynes, Knowledge and Uncertainty,* Aldershot, UK and Brookfield, US: Edward Elgar, pp. 197–210.

Rutherford, M. (1989), 'What is wrong with the new institutional economics (and what is still wrong with the old)?', *Review of Political Economy*, **1** (3), 299–318.

Ryle, G. (1949), *The Concept of Mind,* London: Hutchinson.

Salanti, A. and E. Screpanti (eds) (1997), *Pluralism in Economics: Theory, History and Methodology*, Cheltenham, UK and Brookfield, US: Edward Elgar.

Salazar, C. (1996), 'Between morality and rationality: an analysis of interpersonal economics in rural Ireland', *Economic and Social Review*, **27** (3), 235–52.

Sampson, E. (1993), *Celebrating the Other*, Hemel Hempstead: Wheatsheaf.

Samuelson, P.A. (1939), 'Interactions between the principle of acceleration and the multiplier', *Review of Economics and Statistics*, **21**, 75–8.

Samuelson, P.A. (1947), *Foundations of Economic Analysis*, Cambridge, MA: Harvard University Press.

Samuelson, P.A. (1954), 'The pure theory of public expenditure', *Review of Economics and Statistics*, **37**, 387–9.

Samuelson, P.A. (1968), 'Classical and neo-classical monetary theory', in R. Clower (ed.) (1969), *Monetary Theory*, Harmondsworth: Penguin.

Sardoni, C. (1992), 'Market forms and effective demand: Keynesian results with perfect competition', *Review of Political Economy*, **4**, 377–95.

Sardoni, C. (1996), 'Prices, expectation and investment: a critical assessment of Keynes's marginal efficiency of capital', in S. Pressman and J. Smithin (eds), *The Malvern Conference Ten Years On*.

Sargent, T.J. (1993), *Bounded Rationality in Macroeconomics*, Boston.

Savage, L.J. (1954), *The Foundations of Statistics*, New York: John Wiley and Sons; revised and enlarged edn, New York: Dover, 1972.

Sawyer, M. (1983), *Business Pricing and Inflation*, London: Macmillan.

Sawyer, M. (1985), *The Economics of Industries and Firms*, 2nd edn, London: Croom Helm.

Sawyer, M. (1988), 'Theories of monopoly capitalism', *Journal of Economic Surveys*, **2** (1), 42–76.

Sawyer, M. (1989), *The Challenge of Radical Political Economy*, London: Harvester Wheatsheaf.

Sawyer, M. (1990), 'On the Post Keynesian tradition and industrial economics', *Review of Political Economy*, **2**, 43–68.

Sawyer, M. (1992a), 'Keynes's macroeconomic analysis and theories of imperfect competition', in B. Gerrard and J. Hillard (eds), *The Philosophy and Economics of Keynes*, Aldershot, UK and Brookfield, US: Edward Elgar.

Sawyer, M. (1992b), 'The nature and role of the market', *Social Concept*, **6** (2).

Sawyer, M. (1993), 'The nature and role of the market', in C. Pitelis (ed.), *Transaction Costs, Markets and Hierarchies*, Oxford: Basil Blackwell.

Sawyer, M. (1994a), 'Post-Keynesian and Marxian notions of competition: towards a synthesis', in M. Glick (ed.), *Competition, Technology and Money: Classical and Post-Keynesian perspectives*, Aldershot, UK and Brookfield, US: Edward Elgar.

Sawyer, M. (1994b), 'Post-Keynesian analysis and industrial economics' in M. Sawyer (ed.), *Unemployment, Imperfect Competition and Macroeconomics: Essay in the Post-Keynesian tradition*, Aldershot, UK and Brookfield, US: Edward Elgar.

Sawyer, M. (1995), *Unemployment, Imperfect Competition and Macroeconomics*, Aldershot, UK and Brookfield, US: Edward Elgar.

Sawyer, M. (1996a) 'Money, finance and interest rates', in P. Arestis (ed.), *Keynes, Money and the Open Economy: Essays in Honour of Paul Davidson, Vol. 1*, Cheltenham, UK and Northampton, US: Edward Elgar, pp. 50–68.

Sawyer, M. (1996b), 'New Keynesian macroeconomics and the Determination of employment and wages', mimeo, University of Leeds.

Sayer, S. (1992), 'The city, power and economic policy in Britain', *International Review of Applied Economics*, **6**.

Schmeidler, D. (1982), 'Subjective probability without additivity', working paper, Foerder Institute for Economic Research, Tel Aviv University.

Schmeidler, D. (1986), 'Integral representation without additivity', *Proceedings of the American Mathematical Society*, **97** (2), 255–61.

Schmeidler, D. (1989), 'Subjective probability and expected utility without additivity', *Econometrica*, **57**, 571–87.

Schumpeter, J.A. (1934), *The Theory of Economic Development*, Cambridge MA: Harvard University Press.

Schumpeter, J.A. (1942), *Capitalism, Socialism and Democracy*, New York: Harper and Row.

Schumpeter, J.A. (1955), *Imperialism and Social Classes*, New York: Meridian.

Scruton, R. (1984), *The Meaning of Conservatism*, London: Macmillan.

Seccareccia, M. (1991), 'An alternative to labour-market orthodoxy: the post Keynesian/institutionalist view', *Review of Political Economy* **3** (1), March, 43–61.

Segal, U. (1987), 'The Ellsberg paradox and risk aversion: an anticipated utility approach', *International Economic Review*, **28** (1), 175–202.

Shackle, G.L.S. (1952), *Expectations in Economics*, Cambridge: Cambridge University Press.

Shackle, G.L.S. (1955), *Uncertainty in Economics: And Other Reflections*, Cambridge: Cambridge University Press.

Shackle, G.L.S. (1958), *Time in Economics*, Amsterdam: North-Holland.

Shackle, G.L.S. (1961), *Decision, Order and Time in Human Affairs*, Cambridge: Cambridge University Press.

Shackle, G.L.S. (1967), *The Years of High Theory: Invention and Tradition in Economic Thought, 1926–1939*, Cambridge: Cambridge University Press.

Shackle, G.L.S. (1972), *Epistemics and Economics*, Cambridge: Cambridge University Press.

Shafer, G. (1976), *A Mathematical Theory of Evidence*, Princeton: Princeton University Press.

Shaikh, A. (1980), 'The Laws of International Exchange', in E. Nell (ed.), *Growth, Profits and Property*, Cambridge: Cambridge University Press.

Shaikh, A. (1992), 'Competition and exchange rates: theory and empirical evidence', working paper, Department of Economics, New School for Social Research, New York.

Shapiro, N. (1977), 'The revolutionary character of Post-Keynesian economics', *Journal of Economic Issues*, **XI**.

Shapiro, N. (1995), 'Markets and mark-ups: Keynesian views', in S. Dow and J. Hillard (eds), *Keynes, Knowledge and Uncertainty*, Aldershot, UK and Brookfield, US: Edward Elgar.

Shapiro, N. (1997), 'Imperfect competition and Keynes', in Harcourt and Riach (1997), vol. 1, pp. 83–92.

Shapiro, S.P. (1987), 'The social control of personal trust', *American Journal of Sociology*, **3**, November, 623–58.

Shiller, R.J. (1981), 'Do stock prices move too much to be justified by subsequent changes in dividend?', *American Economic Review*, **71**, 421–36.

Shiller R.J. (1989), *Market Volatility*, Cambridge, MA: MIT Press.

Silberner, E. (1972), *The Problem of War in Nineteenth Century Economic Thought*, New York: Garland.

Simon, H.A. (1957), *Models of Man*, New York: Wiley.

Simon, H.A. (1959), 'Theories of decision making in economic and behavioural sciences', *American Economic Review*, **49**, 253–83.

Simon, H.A. (1976), 'From substantive to procedural rationality', in S. Latis (ed.), *Method and Appraisal in Economics*, Cambridge: Cambridge University Press.

Simon, H.A. (1982), *Models of Bounded Rationality*, Cambridge, MA: MIT Press.

Simon, H.A. (1991), 'Organisations and markets', *Journal of Economic Perspectives*, **5** (2), 25–44.

Simonsen, M.H. and S.R.C. Werlang (1991), 'Subadditive probabilities and portfolio inertia', *Revista de Econometria*, **11**, 1–19.

Sims, C.A. (1980), 'Macroeconomics and reality', *Econometrica*, **48**, 1–47.

Singh, A. (1995), 'Review of wood (1994)', *Economic Journal*, **105** (432), September, 1287–9.

Skidelsky, R. (1992), *The Economist as Saviour, 1920–1937*, New York: Viking Penguin.

Skidelsky, R. (1995), *The World After Communism: A Polemic for our Times*, London: Macmillan.

Skocpol, T. (1979), *States and Social Revolutions*, Cambridge: Cambridge University Press.

Skocpol, T. (1992), *Protecting Soldiers and Mothers*, Cambridge MA: Harvard University Press.

Skott, P. (1991), 'Efficiency wages, mark-up pricing and effective demand', in J. Michie (ed.), *The Economics of Restructuring and Intervention*, Worcestor: Billing and Sons.

Skousen, M. (1992), 'Keynes as a speculator: a critique of Keynesian investment theory', in M. Skousen (ed.), *Dissent on Keynes: A Critical Appraisal of Keynesian Economics*, New York: Praeger.

Smith, A. (1776), *The Wealth of Nations*, reprinted London: Methuen, 1904.

Smith, A. (1976a), *The Theory of Moral Sentiments*, ed. D. Raphael and A.L. Macfie, Oxford: Oxford University Press.

Smith, A. (1976b), *An Inquiry into the Nature and Causes of the Wealth of Nations*, ed. R.H. Campbell, A.S. Skinner and W.B. Todd, Oxford: Oxford University Press.

Smith, A. (1978), *Lectures on Jurisprudence*, ed. R.L. Meek, D. Raphael and P.G. Stein, Oxford: Oxford University Press.

Smith, R. (1994), 'Econometrics' in P. Arestis and M. Sawyer (eds), *The Elgar Companion to Radical Political Economy*, Aldershot, UK and Brookfield, US: Edward Elgar.

Sofianou, E. (1995), 'Post-modernism and the notion of rationality in economics', *Cambridge Journal of Economics*, **19**, 373–88.

Sraffa, P. (1926), 'The laws of returns under competitive conditions', *Economic Journal*, **36**, 535–50.

Steedman, I. (1995), 'Criticising Post Keynesian economics', paper presented at the Post Keynesian Study Group, 5 May 1995; abstract reproduced in the Post Keynesian Study Group Newsletter, September 1995.

Steindl, J. (1952), *Maturity and Stagnation in American Capitalism*, Oxford: Blackwell; reissued with new introduction, New York: Monthly Review Press, 1976.

Steindl, J. (1979), 'Stagnation theory and stagnation policy', *Cambridge Journal of Economics*, **3**.

Steindl, J. (1987), 'Kalecki's theory of pricing: notes on the margin', in G. Fink, G. Pöll and M. Riese (eds), *Economic Theory, Political Power and Social Justice: Festschrift Kazimierz Laski*, Vienna: Springer, pp. 1–18; reprinted in J. Steindl, *Economic Papers 1941–88*, London: Macmillan, 1990, pp. 303–16.

Stekler, H. and R. Fildes (1999), 'The state of macroeconomic forecasting', George Washington University, Center for Economic research discussion paper No. 99–04.

Stettler, M. (1995), 'The rhetoric of McCloskey's rhetoric of economics', *Cambridge Journal of Economics*, **19**, 389–403.

Stigler, G.J. (1961), ' The economics of information', *Journal of Political Economy*, **69**, 213–25.

Stigler, G.J. (1965), *Essays in the History of Economics*, Chicago: University of Chicago Press.

Stigler, G.J. (1976), 'The xistence of x-efficiency', *American Economic Review*, **66** (1), March, 213–16.

Stiglitz, J.E. (1987), 'The causes and consequences of the dependence of quality on price', *Journal of Economic Literature*, **25** (1), March, 1–48.

Stiglitz, J.E. (1994), *Whither Socialism?*, Cambridge, MA: MIT Press.

Stohs, M. (1980), 'Uncertainty in Keynes' General Theory', *History of Political Economy*, **12** (3), 372–82.

Stone, R. (1978), 'Keynes, political arithmetic and econometrics', *Proceedings of the British Academy*, Vol. 64, Oxford: Oxford University Press.

Stumpf, S. (1994), *Philosophy, History and Problems*, 5th edition, New York: McGraw Hill.

Sugden, R. (1983), 'Why transnational corporations?', University of Warwick economics research paper no. 22.

Summers, L. (1989), 'The scientific illusion in empirical macroeconomics', *Scandinavian Journal of Economics*, **93**, 129–48.

Sweezy, P.M. (1939), 'Demand under conditions of oligopoly', *Journal of Political Economy*, **47** (4), August: 568–73.

Tamborini, R (1995), 'Price determination in polypolistic markets and exchange rate changes', *Metroeconomica*, **46**, 63–89.

Targetti, F. and B. Kinda-Haas (1982), 'Kalecki's review of Keynes's General Theory', *Australian Economic Papers*, **21**, 244–60.

Tetlock, P. *et al.* (eds) (1989), *Behavior, Society and Nuclear War, Volume I*, Oxford: Oxford University Press.

Teubner, G. (1993), *Law as an Autopoietic System*, Oxford: Blackwell.

Thompson, E. (1966), *The Making of the English Working Class*, New York: Vintage.

Thweatt, W. (1976), 'James Mill and the early development of comparative advantage', *History of Political Economy*, **8**, 207–34.

Tiao G.C. and R.S. Tsay (1994), 'Some advances in non-linear and adaptive modelling in time-series analysis', *Journal of Forecasting,* **13**.

Tiger, M. (1977), *Law and the Rise of Capitalism,* New York: Monthly Review Press.

Tilly, C. (1992), *Coercion, Capital and European States, AD 990–1992,* Oxford: Blackwell.

Tirole, J. (1988), *The Theory of Industrial Organisation,* Cambridge, MA: MIT Press.

Tobin, J. (1958), 'Liquidity preference as behaviour towards risk', *Review of Economic Studies,* **25**, 65–86.

Tobin, J. (1966), 'Adjustment responsibilities of surplus and deficit countries', in W. Fellner, F. Machlup and R.Triffin (eds), *Maintaining and Restoring Balance in International Payments,* Princeton: Princeton University Press.

Tobin, J. (1974), 'The new economics one decade older', *The Eliot Janeway Lectures on Historical Economics in Honour of Joseph Schumpeter, 1972,* Princeton: Princeton University Press.

Tobin, J. (1978), 'A proposal for international monetary reform', *Eastern Economic Journal,* **4** (3–4), 153–9, reprinted in J. Tobin, *Essays in Economics: Theory and Policy,* Cambridge, MA: MIT Press.

Tobin, J. (1981), *Asset Accumulation and Economic Activity,* Chicago: University of Chicago Press.

Tobin, J. (1982), 'The Commercial banking firm: a simple model', *Scandinavian Journal of Economics,* **84** (4), 495–530.

Tobin, J. (1984), 'James Tobin', in Arjo Klamer (ed.), *The New Classical Economics,* Sussex: Harvester Wheatsheaf.

Tobin, J. (1993), 'Price flexibility and output stability: an old Keynesian view', *The Journal of Economic Perspectives,* **7**, 45–66.

Tobin, J. (1996), 'Prologue', in Haq *et al.* (eds) (1996), pp. ix–xviii.

Torgovnick, P. (1990), *Gone Primitive,* Chicago, University of Chicago Press.

Trotsky, L. (1971), *The Struggle Against Fascism in Germany,* New York: Pathfinder Press.

United Nations Conference on Trade and Development (UNCTAD) (1995), *Trade and Development Report, 1995,* New York and Geneva: United Nations.

United Nations Development Programme (1994), *Human Development Report 1994,* New York and Oxford: Oxford University Press

Usher, D. (1981), *The Economic Prerequisite to Democracy,* New York: Columbia University Press.

van Dieren, W. (1994), 'The disqualification of the Maastricht Treaty', in P.-O. Bergeron and M.-A. Gaiffe (eds), *Croissance, Compétitivité,*

Emploi: à la recherche d'un modèle pour l'Europe, Bruges: Collège d'Europe.

Vautard, R. and M. Ghil (1989), 'Singular spectrum analysis in nonlinear dynamics with applications to paleoclimatic time series', *Physica,* **35B**.

Veblen, T. (1961), 'Why economics is not an evolutionary science?', in *The Place of Science in Modern Civilisation*, New York: Russell and Russel.

Vercelli, A. (1991), *Methodological Foundations of Macroeconomics*: *Keynes and Lucas*, Cambridge: Cambridge University Press.

Vercelli, A. (1992), 'Probabilistic causality and economic analysis: a survey', in A.Vercelli and N.Dimitri (eds), *Macroeconomics: A Survey of Research Strategies,* Oxford: Oxford University Press.

Vercelli, A. (1995), 'From soft uncertainty to hard environmental uncertainty', *Economie Appliquée*, **48**, 251–69.

Vercelli, A. (1996), 'Keynes, Schumpeter and beyond: a non-reductionist perspective', in G.C. Harcourt and P. Riach (eds), *A 'Second Edition' of the General Theory*, London: Routledge.

Vercelli, A. (1999a), 'The recent advances in decision theory under uncertainty: a non-technical introduction', in L.Luini (ed.), *Uncertain Decisions: Bridging Theory and Experiments*, Dordrecht: Kluwer.

Vercelli, A. (1999b), 'The evolution of IS–LM models: empirical evidence and theoretical presuppositions', *Journal of Economic Methodology*, **1**.

Vercelli, A. (2000), 'Financial fragility and cyclical fluctuations', *Structural Change and Economic Dynamics*, **1**, 139–56.

Vercelli, A. (2001), 'Minsky, Keynes and the structural instability of a sophisticated monetary economy', in R. Bellofiore and P. Ferri (eds), *Financial Fragility and Investment in the Capitalist Economy*, Cheltenham, UK and Northampton, MA, US: Edward Elgar.

Vernon, R. (1966), 'International investment and international trade in the product cycle', Quarterly Journal of Economics, **80**, 190–207.

Viner, J. (1931), 'Cost curves and supply curves', *Zeitschrift für Nationalokonomie*, **3**, 23–46.

Visser, H. (1977), 'Marx on money', *Kredit und Kapital*, **10**.

Vromen, J. (1995), *Economic Evolution: An Enquiry into the Foundations of the New Institutional Economics*, London: Routledge.

Wakker, P. (1989), 'Continuous subjective expected utility with non-additive probabilities', *Journal of Mathematical Economics*, **18**, 1–27.

Wallich, H.C. and S. Weintraub (1971), 'A tax-based incomes policy', *Journal of Economic Issues*, **5** (2), June, 1–19.

Walras, L. (1954), *Elements of Pure Economics*, London: Allen and Unwin.

Walters, B. and D. Young (1997), 'On the coherence of Post-Keynesian economics', *Scottish Journal of Political Economy*, **44** (3), August, 329–49.

Walters, B. and D. Young (1999), 'Post-Keynesianism and coherence: a reply to Arestis, Dunn and Sawyer', *Scottish Journal of Political Economy*, **46** (3), August, 346–8.

Walton, J. (1995), 'By the roots', *London Review of Books*, **17**, 26–8.

Waltz, K. (1979), *Theory of International Politics*, Reading, MA: Addison-Wesley.

Wanniski, J. (1989), *The Way the World Works*, Morristown: Polyconomics.

Warren, B. (1980), *Imperialism: Pioneer of Capitalism*, London: New Left Books.

Weber, M. (1983), *Max Weber on Capitalism, Bureaucracy and Religion*, London: George Allen and Unwin.

Weintraub, S. (1956), 'A macroeconomic approach to the theory of wages', *American Economic Review*, **46** (5), December, 835–56.

Weintraub, S. (1963), *Some Aspects of Wage Theory and Policy*, Philadelphia: Chilton.

Weitzman, M. (1982), 'Increasing returns and the foundations of unemployment theory', *Economic Journal*, **92**, 787–804.

Welch, L. (1993), 'Outward licensing by Australian companies', in P.J. Buckley and P.N. Ghauri (eds), *The Internationalisation of the Firm*, London: Academic Press.

Whitley, R. (1984), *The Intellectual and Social Organization of the Sciences*, Oxford: Clarendon Press.

Wickens, M. (1995), 'Real business cycle analysis: a needed revolution in macroeconometrics', *Economic Journal*, **105**, 1637–48.

Will, G. (1983), *Statecraft as Soulcraft*, New York: Touchstone.

Will, G. (1986), *The Morning After*, New York: Collier.

Will, G. (1992), *Suddenly*, New York: Free Press.

Williamson, O.E. (1975), *Markets and Hierarchies: Analysis and Anti-Trust Implications: A study in the economics of internal organisation*, New York: Free Press.

Williamson, O.E. (1979), 'Transaction-cost economics: the governance of contractual relations', *Journal of Law and Economics*, **22**, 233–61.

Williamson, O.E. (1981), 'The modern corporation: origins, evolution, attributes', *Journal of Economic Literature*, **19**, 1537–68.

Williamson, O.E. (1983), 'The economics of governance: framework and implications', Yale University discussion paper no. 153, July.

Williamson, O.E. (1985), *The Economic Institutions of Capitalism: Firms, Markets, Relational Contracting*, London: Macmillan.

Williamson, O.E. (1987), *Antitrust Economics*, Oxford: Basil Blackwell.

Williamson, O.E. (1993), 'Calculativeness, trust and economic organization', *Journal of Law and Economics*, **36**, 453–86.

Williamson, O.E. and S.G. Winter (eds) (1993), *The Nature of the Firm: Origins, Evolution, and Development*, Oxford: Oxford University Press.

Willinger, M., (1990), Irréversibilité et cohérence dynamique des choix, *Revue d' Economie Politique*, **100** (6), 808–32.

Winslow, E.G. (1986), 'Human logic and Keynes's economics', *Eastern Economic Journal*, **12**, 423–30.

Winslow E.G. (1995), 'Uncertainty and liquidity preference', in S. Dow and J.V. Hillard (eds), *Keynes, Knowledge and Uncertainty*, Aldershot, UK and Brookfield, US: Edward Elgar, pp. 221–24.

Winslow, T. (1989), 'Organic interdependence, uncertainty and economic analysis', *Economic Journal*, **99**, 1173–82.

Winston, G.C. (1988), 'Three problems with the treatment of time in economics: perspectives, repetitiveness, and time units', in G.C. Winston and F. Teichgraeber III (eds) (1988), *The Boundaries of Economics*, Cambridge: Cambridge University Press.

Wiseman, J. and S.C. Littlechild (1990), 'Crusoe's kingdom: cost, choice and political economy', in S.F. Frowen (ed.), *Unknowledge and Choice in Economics*, Basingstoke: Macmillan.

Wolf, B. and M. Smook (1988), 'Keynes and the question of tariffs', in O. Hamouda and S. Smithin (eds), *Keynes and Public Policy After Fifty Years, Vol. 2: Theories and Method*, Aldershot, UK and Brookfield, US: Edward Elgar.

Wood, A. (1978), *A Theory of Pay*, Cambridge: Cambridge University Press.

Wood, A. (1994), *North–South Trade, Employment and Inequality: Changing Fortunes in a Skill-Driven World*, Oxford : Clarendon Press.

Woodford, M. (1990), 'Learning to believe in sunspots', *Econometrica*, **58**, 277–307.

Worswick, D. and J. Trevithick (eds) (1983), *Keynes and the Modern World,* Cambridge: Cambridge University Press.

Worswick, G.D.N. (1972), 'Is progress in economic science possible?', *Economic Journal*, **82**, 73–86.

Wray, L.R. (1990), *Money and Credit in Capitalist Economies: The Endogenous Money Approach*, Aldershot, UK and Brookfield, US: Edward Elgar.

Wray, L.R. (1995), 'Keynesian monetary theory: liquidity preference or black box horizontalism?', Journal of Economic Issues, **29**, 273–83.

Wren-Lewis, S. (1990), 'Nominal inertia and Keynesian effects', *National Institute of Economic and Social Research*, discussion paper no. 174.

Wrong, D. (1979), *Power*, Oxford: Blackwell.

Young, W. (1987), *Interpreting Mr Keynes: The IS–LM Enigma*, Cambridge: Polity Press.

Zadeh, L.A. (1965), 'Fuzzy sets', *Information and Control*, **8**, 338–53.

Zarnowitz, V. and P. Braun (1992), 'Twenty-two years of the NBER-ASA quarterly outlook surveys: aspects and comparisons of forecasting performance; NBER Working paper 3965.

Zucker, L.G. (1986), 'Production of trust: institutional sources of economic structure, 1840–1920', *Research in Organizational Behaviour*, **8**, 53–111, Greenwich, Connecticut: JAI Press.

Index

Shell 10
Shin, Y. 198
short-run unemployment relationship
   200–1
short-term expectations 105–6
Simon, H.A. 54, 62, 67, 72
Sims, C.A. 113, 122–3, 152, 154
singular value decomposition 137–9
skills 8–10
Sklivas, S. 177
Skott, P. 193
Smith, A. 8, 10–11, 12, 21, 22, 24, 25,
   81, 85
Smith, R. 130
social anthropology 45–7, 52
software 20
software operating systems 21
spatial comparison 47
specification problems 121, 127
speculative demand 169
stability 18–19
static equilibrium 23
statistical analysis 171
statistical generating mechanism
   (SGM) 125, 130
Steedman, I. 145
Stekler, H. 134
Stigler, G.J. 65
Stiglitz, J. 163
Stone, R. 166
strategy 60–1, 67–70, 70–2, 77–9
strikes 197–8
structural instability 130
structural models 139–40
structural relationships 140–3
structural VAR approach 124
stylized facts 187
subjective priors 152–4
subsidies 27, 28
Sugden, R. 60–1, 66–70, 70, 71, 72, 74,
   75
Summers, L. 177
surprises 13
Sweezy, P.M. 69
sympathy 10–11
systems trust 92

tacit knowledge 90
taxes 27, 28
  cuts 180

wages and unemployment 195, 197,
   199
team working 95
technical progress 162–3, 175
tendency to equilibrium 22–4
Teubner, G. 52
textbook/AER approach 119–22,
   127–8, 131, 150
theory appraisal methods 110–11
Thurwell, J. 45
Tiao, G.C. 137
time 172
  importance and trust 86–90
Tinbergen, J. 113, 129, 150, 171
transaction costs 3, 44–59
  clarifying 65–6
  language, information and
    managerial judgment 54–6
  longitudinal and comparative
    research 44–7
  managerial perceptions 49–52
  measurement of 48–51
  realism and 33, 38, 39–40
  theory of the firm 62–6, 66–7, 73,
    78
  uncertainty 56–7
transcendental realism 118–19
  see also critical realism
Treasury model 135
Treatise on Probability, A (Keynes)
   97–103, 107–8, 165–7
trust 3, 53–4, 81–96
  economics and 83–5
  importance of time 86–90
  significance 93–5
  types 90–3
Tsay, R.S. 137
two-level brain 11, 13

uncertainty 3, 103
  information and a source of 103–7
  Keynes's analytical framework for
    behaviour under 97–100
  long-term expectations of
    investment return 28–9, 169
  Post Keynesian economics 172
  theory of the firm 60–1, 65–6, 70–6,
    77–9
  transaction costs and 56–7
  trust and 88–90, 93–5